Selected Poems of
Jacint Verdaguer

1. Oil painting of the young Verdaguer at the Willow
Fountain, by Marià de Picó (1871).

A BILINGUAL EDITION

Selected Poems of
Jacint Verdaguer

Edited and Translated from Catalan by
Ronald Puppo

With an Introduction by
Ramon Pinyol i Torrents

THE UNIVERSITY OF CHICAGO PRESS

CHICAGO AND LONDON

JACINT VERDAGUER was born in 1845 in the village of Folgueroles (near Vic, a county capital in provincial Catalonia in Spain). The author of more than thirty books, he was a poet, a patriot, and a priest. He died of tuberculosis in 1902.

RONALD PUPPO is associate professor of English studies and head of the Department of Foreign Languages, Translation School, University of Vic, Catalonia, Spain.

RAMON PINYOL I TORRENTS is professor of Catalan and Spanish, Translation School, University of Vic.

The University of Chicago Press, Chicago 60637
The University of Chicago Press, Ltd., London
© 2007 by The University of Chicago
All rights reserved. Published 2007
Printed in the United States of America

16 15 14 13 12 11 10 09 08 07   1 2 3 4 5

ISBN-13: 978-0-226-85300-0 (cloth)
ISBN-10: 0-226-85300-4 (cloth)

ᒪᒪᒪᒪ institut
ramon llull

The translation of this work has been supported by a grant from the Institut Ramon Llull.

Library of Congress Cataloging-in-Publication Data

Verdaguer, Jacinto, 1845–1902.
[Poems. English & Catalan. Selections]
Selected poems of Jacint Verdaguer : a bilingual edition / Jacint Verdaguer ; edited and translated by Ronald Puppo ; with an introduction by Ramon Pinyol i Torrents.
p. cm.
Includes bibliographical references and index.
ISBN-13: 978-0-226-85300-0 (cloth : alk. paper)
ISBN-10: 0-226-85300-4 (cloth : alk. paper) 1. Verdaguer, Jacinto, 1845–1902—
Translations into English. I. Puppo, Ronald. II. Title.
PC3941.V4A2 2007
849'.914—dc22

2007013786

CONTENTS

2. Portrait of Verdaguer by J. M. Marqués (1880), displayed
at the Barcelona World's Fair 1929-30.

ILLUSTRATIONS

ACKNOWLEDGMENTS

I am indebted to a number of Verdaguerian scholars who have helped
me in countless ways during the preparation of this volume, particularly
Ricard Torrents, Ramon Pinyol, M. Àngels Verdaguer, Francesc Codina,
M. Carme Bernal, and Llorenç Soldevila. More generally, I am grateful
for support at various stages of the project from Víctor Obiols, Joan Solà,
Carme Sanmartí, Martha Tennent, Lawrence Venuti, Rosa Flotats, Mary
Ellen Kerans, Montserrat Obiols, Ifan Lloyd, Montserrat Manent, Josep
Ferrer, Alfons van Campen, Jordi van Campen, Kathleen McNerney,
Patricia Hart, Gregory H. Davis, Daniel Olsen, Monica Cowell, Dolors
Vall, and Roger Rapp. Further, I am deeply indebted to both the late
Arthur Terry of the University of Essex and the late Segimon Serrallonga
of the University of Vic for their generous scholarly guidance during the
early years of my encounter with Verdaguer.

Throughout this book's introductory matter and notes, scholars' state-
ments and other prose materials are provided in English rather than the
original Catalan. The translations are my own.

For their invaluable archival and technical assistance with the illus-
trations in this volume, I would like to express my thanks to Carme Tor-
rents and Pilar Canudas of the Casa Museu Verdaguer in Folgueroles; to
M. Victòria Casals, Marta Riera, Oriol Miralles, and Cebrià Vicente of the
Biblioteca de Catalunya, Barcelona; to Àngels Rius of the Biblioteca de
Montserrat; to Miquel Pérez of the University of Vic; and to Anton Granero,
Marta Prat, and Jordina Bartomeus of Eumogràfic, Vic.

Finally, a special thanks to Randolph Petilos and Ruth Goring of the University of Chicago Press, and last but certainly not least, to Teresa Vall i Folgarolas for her unflagging encouragement, faith, and wise counsel from start to finish.

INTRODUCTION

The literary achievement of Jacint Verdaguer (1845-1902), widely acclaimed in Catalonia and throughout Spain since the last quarter of the nineteenth century, lies not only in his masterful epics of Spain and Catalonia—*L'Atlàntida* and *Canigó*—but also in his splendid lyric poetry that effectively tapped the popular sentiment of his day. Further, the success of his works gave the nineteenth-century Catalan literary renaissance, the Renaixença, the burst of vitality needed to unleash the literary potential of the Catalan language at a critical moment in its history. At the same time, enthusiasm for Verdaguer's works abroad signaled the existence of a literature that, despite its renown in the Middle Ages, had for centuries ceased to exist for the rest of Europe; the triumph of *L'Atlàntida* at the 1877 Jocs Florals (Floral Games, medieval literary competitions that had been revived in Barcelona in 1859) spotlighted not only Verdaguer but the Catalan Renaixença itself, redoubling its strength and reach. Embraced by the Church as the ideal man of letters and by writers of other renascent non-nation-state literatures such as Frédéric Mistral of Provence, Verdaguer enjoyed a rapid international reception of his works, despite the loss of support resulting from his bitter conflict with the Catholic hierarchy in the mid-1890s. Thirteen of Verdaguer's works have been translated into about a dozen languages, totaling some one hundred editions. After medieval poet and philosopher Ramon Llull and fifteenth-century writer Joanot Martorell (author of *Tirant lo Blanc*), Verdaguer is probably the most widely translated of Catalan authors.

It may seem surprising that until now very little of Verdaguer has been available to English readers. The translation of *L'Atlàntida* into English by

Verdaguer's Irish contemporary William Bonaparte-Wyse was left unfinished with the death of the translator; perhaps the fact that Wyse had undertaken the task discouraged others. In any event, as Harold Bloom—reader of Verdaguer in French and German—remarked in an interview commemorating Verdaguer at the centennial of his death (2002), translating Verdaguer into English can only restore to a major figure in the Western literary tradition the place he rightfully held a century ago.

Life

Jacint Verdaguer i Santaló was born on 17 May 1845 in the village of Folgueroles, near Vic, a county capital in provincial Catalonia some forty-five miles from Barcelona and seat of an extensive Catholic diocese. The third of eight children (of whom only three survived), he grew up in a modest family that valued learning. His father, who worked as a brick mason and farmer, and his mother in particular, a deeply religious woman, earmarked the young Jacint for seminary studies, commonly expected of a son who under the system of primogeniture must make his livelihood outside the family. So at age ten the boy began his studies at the seminary, walking

3. Can Tona (postcard, 1945). Courtesy of the Biblioteca de Catalunya.

the three miles to and from Vic each day. There, at age fifteen, he began showing an active interest in literature and writing his first poems. Classes in rhetoric and poetics opened up to him the world of classic literature in Greek and Latin, the great European writers, and the Spanish baroque. Later he would discover the French Romantics; meanwhile, throughout his youth, he gleaned a remarkable wealth of popular prosody and lore from his vital surroundings. Verdaguer lived with his family until age seventeen, then took up residence at Can Tona, a farmhouse on the road to Vic where the householders often employed a student of modest means to instruct younger children in the family and help out on the farm.

Verdaguer's earliest compositions were poems of love, Christian devotion, and satire. Soon he began work on poems of broader scope, such as the epic *Dos màrtirs de ma pàtria* (Two Christian Martyrs of Ausona), published in Vic in 1865, and *Colom* (Columbus), unfinished but later developed into *L'Atlàntida* (Atlantis, 1878). In 1865 and 1866 Verdaguer was awarded prizes at the Jocs Florals in Barcelona, Catalonia's foremost literary competition and springboard to renown for aspiring authors. The awards bolstered his dedication to writing and put him in contact with leading scholars, poets, and critics of the day such as Manuel Milà i Fontanals, Marià Aguiló, and others who advised and encouraged him. To be sure, the Renaixença, the cultural revival ushering in the modern age of Catalan literature, was still getting under way. No great work or author of remarkable talent had yet emerged—that rank to be earned by Verdaguer some years later. In 1867 Verdaguer founded l'Esbart de Vic (the Vic Group) with other literary-minded friends; the group held meetings and readings (modeled on the Félibrige, the linguistic-literary revival movement launched in Provence in 1854) at the fountain they dubbed "the Willow" near Can Tona. Meanwhile, Verdaguer continued at the seminary in preparation for the priesthood.

Verdaguer was ordained on 24 September 1870 and assigned as parish priest to the church in Vinyoles d'Orís, a small village a few miles north of Vic. Thereafter, while maintaining a full schedule of churchly duties, he advanced his poetic production on three fronts, composing devotional poetry of popular stamp, writing mystical poetry, and pursuing his poem of Atlantis begun some years earlier. These were creative but difficult years. The country was torn by civil war (the third of the Carlist Wars), and Vinyoles d'Orís happened to be situated on the line dividing the warring sides; at one point Verdaguer narrowly escaped being shot to death by a band of Liberals. Finally, suffering severe cephalalgias, Verdaguer was obliged to give up his parochial assignment. Seeking a cure for his health problem, no doubt aggravated by isolation from literary hubs and friends—most of whom lived in Barcelona—he spent part of 1873 and 1874 seeing doctors in Barcelona and living in bare subsistence. Thanks to friends, he was assigned the post of ship's chaplain for the Transatlantic Company and set sail in late 1874. During the next two years he made nine crossings to Cuba and Puerto Rico, then Spanish colonies. In addition to recovering his health, Verdaguer all but finished his epic poem *L'Atlàntida* and came into the good graces of the López family, owners of the Transatlantic Company, into whose service he entered as family chaplain protected by Antonio López, the first marquis of Comillas. At the death of the marquis in 1883, Verdaguer would pass into the service of his son Claudi. Under their patronage, Verdaguer made Barcelona his home and succeeded in reconciling his twofold vocation of priest and writer.

The marquis, a financier who possessed the largest personal fortune in Spain, was a powerful player and kinsman to both the Spanish aristocracy and the wealthy Barcelona bourgeoisie, wielding influence at every turn: the monarchy, the wheels of government, Vatican diplomacy, the business world, and the banks. (He was also father-in-law to Eusebi Güell, patron of Antoni Gaudí.) Between the marquis and the poet there developed a perfect symbiosis, recalling the patron-artist couplings of the Renaissance. The millionaire aristocrat shone brightly in society at home and abroad with the dazzle of the great poet taken under his wing; the poet, in turn, gave himself over to his creative labor, basking in the prestige added by his protector.

With the triumph of *L'Atlàntida* at the 1877 Jocs Florals in Barcelona, Verdaguer established himself as the towering figure of the Renaixença. He traveled often with his patrons throughout Spain, mingling with Spain's royal family. Soon he would travel throughout Europe (France, Switzerland, Germany, Italy, Russia) and then to the Balearic Islands, North Africa, and the Holy Land. During summers he would enjoy long holidays, walking the Catalan Pyrenees to become intimately acquainted with their spirit-stirring landscape and lore.

Between 1877 and 1889, the most productive years of his career, Verdaguer published *Idil·lis i cants místics* (Idylls and Mystic Songs, 1879), *Llegenda de Montserrat* (Legend of Montserrat, 1880), *Cançons de Montserrat* (Songs of Montserrat, 1880), *Caritat* (Charity, 1885), *Canigó* (Mount Canigó, 1886), *Lo somni de sant Joan: Llegenda del Sagrat Cor de Jesús* (The Dream of Saint John: Legend of the Sacred Heart of Jesus, 1887), *Excursions i viatges* (Excursions and Travels, 1887), *Pàtria* (Country, 1888), *Dietari d'un pelegrí a Terra Santa* (Diary of a Pilgrim in the Holy Land, 1889), and others. Having attained renown and recognition as Catalonia's leading poet and being well regarded throughout all Spain, Verdaguer in-

4. The yatch *El Vanadis*, on which Verdaguer accompanied the López and Güell families and friends in the Mediterranean in 1883 (photo, nineteenth century).

volved himself in numerous projects of religious, patriotic, and literary character, taking an especially active role in the recovery of the waning prestige of the Catholic Church. At the same time, he took part in the pro-Catalan social resurgence without involving himself directly in politics; nor, to his credit, did he ever act out of self-interest, as he turned down both a canonicate at Barcelona's cathedral and a royal chaplainship.

In 1886, in the wake of his pilgrimage to Palestine, Verdaguer began suffering a personal crisis that compelled him to turn his life around and, all but giving up writing completely, to pursue a path of holy living—more prayer, fasting, confession, and almsgiving. When, in carrying out his duties as almoner for the marquis, he saw that the charitable allotments failed to meet the needs he confronted, he tried to fill the gap by digging into his own pockets. Separately, he came into contact with a group of fervent devotees who were privy to supernatural visions and organized unauthorized exorcisms. Verdaguer, drawn to the group, was thereby linked to practices that were distasteful to his patron Claudi López, the second marquis of Comillas. Finally, anxious to cut his ties with the man whose unorthodox associations might besmirch his good name, the marquis enlisted the cooperation of the bishops of Barcelona and Vic to have Verdaguer sent away from Barcelona, on the pretext he needed a rest.

Bishop Morgades of Vic, Verdaguer's immediate superior, reassigned him to the church at La Gleva, some five miles outside Vic. There he took up writing once again, only to realize, little by little, that he had fallen out of favor and was in fact *confined* to La Gleva. To make matters worse, Verdaguer had run out of money and was unable to pay back his creditors for the purchase of a piece of property in Vallcarca on the outskirts of Barcelona, where his unorthodox friends met. After two years of isolation at La Gleva, Verdaguer, in defiance of his superior, returned to Barcelona to take up residence at the home of Deseada Martínez, widow of a friend, whose daughter was among those who saw visions. This family—former beneficiaries of the marquis—added to Verdaguer's problems.

The bishop took vigorous measures, suspending Verdaguer's duties and functions as a priest. Verdaguer counterattacked with two series of articles, *Un sacerdot calumniat* (A Priest Slandered, 1895) and *Un sacerdot perseguit* (A Priest Persecuted, 1897), published in Barcelona by the left-leaning press and brought together under the single title *En defensa pròpia* (In Self-Defense, 1895; later expanded to include the second series), in which he accused his persecutors of plotting his downfall. The plotters were Bishop Morgades, Claudi López, lifelong friend Jaume Collell, and attorney Narcís Verdaguer i Callís, the poet's cousin. The ensuing controversy sparked by the highly publicized Verdaguer-Morgades clash sent repercussions rippling throughout Spain and abroad, polarizing Catalan public opinion into two camps: those in favor of Verdaguer and those against. Allegations were made against Verdaguer's sanity—including a medical report made public—and his moral integrity was called into question because he lived with the Duran widow (Deseada Martínez) and her family.

Most of Verdaguer's friends in the Church turned away from him, as did a considerable part of the Catalan literary movement. His economic situation desperate, Verdaguer was shut out from literary, social, and ecclesiastic life. Despite attempts by various interests (including the Vatican) at reconciliation, the breach remained unhealed. The staunchly devout Verdaguer, convinced of his innocence, believed himself unjustly persecuted and refused to submit to the bishop. The bishop, a leading figure both in Catalonia's Catholic Church and among pro-Catalan conservatives, would settle for nothing less than full capitulation.

The matter was finally put to rest in 1897 in Madrid, thanks largely to the Augustinian friars at El Escorial, who arranged an agreement whereby Verdaguer signed a statement acknowledging the bishop's authority and apologizing for any harm done to the Church, while the bishop agreed to restore Verdaguer's functions as an active priest—now under the jurisdiction of the bishop of Barcelona.

Verdaguer was assigned to the Bethlehem church on La Rambla, located, as it turns out, just in front of the Comillas residence, Palau Moja, though the marquis now lived in Madrid most of the time. Still burdened with debts and with his author's rights impounded, Verdaguer found himself having to supplement his stipend with extra duties such as officiating funerals. Above all, he threw himself into literary activity with renewed vigor, writing several more volumes (some of which were never published), editing three literary magazines, publishing articles, presiding over competitions, and socializing in literary circles. Still, he never recovered all his former friendships nor entirely reclaimed his privileged place in Catalan letters. He now worked mostly with young writers, particularly the *modernistes*, who saw in Verdaguer the misunderstood genius spurned by bourgeois society. Such a vision inspired Santiago Rusiñol's play *El místic* (The Mystic, 1904) and Benito Pérez Galdós's *Nazarín* (Nazarene, 1895), which appeared as a film directed by Luis Buñuel in 1958.

Aged before his time and his health failing, Verdaguer fell seriously ill in March 1902, probably with tuberculosis, and was taken to Vil·la Joana, a house in Vallvidrera, in the hills above Barcelona, where he died on 10 June. After lying in state in the hall of Consell de Cent (where he had once received his first prizes), Verdaguer's body was transported to the cemetery at Montjuïc overlooking Barcelona and the sea. Along the way, 300,000 mourners turned out to bid farewell—the most ever in Barcelona—a consummating spontaneous testimony to the huge popularity of Catalonia's national poet.

Verdaguer's Works

Written over a period of some forty years, Verdaguer's essentially Romantic literary production consists primarily of more than thirty volumes of poetry (including those published posthumously), several works of excellent prose, and various prose and verse translations. Works left unpublished during Verdaguer's lifetime have been appearing since his death, yet among the thousands of pages of extant manuscripts are numerous works of poetry and prose which—some completed, others unfinished—have yet to appear in print. Topping it all off are his more than fifteen hundred letters, most of them published.

Verdaguer's works are usually divided into three stages. These stages, summarized below, can be followed in further detail in the headnotes to the sections of this volume.

Early Works (1860–78)

Verdaguer probably penned his first poems at age fifteen. At the seminary in Vic he dabbled briefly in humorous and satirical poetry, a sample of which survives under the title "Goigs de Sant Taló" (Praises to Sant Taló), where Sant Taló (Saint Heel) derives from the poet's second surname, Santaló. He soon began composing pastoral and amatory poetry of the popular variety—some compiled in the posthumous *Jovenívoles* (Poems of Youth, 1925)—notably *Amors d'en Jordi i na Guideta* (Loves of Jordi and Guideta), written in 1865, in which Verdaguer imitates Frédéric Mistral's long poem *Mirèio*. When ordained a priest, he gave up amatory poetry and hid the manuscripts; luckily, they were not destroyed. He also began to write religious and patriotic poetry during this stage—winning prizes at the Jocs Florals in 1865 and 1866—and his first epic poem, *Dos màrtirs de ma pàtria* (Two Christian Martyrs of Ausona, 1865), composed in rhyme royal and dedicated to Vic's legendary saints, Llucià and Marcià. During this same period he also drafted his early versions of *L'Atlàntida* (Atlantis, 1878), one of which, submitted to the Jocs Florals in 1868, won no prize. Finally, he wrote the unfinished *Colom* (Columbus) and several autobiographic essays.

Once ordained, Verdaguer focused on religious poetry (both popular and refined in form), historical and patriotic poetry, and his epic *L'Atlàntida*. Returning home after two years' steaming across the Atlantic as ship's chaplain (1874–76), Verdaguer had practically completed *L'Atlàntida*, which triumphed the following year at the Jocs Florals and established its author as Catalonia's foremost poet of the Renaixença. The poem, with its ten cantos embedded between an introduction and conclusion spotlighting Columbus, narrates the sinking of the mythic continent Atlantis, the formation of Spain, and the emergence of a New World. To be sure, the poem is not a heroic account in the classic sense, and the cataclysmic descriptions sometimes stifle the narrative flow. As Arthur Terry has remarked:

> The story of Hercules and the destruction of Atlantis is told to the young Columbus, so that the discovery of the New World appears to restore the cosmic unity which was broken by the legendary disaster. Read purely as a narrative, the poem has its faults: its protagonists—Hercules, Hesperis and Columbus—are insufficiently characterized, and the Columbus episode is joined awkwardly to the central myth. But the real unity of the poem, one can argue, lies deeper: in a sense, its underlying theme is power, and Verdaguer's Romantic affinities are nowhere clearer than in his attempt to fuse the pagan and Christian worlds in a pattern of cosmic retribution and renewal. (2003, 63)

Despite its flaws, Verdaguer's epic stands as a great work without precedent in Catalan literature, striking in its power of description and imagination, the originality and beauty of its images and its extraordinary use of language. Finally, with its exponential impact on its cultural context, the poem ushered in the full recovery of Catalan literature at a decisive crossroads in its history.

Verdaguer at the Height of his Powers (1879–89)

Crowning his early years and stirring up recognition both at home and abroad, *L'Atlàntida* opened the way to Verdaguer's most powerfully productive period. To accusations that *L'Atlàntida* was an unpriestly work, Verdaguer responded with a new book, *Idil·lis i cants místics* (Idylls and Mystic Songs, 1879), dispelling any doubt whether Verdaguer was Catalonia's leading religious—as well as epic—poet. The two fundamental elements that run consistently through his poetry—religion and country—combined in his next two works, published in 1880: *Llegenda de Montserrat* (Legend of Montserrat) and *Cançons de Montserrat* (Songs of Montserrat). In 1882 he published another religious poem, *Lo somni de sant Joan* (The Dream of Saint John; revised and republished in 1887), dedicated to the Sacred Heart of Jesus, one of the leading devotions of the Catholic Church. For the 1883 Jocs Florals, Verdaguer submitted one of his shortest epics, an ode titled "A Barcelona" (To Barcelona), praising the city's vitality and, *pari passu*, the vim and vigor of Catalonia's industrial bourgeoisie. The poem's high eloquence avoided the elegiac tone formerly prevalent in Catalan patriotic poetry, and its huge success prompted city hall to print 100,000 specially designed copies of the poem. In 1885 Verdaguer published the poetic anthology *Caritat* (Charity) in response to a devastating earthquake that struck Andalusia; the proceeds from this volume were added to relief funds.

In December 1885, but dated 1886, Verdaguer's second great epic appeared, closer in mold to the earlier Romantics than was *L'Atlàntida* since, somewhat reminiscent of the chanson de geste, it deals with the legendary origins of Catalonia. Like *L'Atlàntida*, however, *Canigó*—regarded as the epic poem of the mature Verdaguer—must come to terms with Catalonia's Christian and non-Christian legacies. The poem's twelve cantos and epilogue (the elegy "The Two Bell Towers") bring together a number of loosely woven narratives drawn from popular lore, legend, and history framed in a series of extraordinary descriptions of the Pyrenees Mountains. Set in the year 1000, the poem celebrates the historic birth of Catalonia symbolized in

Mount Canigó, where Christendom triumphed over pagandom (represented by fairies driven from the mountain) and, separately, where the Catalan counts launched an attack against the invading Saracens, securing Christendom's foothold in the Spanish March (Catalonia). More human and realistic in scope than *L'Atlàntida*, and despite its digressions, the poem holds together through various symmetries and alternations in meter that separate the historical drama (the fighting of battles and the founding of Sant Martí del Canigó) from a legendary tragedy (the love between the newly knighted Gentil and the shepherdess Griselda, crossed by the scheming Flordeneu, queen of the fairies). With *Canigó*, Verdaguer took on the task of writing the Catalan national epic and, at the same time, sought to overcome the flaws that critics had uncovered in his previous epic. To quote Terry once again: "Between them, *Canigó* and the *Atlàntida* represent the height of Verdaguer's achievement in the long poem. The range of their language and vocabulary are unequaled in later Catalan poetry, and their appearance in the last quarter of the nineteenth century established beyond any doubt the possibilities of Catalan as a modern literary language" (2003, 65).

During the 1880s, Verdaguer composed more devotional poems, many of which were printed on single sheets and later anthologized in *Càntics* (Songs, 1882, 1889), in addition to patriotic and civil poetry, much of which appeared in *Pàtria* (Country, 1888), containing poems written over the previous twenty-five years. Verdaguer's travels during this period gave rise to two prose volumes, *Excursions i viatges* (Excursions and Travels, 1887)—compiling his notes while traveling through Europe, North Africa, and the Pyrenees—and *Dietari d'un pelegrí a Terra Santa* (Diary of a Pilgrim in the Holy Land, 1889).

Later Works (1890–1902)

By the end of the 1880s, Verdaguer had reached the height of his literary career and enjoyed wide acclaim. Still, his worldly triumphs ended up clashing with his deep-felt need for spiritual perfection, giving rise to an overwhelming sense of dissatisfaction that touched his writing. As noted, this personal crisis would lead to his confrontation with the Church hierarchy and his patron the marquis of Comillas. Verdaguer's works published at the outset of the 1890s consisted almost entirely of his trilogy *Jesús Infant* (Child Jesus), which seems to have influenced architect Antoni Gaudí in his conceiving the idea of the Holy Family temple of Barcelona: *Natzaret* (Nazareth, 1890), *Betlem* (Bethlehem, 1891), and *La Fugida a Egipte* (The Flight to Egypt, 1893). In 1893 Verdaguer was banished to La Gleva, where at first

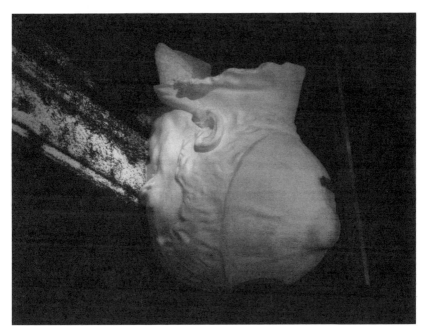

5. *Relief: Chalking with the Head*, mural and bust by Perejaume (2005) re-creating Joan Borrell i Nicolau's 1924 sculpture of Verdaguer. University of Vic.

he enjoyed the peace and quiet needed to return to his writing. But now his writing had changed. Putting aside historical and patriotic epics, he delved into religious themes, writing shorter, more intimate poems. He composed *Roser de tot l'any* (The Rose Almanac)—a collection of religious thoughts for each day of the year, which were first published weekly in the magazine *La Veu de Catalunya* (The Voice of Catalonia)—and *Veus del Bon Pastor* (Voices of the Good Shepherd), both published in 1894. The following year he moved to Barcelona, committing the breach of authority that resulted in the suspension of his duties and functions as a priest. It was during these bitter years that he wrote the series of articles collected in *En defensa pròpia* (In Self-Defense, 1895, 1897), the long poem *Sant Francesc* (Saint Francis, 1895)—the saint's exemplary suffering served as comfort—and *Flors del Calvari* (Flowers of Calvary, 1896), subtitled *Llibre de consols* (Book of Solace), in which a striking depiction of Verdaguer's suffering gives way to the realization that his Christian values are being put to the test.

Reinstated as a full-fledged priest early in 1898, Verdaguer redoubled his literary activity in hopes of redressing his worn prestige. He collaborated with a number of publications, took part in social and literary events, worked on new books and revised old ones—for example, bringing all his Montserrat poems (except for the *Legend*) into a single volume titled *Montserrat: Llegendari, cançons, odes* (Montserrat: Legends, Songs, Odes, 1899)—published others, such as *Santa Eulària* (Saint Eulària, 1899, sketching the life and martyrdom of Barcelona's patron saint), *Aires del Montseny* (Airs of Montseny, 1901, containing poems written between 1871 and 1900 on civil and autobiographic themes), and *Flors de Maria* (Flowers of Mary, 1902), published just before the poet's death.

A number of volumes Verdaguer prepared before his death appeared posthumously: *Al cel* (To Heaven, 1903), *Eucarístiques* (Eucharist Poems, 1904), *Càntic dels càntics* (Song of Songs, 1907), *Perles del "Llibre d'Amic e d'Amat" d'en Ramon Llull* (Pearls of the *Book of the Lover and the Beloved* by Ramon Llull, 1908), and, much later, *Brins d'espígol* (Sprigs of Lavender, 1977). Various publishers have come out with volumes of any number of Verdaguer's unfinished works from his youth or his later years, including *Rondalles* (Folk Tales, 1905), *Colom* (Columbus, 1907), *Jovenívoles* (Poems of Youth, 1925), *Barcelonines* (Barcelona Poems, 1925), and *Escrits inèdits* (Unpublished Writings, 1958). Previously unpublished works by Verdaguer have appeared as recently as 2006 or were in preparation as this book went to press: *Jesús-Amor* (Jesus-Love), *Cor de Jesús* (Heart of Jesus), *Espines i flors* (Thorns and Flowers), and *Barcelona* (Barcelona).

General Features of Verdaguer's Works

Epic Poetry

The nineteenth century confirmed the novel as foremost among literary genres, seen as the evolutionary result of the epic and, indeed, as the modern epic. Given this, it may seem puzzling that Verdaguer would take on the troublesome task of writing epic poetry in Catalan at all. The answer lies partly in Verdaguer's literary upbringing and partly in the situation of Catalan literature during his time. In the academic environment at the seminary in Vic during the early years of the Renaixença (the nineteenth-century Catalan cultural revival), epic poetry was highly esteemed. We know that Verdaguer read Virgil's *Aeneid*, Torquato Tasso's *Gerusalemme liberata*, John Milton's *Paradise Lost*, and Friedrich Gottlieb Klopstock's *Der Messias*. He was also familiar with more contemporary authors such as Johann Wolfgang von Goethe, Frédéric Mistral, Sir Walter Scott, Alphonse de Lamartine, Victor Hugo, and François-René Chateaubriand, all of whom had taken steps toward revitalizing the epic. As for the Catalan context, there prevailed the idea that any full-fledged national literature needed some sort of epic to stand as an artistic and linguistic landmark. A few Catalan Romantics had already attempted the task without result, and one of the most influential thinkers of his day, Professor Manuel Milà i Fontanals of the Universitat de Barcelona, had advanced the idea that the epic could no longer be fashioned along classic lines and must be adapted into a less ambitious genre such as the simple narrative poem, heroic or idyllic.

At first Verdaguer, following Milà, emulated Mistral in composing the long narrative (over a thousand lines in length) *Amors d'en Jordi i na*

6. Scene from *L'Atlàntida* by Antoni Vilanova, published in *La Llumanera*, New York (1878). Courtesy of the Biblioteca de Catalunya.

Guideta, which he never published. At the same time he wrote—following the neoclassic model—an epic story set in Vic during Roman times, *Dos màrtirs de ma pàtria*, published in 1865. From that year until 1868 he made an unsuccessful attempt to write a Renaissance-style epic about the emergence of the New World, *Colom* (Columbus). This would be the germ of *L'Atlàntida* (1877), written over ten years and following the classic model, which is considered the most enduring, though as Pere Farrés (2002) points out, certain Romantic techniques were added, such as the incorporation of separate poems and the chorus in canto 7. The epic *L'Atlàntida* sings, as was de rigueur, of mythic origins, though of the entire Iberian Peninsula rather than a single nation. Again, the resounding triumph of the poem at home and abroad assured the success of the Renaixença's overarching aim: Catalan literature's long-awaited recovery.

Soon afterward Verdaguer wrote *Llegenda de Montserrat* (1880), continuing the process of adapting the epic form begun in *L'Atlàntida*, now modeled on the "Romantic legend" popular in his day and taking as theme the traditional origin of the Montserrat monastery, which along with the mountain on which it perched had become a powerful symbol of Catalan identity. Verdaguer then spent the first half of the 1880s conceiving and writing what for many critics would be his finest epic: *Canigó* (1886). Singing of the birth of Catalonia in both national and Christian terms thanks to the defeat of the Saracens and, subsequently, the unseating of the fairies inhabiting Mount Canigó, this epic is unique in structure, composed as an extraordinary ensemble of shorter poems of metric variety—separate from each other yet blending eloquently into a single, superbly woven long poem. With *Canigó* Verdaguer reached the topmost summit of Catalan epic poetry, confirming his place as Catalonia's outstanding nineteenth-century poet.

Civil Poetry

Despite the fact that in Verdaguer's poetry faith and country are always closely interblended, a number of his poems appear unmotivated by religion. These works, which Joaquim Molas has categorized as "civil poetry" (1986, 265–79), are found especially in two of Verdaguer's books: *Pàtria* (1888) and *Aires del Montseny* (1901). The Verdaguerian notion of *pàtria* (homeland or country) can be understood in the most immediate, traditional, and etymological sense of the word: the country of one's fathers. To be sure, this country was for Verdaguer, as distinguished poet and critic Carles Riba once noted, "a work and gift of God" (1922, 20). Within this notion are contained all those aspects that, in his view, come together to form a particular country: landscape, inhabitants, history, religion, and myth.

It is important to define the territorial limits of the Verdaguerian homeland. On one level, it comprises all the historically linked Catalan-speaking areas. This notion of Catalan identity underlies all Verdaguer's works, and in certain poems in *Pàtria* it is stated with an unequivocal ring not always heard among Verdaguer's contemporaries. This is not to say that Verdaguer ever suggested anything beyond linguistic, historical, and cultural unity, together with a desire for a resurgent awareness of identity. The focal point of Verdaguer's civil poetry is Vic and its surrounding area, and further, Catalonia proper (including French Catalonia), extending outward to all Catalan-speaking territories only in the historical and cultural sense (including also the former kingdom of Aragon) or else within the politicohistorical apparatus of the Spanish State, where a shared destiny—especially religious—enters into play.

Two prevailing concepts arise in connection with Verdaguer's notion of *pàtria*: history and *enyorança*, or longing for homeland. History comes to the fore particularly in the early poems, where patriotic and bellicose spirits may rub shoulders, taking aim either at France or at Castile, depending on the case. Verdaguer will later take the edge off this historical zeal (short of stamping it out altogether) in his mature works and revisions of early poems. Cast in the Romantic mold, Verdaguer devoted poems to Catalan medieval history but also undertook contemporary historical topics laden with ideological import, as in his two long poems depicting Barcelona as a symbol of the whole of Catalonia: "A Barcelona" (To Barcelona, 1883) and "La palmera de Jonqueres" (The Palm of Jonqueres, 1881). These poems represent, as Verdaguer saw it, opposing visions of Catalonia under the Bourbon Restoration. Thus "A Barcelona" sings optimistically of an industrious, flourishing Catalonia and its European-style bourgeoisie, while "La palmera de Jonqueres" (not included in this selection) depicts an altogether different state of affairs. Verdaguer wrote "La palmera de Jonqueres" upon learning that the city's reputedly oldest living palm tree had died after being removed from the Jonqueres convent; the poem alludes allegorically to the destruction of Barcelona's religious buildings during the social upheavals of the nineteenth century. Verdaguer attributes this destruction to revolutionary acts ("torches" and "rifles") and the "golden calves" of progress (where convents and monasteries once stood one now sees streets, squares, theaters, and brothels). Of all the poems in *Pàtria*, "La palmera de Jonqueres" is the most explicitly ideological, elegiac in evoking the passing of the old world to the march of nineteenth-century social and political change alongside the growing concern in Catholic quarters to recover what may be restored of the old order while vigorously adapting to the new.

In addition to history, the sentiment of *enyorança*, or longing for homeland, arises as a distinctly Romantic element throughout Verdaguer's works. Closely linked to memory and dream, it projects over Catalonia's past (particularly the splendor of the medieval period), the poet's past (childhood and youth), his native landscape (both Verdaguer's home county of Osona and all of Catalonia), and, in the mystic sense, the "celestial paradise." The landscape itself is a powerful Verdaguerian theme, particularly in connection with memory; other motifs touch on tradition, crafts in decline, prominent figures in the Church, and Marian devotions throughout Catalonia. Finally, Verdaguer's handling of patriotic themes generally stands above that of his contemporaries or previous Romantics, whose grandiose eloquence often rings cumbrous beside Verdaguer's effective rhetorical balance and engaging narrative flow.

Religious Poetry

From the moment Verdaguer resolved to become a priest, he devoted the bulk of his poetry to religious themes, writing in the service of the Catholic Church. His religious production is vast and uneven and was widely disseminated among the faithful by means of circulars, leaflets, pamphlets and holy cards in addition to book printings. Verdaguer responded to the need of the Church for instructive, devout, and vindicative religious literature by writing a vast amount of such poetry, though it has not withstood the test of time as well as his other works. Nevertheless, there is more to Verdaguer's religious poetry than devotional and instructive works of this sort (these were often written for a particular purpose such as some recent controversy, canonization, or clerical initiative). A number of Verdaguer's religious works clearly rise above the rest in ambition and stature.

As mentioned earlier, the appearance of *Idil·lis i cants místics* (1879) in the wake of the triumph of *L'Atlàntida* confirmed Verdaguer as a religious poet of accomplishment, as renowned critic Marcelino Menéndez Pelayo affirmed before fellow members of the Real Academia Española (see corresponding headnote in this selection). Verdaguer's mystic poetry, though influenced by the Song of Solomon, Ramon Llull, Thomas à Kempis, St. John of the Cross, and St. Teresa, takes up where these left off by developing and updating the genre. Other of Verdaguer's outstanding religious works from the same period, though not mystic, include the two volumes written for the 1880 millennial celebrations of the founding of Montserrat monastery

(*Cançons de Montserrat* and *Llegenda de Montserrat*) and *Caritat* (1885), the volume of miscellaneous poems whose proceedings went to relief funds for victims of the earthquake that had just struck Andalusia.

Over the next few years Verdaguer published a number of major religious volumes conceived as long poems, though loosely structured, ideological in character, and connected with modern devotions promoted by the Church such as *Lo somni de sant Joan* (1887) and the Holy Family trilogy *Jesús Infant* (1890–93) or, alternatively, more intimist such as *Sant Francesc* (1895). Finally, with the hardship resulting from Verdaguer's confrontation with the Church hierarchy there emerged a new religious poetry of particular interest that Pere Ramírez Molas has described thus: "The static, idyllic contemplation faded away [and] the dynamic tensions gave rise to an intimate expression, the yearning of the *homo viator* [wayfaring man] who, finding no haven in a hostile world, nor even in . . . the tortured self, seeks refuge and solace in divine love's transcendence" (see J. Molas 1986, 283). The finest among these works are *Roser de tot l'any* (1894), *Flors del Calvari* (1896)—the most striking example of the poet's personal drama—*Flors de Maria* (1902), and the posthumous *Al cel* (1903), *Eucarístiques* (1904), and *Perles del "Llibre d'Amic e d'Amat" d'en Ramon Llull* (1908).

The Verdaguerian Legacy

Verdaguer stands as the towering nineteenth-century Catalan author and one of Catalonia's all-time classics. To his outstanding literary production must be added his historic role in consolidating the Renaixença and providing the linguistic foundations for subsequent Catalan writing. His prestige in the world of letters prompted international recognition of renascent Catalan literature. Still, though Verdaguer continues to spark interest and delight readers to this day, he remains a controversial figure. Not only does his clash with Church authorities raise concern for some, his style has been superseded by more recent trends in poetry. Political and ideological factors also enter the picture. In 1924 when King Alfonso XIII and dictator General Primo de Rivera (representing the upper ecclesiastic and military echelons) unveiled a monument to Verdaguer in Barcelona, the populace boycotted the event, though a widely representative delegation of Catalan writers paid homage to Verdaguer by placing a wreath on his tomb with the message "To the Rev. J. Verdaguer. From his own." This double-edged appropriation of Verdaguer by Spain's prevailing powers on the one hand and the pro-Catalan base on the other resurfaced in 1945 at the centennial of the poet's birth. As the powers-that-be paid public homage, the Catalan

7. Five-hundred-peseta bill (1971, no longer in circulation) with Verdaguer wearing a *barretina* (obverse) and the French town of Vernet below Mount Canigó (reverse).

cultural resistance did so clandestinely, while intellectuals and politicians in exile spoke out in symbolic accord. The Francoist dictatorship, in a typical display of institutionalized cynicism, banned public use of Verdaguer's language and repressed his culture even as it paid him homage, going so far as to authorize an edition of his works in the archaic spelling (predating standard Catalan) in an attempt to treat Catalan literature as a relic of the past and demotivate new readership.

A few years later, as the fiftieth anniversary of Verdaguer's death approached, the divide between official and pro-Catalan sectors eager to embrace the bard reopened. In the wake of several published biographies, heated debate erupted regarding the precise significance of Verdaguer's life and works. During the 1950s and 1960s, interest in Verdaguer's works fell off, though the attraction to his life drama held steady. With few exceptions (such as the case of scholar and publisher Josep M. de Casacuberta), only with the return of democracy and the teaching of Catalan language and literature in elementary schools, high schools, and universities did Verdaguer again become an object of academic study and research, his works published and republished in popular and scholarly editions.

During the early twentieth century, the most dynamic and innovative circles in Catalan letters felt in some sense removed from Verdaguer. The *modernistes*, in part his contemporaries, took interest above all in Verdaguer the man, embodying the *fin-de-siècle* hero at loggerheads with bourgeois society and its stifling of the artistic spirit. They were also indebted to Verdaguer's contribution to literary language. Aesthetically, however, they felt estranged from him. Subsequent literary trends such as Noucentisme (classicist and anti-Romantic) and the avant-gardists prevalent until the 1930s passed over Verdaguer almost altogether—admiring the craftsman of prose but disregarding the poet. Yet during these years many of Verdaguer's works were published—some for the first time—including a number of collections of Verdaguer's complete works.

It is important to keep in mind that—critical assessments of all kinds aside—Verdaguer has always enjoyed immense popularity, from which stems a sort of poet-populace symbiosis that has made many of his poems (such as "L'emigrant," "El virolai," and "La mort de l'escolà") into popular songs known throughout Catalonia (though some people may have difficulty identifying the author). Musical compositions that have been written to accompany Verdaguerian poems number upward of a thousand (see F. Cortès, 1999). This, along with the hundreds of streets and avenues throughout Catalonia that bear his name and the dozens of monuments that stand in his honor, are testimonial to Verdaguer's literary and cultural achievement, his enduring popularity, and his unique place of privilege in Catalan letters.

Ramon Pinyol i Torrents

TRANSLATOR'S NOTE

Our aim has been to render Verdaguer into rhythmic, readable, modern English verse. The choice of meter and rhyme in the translations varies, as in the original works, with the form and content of each poem. For instance, consistent with the epic tone of *Canigó*, we have used iambic pentameter combined with trimeter in "La Maladeta" and blank verse in "Guisla." On the other hand, the faster-paced *Dos màrtirs de ma pàtria* uses tetrameter for Verdaguer's feminine decasyllables, and in "Discovery of the Virgin" we have used pentameter combined with tetrameter to achieve a natural narrative flow. For "The Two Bell Towers," elegiac in tone, and the sustained exaltation of the ode "To Barcelona," we have used rhyming iambic pentameter (with some metrical variation) to render Verdaguer's decasyllables in the former and, in the latter, his masterful dodecasyllabic alexandrines, feminine at the caesura (that is, with an unstressed, uncounted seventh syllable). Verdaguer uses these same alexandrines in "La Maladeta," rhyming *aabcc*, with a final half-alexandrine *b* rhyme:

> Passaren anys, passaren centúries de centúries
> abans que s'abrigassen de terra i de boscúries
> aqueixes ossamentes dels primitius gegants,
> abans que tingués molsa la penya, flors les prades,
> abans que les arbredes tinguessen aucellades,
>   les aucellades cants.

rendered in English by iambic pentameter (with some variation) and a final trimeter:

Years passed, centuries piled on centuries
Before this bone-frame of primeval giants
Dressed itself in topsoil and timberland,
Before the crags grew moss, the meadows flowers,
Before the forests filled with thronging birds,
    The thronging birds with song.

Here, and throughout the translations, internal rhyme, weak rhyme, slant
rhyme, alliteration, assonance, and other rhythmic elements combine to
balance and compensate where it has not always been possible to reproduce
the Catalan end rhyme. (Indeed the epic and narrative tradition in English
poetry does not always feature end rhyme, as in Milton, Longfellow, and
Tennyson.)

Similar criteria hold for Verdaguer's lyric poetry. The feminine decasyl-
lables of "The Harp" are rendered in iambic/trochaic tetrameter; the shorter
hexasyllables of "The Rose of Jericho" and pentasyllables of "Thorns" are
concisely rendered in English dimeter; and the modern ironic tone of "Beg-
ging," conveyed in octosyllables by Verdaguer, finds an English correspon-
dence in stanzas of alternating tetrameter/trimeter rhyming *ababcdcdee*
with final tetrameter couplets. Similar metrical considerations hold for the
Roser de tot l'any, *Sant Francesc*, and *Flors del Calvari* poems, devotional
and intimist yet surprisingly modern in tone. In "Sum vermis" Verdaguer's
desperate resolve is conveyed in blank verse, rendered in English by lines
of varying length to suggest the rhythms of ordinary speech. In the more
lyrical "By the Sea" and "What Is Poetry?" the English versions adhere
once again to fixed metrics and rhyme, and while the predominantly blank-
verse metrics of "The Milky Way" are translated into nonrhyming English
tetrameter, Verdaguer's five-line stanzas of decasyllables with fourth-line
hexasyllables in "The Moon" find their equivalent English rhythm in te-
trameter and dimeter, respectively. Finally, the heptasyllabic romance "To
a Nightingale from Vallvidrera" is rendered in English combining tetram-
eter and trimeter to convey the poet's heartfelt complaint with appropriate
concision and rhythm.

The fragments of *L'Atlàntida* translated by Verdaguer's contemporary
William Bonaparte-Wyse—reproduced here with minor revisions (see
endnotes)—have been included as testimony to the far-reaching impact of
Verdaguer's work in his day. Antoinette Ogden's translation of "A Mother's
Love" and Deems Taylor and Kurt Schindler's translation of "A Choirboy
Died" (in the endnotes) have been included for the same reason.

Not all considerations have been purely poetical. Lexical and lexico-graphic issues come into play too. The field of significations of the Catalan loanword *sardana* is narrower in English (referring only to the dance or its music), while the Catalan phrase *feien . . . la sardana* in "The Harp" con-veys the extended meaning "joined hands in play." The Catalan *barretina*, in the same poem, remains for English lexicographers an exoticism—de-spite popularization of this traditional hat by Catalan painter Salvador Dalí—and therefore appears in italics. Morphology frequently enters the picture as well; for instance, the Catalan *aucell* (bird) forms a collective noun with addition of the suffix *-ada* (*aucellada*), rendered in my transla-tion of an excerpt from *Dos màrtirs de ma pàtria* as "birdthrong" and in "La Maladeta" as "thronging birds."

George Steiner once described translating as "an exact art," which when most effective "bestows on the original *that which was already there.*" The creative challenge of the translator lies in *re*-creating the work—outside the symbolic universe from which it sprang—so that after all the semantic, syn-tactic, rhetorical, and rhythmic reshuffling it is once again seen for what it is, only now through a prism that refracts its light and disperses it in new di-rections. It is our hope that through these translations, with all their textual refraction and dispersion, English readers might catch a glimpse of many Verdaguerian rainbows.

8. Verdaguer circa 1878, at the time of the success of *L'Atlàntida*.

CHRONOLOGY ❧

1845   Birth of Jacint Verdaguer Santaló (hereafter "JV"), the third of eight children of Josep Verdaguer and Josepa Santaló, in Folgueroles (county of Osona, Barcelona province) on 17 May.

1859   Begins studies in rhetoric at the seminary in Vic, county capital and seat of an extensive Catholic diocese.

1863   Stays on at the seminary to study theology, taking up residence at Can Tona, a large farmhouse halfway between Folgueroles and Vic, where he tutors the family's children. Writes amatory poems, later collected and published posthumously as *Jovenívoles* (Poems of Youth) and *Amors d'en Jordi i na Guideta* (Loves of Jordi and Guideta).

1865   Awarded various minor prizes at the Jocs Florals in Barcelona. First work published: *Dos màrtirs de ma pàtria, o siga Llucià i Marcià* (Two Martyrs of My Fatherland, or Llucià and Marcià; in this selection, Two Christian Martyrs of Ausona).

1866   Awarded four second-place prizes at the Jocs Florals. Writes the unfinished poem *Colom* (Columbus).

1868   Submits the epic poem *L'Atlàntida enfonsada i l'Espanya naixent de ses ruïnes* (The Sinking of Atlantis and the Rise of Spain from Its Ruins) in the Jocs Florals but wins no prize. Meets Frédéric Mistral.

1870   Ordained a priest and assigned to a small rural parish, Vinyoles d'Orís, near Vic.

1873   Awarded another prize at the Jocs Florals. Publishes *Passió de Nostre Senyor Jesucrist* (Passion of Our Lord Jesus Christ). Diagnosed as suffering from "cerebral anemia."

1874   Takes up residence in Barcelona, seeking a remedy for his illness and taking part in the city's literary life. Accepts the post of ship's chaplain for the Transatlantic Company and embarks on his first crossing to the Antilles.

1876   After nine round-trip voyages across the Atlantic, his health recovered, JV completes *L'Atlàntida* (Atlantis) and determines to remain in Barcelona.

1877   Takes employment as family chaplain for Antoni López, the first marquis of Comillas and title to the largest fortune in Spain. *L'Atlàntida* triumphs at Barcelona's Jocs Florals.

1878   Publication of *L'Atlàntida* after revision. JV is received by Pope Leo XIII in Rome.

1879   Walks part of the French-Catalan Pyrenees, visiting its majestic Romanesque abbeys and conceiving his epic *Canigó* (Mount Canigó). Publishes *Idil·lis i cants místics* (Idylls and Mystic Songs).

1880   Publishes two books, *Cançons de Montserrat* (Songs of Montserrat) and *Llegenda de Montserrat* (Legend of Montserrat), for the millennial celebrations of the founding of Montserrat Abbey, Catalonia's foremost pilgrimage site and cultural symbol.

1882   Continues work on *Canigó*. Walks the central Pyrenees area and ascends its highest peak, Aneto. Publishes religious poems *Càntics* (Songs) in fascicles.

1883   Travels the coasts of Morocco and Algeria. The ode "A Barcelona" (To Barcelona) triumphs at the Jocs Florals, and Barcelona's city hall publishes 100,000 copies. JV undertakes another expedition in the Pyrenees.

1884   Travels with Count Eusebi Güell (architect Antoni Gaudí's patron and brother-in-law to the second marquis of Comillas) throughout central and northern Europe. Continues working on *Canigó*. Turns down a canonicate at the cathedral of Barcelona.

1885   Publishes *Caritat* (Charity), a volume of poems whose proceeds add to relief funds for the victims of the Andalusia earthquake. Publishes a prose translation in Catalan of Mistral's long narrative poem *Nerto*.

1886   Publishes his second great epic, *Canigó: Llegenda pirinaica del temps de la Reconquesta* (Mount Canigó: Pyrenean Legend of the Days of the Reconquista), marking the highest point in JV's career. Makes a pilgrimage to the Holy Land, traveling through Palestine, Lebanon, Syria, and Egypt.

1887   Publishes two new books: *Lo somni de sant Joan: Llegenda del Sagrat Cor de Jesús* (The Dream of Saint John: Legend of the Sacred Heart of Jesus), with an accompanying self-translation into Spanish, and *Excursions i viatges* (Excursions and Travels), JV's first volume of prose.

1888   Publishes *Pàtria* (Country), a collection of poems (some of which had already appeared, others previously unpublished) categorized as civil poetry. Publishes his second book of prose, *Dietari d'un pelegrí a Terra Santa* (Diary of a Pilgrim in the Holy Land), in which the spiritual crisis he will undergo in the following years begins to suggest itself.

1889   Intensification of JV's spiritual life. Publishes *Col·lecció de càntics religiosos pel poble* (Collection of Religious Songs for the Populace).

1890   Publishes *Jesús Infant: Natzaret* (The Child Jesus: Nazareth). Comes into contact with peripheral Catholic activists who perform exorcisms.

1891   Publishes *Jesús Infant: Betlem* (The Child Jesus: Bethlehem).

1893   The bishop of Barcelona expels JV from the diocese, and the second marquis of Comillas terminates his services as family chaplain and almoner. The bishop of Vic confines him to the sanctuary at La Gleva. Publishes *La fugida a Egipte* (The Flight to Egypt), completing the Child Jesus trilogy.

1894   Publishes two new volumes: *Roser de tot l'any: Dietari de pensaments religiosos* (The Rose Almanac: Diary of Religious Thoughts) and a collection of religious songs, *Veus del Bon Pastor* (Voices of the Good Shepherd). Visits Barcelona and Mallorca, temporarily breaking his confinement at La Gleva.

1895   Abandons La Gleva and takes up residence in Barcelona at the home of the widow of a late friend and her children. An ecclesiastic tribunal in Vic suspends JV's duties and functions as a priest. Refusing to submit to the bishop's authority, JV denounces his mistreatment in the Barcelona press through a series of articles known as *En defensa pròpia* (In Self-Defense). Publishes a new book of poetry, *Sant Francesc* (Saint Francis).

1896   Publishes *Flors del Calvari: Llibre de consols* (Flowers of Calvary: Book of Solace). Without means of livelihood and pursued by creditors, JV sells his copyrights. Writes *La Pomerola* (The Shadbush), a long poem rebuffed at the Jocs Florals.

1897   The Verdaguer affair sharply divides public opinion at home and abroad. JV writes a second series of articles in the press. Travels to Madrid, where the Augustinian friars at El Escorial intervene on his behalf, arranging a compromise between JV and the bishop of Vic.

1898   JV's duties and functions as a priest are fully restored. Given permission to take up residence in Barcelona under the authority of its bishop, he devotes himself to writing with renewed vigor. Republishes Montserrat poems, adding new ones, under the title *Montserrat*.

1899   Publishes *Santa Eulària: Poemet* (Saint Eulària: A Short Poem). Steps up literary activities and edits the magazine *La Creu del Montseny* (The Cross of Montseny).

1900   Founds and edits the weekly magazine *Lo Pensament Català* (Catalan
        Thought). Prepares new books, anthologies, and republished editions.

1901   Publishes *Aires del Montseny* (Airs of Montseny). His tableau *L'adoració
        dels pastors* (The Adoration of the Shepherds) is performed.

1902   Publication of JV's last work during his life, *Flors de Maria* (Flowers of
        Mary). Dies of tuberculosis on 10 June at Vil·la Joana, house in the Coll-
        serola hills overlooking Barcelona.

EPIC POEMS

9. Cover of Melcior de Palau's Spanish translation of *L'Atlàntida*, designed by
Lluís Domènech i Montaner (1878). Courtesy of the Biblioteca de Catalunya.

FROM

L'Atlàntida
(Atlantis, 1878)

The spark set off in Verdaguer's imagination by the ancient tale of the de-
struction of Atlantis and, at the same time, Columbus's first voyage and the
emergence of an uncharted world to the west began to take poetic form in
his days as a seminarian in Vic. As noted by Pere Farrés (2002, 15–16), the
lost continent of Atlantis was first depicted by Verdaguer in *Colom* (Colum-
bus, begun in 1866 but abandoned the following year) and developed into
a separate poem submitted in Barcelona's 1868 Jocs Florals under the title
L'Atlàntida enfonsada i l'Espanya naixent de ses ruïnes (The Sinking of At-
lantis and the Rise of Spain from Its Ruins). The poem won no prize.

Nine years later, after doing long and substantial revision—the poem's
length more than doubled, its five cantos expanded to ten—and two years
serving as chaplain on the transatlantic ships of his patron and employer
Antoni López, the first marquis of Comillas, Verdaguer received the
"Extraordinary Prize" for *L'Atlàntida* (Atlantis) in the 1877 Jocs Florals.
Hailed as the epic that would restore Catalan literature's place among the
literatures of Europe after a hiatus of some three centuries (Frédéric Mistral
compared it to Milton's *Paradise Lost* and Lamartine's *La chute d'un ange*),
the poem was slated for editing and publication (together with a separate
Spanish prose translation by Melcior de Palau), expenses to be paid by
the marquis—to whom Verdaguer dedicated the poem. With a view to this
first edition (1878), Verdaguer made significant revisions, most notably—
on the advice of friend and fellow clergyman Jaume Collell—the recasting
of canto 7 (displacing its original verses into cantos 6 and 8) under a new
title, "Chorus of Greek Isles," which came to be regarded by many, such as
renowned Spanish critic Marcelino Menéndez Pelayo (1856–1912), as the

poem's best. Subsequent editions of *L'Atlàntida* (1886, 1897) entailed no significant revisions.

L'Atlàntida, Verdaguer's foundational epic of Spain, fuses the classic heroism of Hercules with the Judeo-Christian providentialism culminating in Columbus's first voyage. On the one hand, the poem recasts Hercules' labors associated with the Iberian Peninsula—the encounter with Geryon, Hesperides and the golden apples (in Verdaguer's account an orange tree), the opening of the Strait of Gibraltar, and, in addition, the founding of Barcelona. Moreover, by wedlock with Hesperis (the widowed queen of Atlantis), Hercules appears as the progenitor of a new Iberian people. On the other hand, Columbus's bridging of the Atlantic opens new horizons for the spread of Catholicism, which, following Ricard Torrents, is "the first ideology of globalization" (2004, 105). With the destruction of Atlantis, providentialism holds sway even in the pre-Christian punishment the gods inflict on the Atlanteans for presuming to rival them; in his ideological synthesis of the ancient classic and the Judeo-Christian traditions into one universe where the latter prevails, Verdaguer gives voice to Jehovah (4.145–48):

> I joined the continents, drawing back the waters,
> So in my glory all might gather in one song;
> But to my grief, their sin compels them to be scattered;
> What have I done, Eve's children, that you should do me wrong?

With the continents united once more by Columbus, the "pattern of cosmic retribution and renewal" is, following Arthur Terry (2003, 63), now complete, and Spain, as Farrés observes, has fulfilled "[its] destiny in the transmittance of Christianity" (2003, 70).

Verdaguer implants this fusion of classic and Christian elements into the very structure of the poem. Following the example of the embedded narrative used in the *Odyssey*, the *Aeneid*, and Lamartine's *La chute d'un ange*, the "Introduction" relates how a young man who turns out to be Columbus is rescued from shipwreck off the Portuguese coast by an aging hermit, who tells him the story of Atlantis; cantos 1 through 10 constitute the hermit's narrative, ordered around the central figure of Hercules; in "Conclusion: Columbus," after Isabella's curious dream, Columbus's westward-sailing ships are seen by the hermit, whose heart is put at ease.

The ten cantos (2,256 lines) forming the bulk of the poem are written mostly in quatrains of dodecasyllabic alexandrines that are feminine at the caesura (that is, with an unstressed, uncounted seventh syllable) and feature alternating feminine-masculine (*abab*) rhyme. However, for the "Chorus of

Greek Isles" (canto 7) Verdaguer used longer, more lyrical poem–like stanzas of varying length featuring decasyllables in combination with hexasyllables, feminine throughout, and a variety of rhyme schemes, for instance, *abaabbcdecedfgffg*. Other passages in cantos 3, 6, and 10 feature decasyllables combined either with hexasyllables or pentasyllables to highlight discursive or thematic shifts. "Introduction" (156 lines) features six-line stanzas of decasyllables rhyming *aabccb* (*a* and *c* lines are feminine, *b* are masculine); "Conclusion: Columbus" (179 lines) takes up once again this same decasyllabic pattern in six-line stanzas, except for the seventeen stanzas of "Isabella's Dream," which feature quatrains of heptasyllables alternating feminine-masculine *abab* rhyme and a singular final seven-line stanza rhyming *aabcccb*, that is, with an additional triplet deferring the completion of the final couplet.

Numerous translations of *L'Atlàntida* soon appeared in several European languages. After the 1878 Spanish prose translation came the first verse translation into Spanish in 1884 by Francisco Díaz Carmona, followed by several others, most notably the 1930 verse translation by Juan Ots y Lleó (the most recent edition published in 1992). Translations into French followed suit: Albert Savine's 1883 prose translation was followed by the verse translation by Justin Pépratx (Paris: 1884, 1887; Montpelier: 1890, 1892, 1894, 1900, the last with a prologue by Mistral); then came prose and verse translations into Italian by Luigi Suñer in 1885 and Emmanuele Portal in 1916; a verse translation into German by Clara Commer appeared in 1897 (republished in 1911), a prose translation into Provençal by Jan Monné in 1888, a verse translation into Czech by Jaroslav Vrchlický in 1891, and a verse translation into Portuguese by Josep M. Gomes Ribeiro in 1909. In English, the two texts in this selection ("Introduction" and "Isabella's Dream") translated by Verdaguer's Irish contemporary William Bonaparte-Wyse are the only ones available to date. Verdaguer's enthusiasm for the project can be seen in his correspondence with Wyse between 1881 and 1885; unfortunately, Wyse died before finishing the translation. The English texts appeared in Narcís Garolera's article "Dos fragments d'una versió anglesa, inèdita, de *L'Atlàntida*" in *Homenatge a Arthur Terry, 2*, Estudis de llengua i literatura catalanes 38 (Barcelona: Publicacions de l'Abadia de Montserrat, 1999); the original manuscript Wyse sent to Verdaguer is kept in the Biblioteca de Catalunya, Catalonia's national library.

The powerful appeal of *L'Atlàntida* gave rise to the cantata *Atlàntida* composed by Manuel de Falla, featuring Victòria dels Àngels and Raimon Torres and performed in 1961 at Barcelona's Liceu opera house, then in Cádiz, and the following year in Milan, Granada, Edinburgh, Santander, Donostia (San Sebastián), New York, and Madrid.

10. Title page and fragment of score from program for "Atlàntida," cantata by Manuel de Falla, performed in 1961 at Barcelona's Liceu opera house before its world tour.

Introducció

S'encontren en alta mar un bastiment de Gènova i altre de Venècia, i s'escometen en batalla. Sobrevé gran temporal i un llamp encén lo polvorí d'un d'ells, que, esberlant-se, arrossega també l'altre a l'abisme. Soldats i mariners se'n van a fons; sols amb prou feines se salva un jove genovès que, abraçat amb un tros de pal, pot prendre terra. Un savi ancià, que, retirat del món, vivia vora la mar, surt a rebre al nàufrag; lo guia a un rústic altar de la Verge i tot seguit a sa balma, feta de branques i roca, aon lo retorna. Dies aprés, veient al mariner capficat mirant aquelles aigües, li conta llur antiga història per distraure'l del passat naufragi.

Vora la mar de Lusitània un dia
los gegantins turons d'Andalusia
veren lluitar dos enemics vaixells;
flameja en l'un bandera genovesa,
i en l'altre ronca, assedegat de presa,
lo lleó de Venècia amb sos cadells.

Van per muntar-se les tallantes proes,
com al sol del desert enceses boes,
per morir una o altra a rebolcons;
roda com un carro el tro de guerra,
fent en sos pols sotraquejar la terra,
temerosa com ells d'anar a fons.

Així d'estiu en tarda xafogosa
dos núvols tot just nats, d'ala negrosa,
s'escometen, al veure's, amb un bram,
i atrets per l'escalfor de llurs entranyes,

Introduction

On the high seas, two ships, one Genoese and the other Venetian, engage in battle. Meanwhile, a mighty tempest arises, and a thunderbolt sets fire to the powder-store of one of them, which thereupon, being shivered to fragments, drags down the other along with it into the abyss. Soldiers and seamen are instantaneously drowned; one alone escapes after desperate efforts, a youth of Genoa, who, having clutched at a piece of floating spar, is enabled to reach the shore. A venerable sage, who was dwelling hard by the sea, retired from the world, comes forth to receive the shipwrecked man, conducts him to a rustic altar of the Virgin, and immediately after to his habitation, constructed of boughs and rock-work, where he offers him refreshment. A few days subsequently, on his chancing to see the mariner thoughtfully contemplating the waves from which he had been rescued, he relates to him their primeval story, as a means of diverting his attention from his recent peril.

Hard by the Lusian Sea, far back in time,
Fair Andalusia's giant hills sublime
    Beheld two hostile ships in fight engaged;
Fluttered the flag of Genoa from one,
Venetia's lion on the other shone,   5
    Near to her cubs, loud-roaring and enraged.

The slashing prows are eager for the fray,
Like boas frenzied by the desert-ray,
    Either determined or to do or die;
And, chariot-like, of strife the thunder rolls,   10
Causing the earth to quake in both her poles,
    Fearful alike to founder utterly.

So, on a misty eve of middle June,
Two black-winged storm-clouds, but just formed, soon
    As they perceive each other, bellowing crash,   15
And close-attracted by their inward heat,

s'eixamplen acostant-se, les muntanyes
fent estremir a l'espetec del llamp.

Amb cruixidera i gemegor s'aferren,
com espatlludes torres que s'aterren
trinxant amb sa caiguda un bosc de pins;
i entre ais, cridòria i alarit salvatge,
ressona el crit feréstec d'abordatge,
i cent destrals roseguen com mastins.

A la lluita carnívora i feresta
barreja sos lladrucs negra tempesta
congriada a garbí sobtadament,
i revinclades ones s'arrastellen
damunt les naus, que cruixen i s'estellen,
com un canyar dins esverat torrent.

L'espantosa abraçada més estrenyen,
i es topen, se rebolquen i s'empenyen,
acarades ses boques de volcans;
de l'hòrrida tormenta no s'adonen,
i escopint foc i ferre, s'abraonen
a la gola d'abismes udolants.

Tal un recer de roures muntanyesos
en temps d'estiu pel llenyataire encesos,
de l'huracà al ruflet devorador,
fa ressonar per conques i cingleres
plors i crits i grinyols d'homes i feres,
aspre gemec d'un petit món que es mor.

Ofegant lo brogit de la batalla,
un llamp del cel espetegant davalla
de la nau veneciana al polvorí;
se bada i roda al fons feta un vesuvi,
mentres romp la de Gènova un diluvi
d'escumes, foc i flama en remolí.

Càrrega i naus les ones engoliren,
i amb elles los taurons s'ho compartiren;

Each seeks the other, causing, when they meet,
    The hills to tremble 'neath the mighty clash.

They grapple grim with many a yell and groan,
Like to two towers unwieldly, overthrown,   20
    Which, crackling, split a pine-wood in their fall:
A hundred axes like fierce bull-dogs bite;
And midst of loud lament and wild delight,
    "*No quarter! Death!*" clangs awful over-all.

With such a man-devouring conflict fell,   25
Fresh from the South, a tempest terrible
    Mingles obstreperous its roarings hoarse;
And mountain-waves in cataract volumes race
Sheer o'er the ships, which snap and split apace,
Like reeds beneath a sudden torrent's force.   30

Their mouths volcanic pitted face to face,
They closer strain their horrible embrace,
    And clash, and butt, and round each other sweep;
And they the tempest heed not, blinded they!
But, belching fire and iron, cleave their way   35
    Into the howling gulfs of the black deep.

Even as a tract of mountain-oaks sublime,
Fired by the woodman in lush summer-time,
    Amid the hurricane's devouring blast,
Makes to reverberate thro' hill and dale   40
Of men and beasts the growls and desperate wail—
    Harsh groan of a wee world that breathes its last!

Utterly deadening the battle's din,
A thunderbolt, descending, crashes in
    The powder-store of the Venetian bark: 45
She splits and founders, like an Etna shown,
Whilst o'er the Genoese a cloud is blown,
    Of foam and flames, wild-whirling thro' the dark.

Cargo and craft are swallowed by the tide
Whose spoil with it the ravenous sharks divide;   50

de mil guerrers sols lo més noi roman;
entre escuma a flor d'aigua un pal obira,
i quan lo braç per amarrar-s'hi estira,
altra onada el sepulta escumejant.

Mida l'abisme bracejant i, destre,
ne surt muntat a un tros de l'arbre mestre,
que gira on bé li plau com un corser,
i al terbolí es rebat de les zumzades,
com vell pastor al mig de ses ramades
de banyegaires bous que abeura el Ter.

Los cetacis aflairen carn humana,
que l'àliga de mar també demana,
fent parella amb lo corb; pertot arreu
l'escometen records del cataclisme;
a cada pas lo xucla un nou abisme.
Qui el traurà de sa gola? Sols un Déu.

Al cim d'un promontori que roseguen
les ones que a ses plantes s'arrosseguen,
fugint del món dolent la vanitat,
vivia un religiós de barba blanca,
de l'arbre del saber mística branca
que floria en la dolça soletat.

Llàntia un dia del món, al cel suspesa,
l'enlluernà amb sos raigs, i en sa vellesa,
com per més bell renàixer mor lo sol,
deixat havia el món i ses corones,
i nià com alció sobre les ones,
de sa infantesa falaguer bressol.

I quan de nits la tempestat brogia,
dant far als pobres nàufrags, encenia
la trèmula llanterna de l'altar;
i els que amb ull ple de llàgrimes la veien:
«Ja som a port», agenollant-se deien,
«veu's(e)-la allí l'Estrella de la mar».

One lad remains from many men of war:
Floating in foam a spar attracts his sight,
And when he thrusts an arm to clutch it tight,
    Another billow hurries it afar.

He threads the abyss, but issues thence at last,   55
Set on a splinter of the mizzen-mast,
    Which whither he would he guides like any steed;
And at the soaring surges dashes strong,
Like to a tough old hind amid his throng
    Of horned herds the Ter with plenty feeds.   60

The sea-beasts sniff the scent of human flesh,
For which the ocean-osprey screams afresh,
    With the gaunt raven paired: on all sides shown,
Mementoes meet him of the cataclysm;
At every moment yawns a new abysm: 65
    Who now can rescue him? God, God alone!

High on a craggy cape whose furrowed base
Of ever-chafing billows bear the trace,
    Far from the world's vain melancholy scene,
There dwelt an anchorite with beard of snow,   70
Bough of the knowledge-tree whose branches blow
    With mystic bloom in solitude serene.

Once shining in the sky as lamp of gold
His light shone on the world, but, waxing old,
    As sets the sun to rise with brighter blaze,   75
The world and its rewards he dared to flee,
And, like a halcyon, settled on the sea—
    The darling cradle of his earliest days.

And when the tempest raved at dead of night,
To save poor sailor-folk, he used to light   80
    The altar-lamp's far-flickering taper-spark.
And they who saw it, with wet eyes enflamed,
"Behold the haven!" on their knees exclaimed,
    "Our Star o' the Sea, sweet-shining thro' the dark!"

Maria! Ella és lo nord del jove tendre,
que, sentint en son cor la vida encendre,
amb més coratge rema i més delit;
i al raig creixent de la celístia hermosa,
veu de més prop la terra somiosa,
com verge a l'ombra d'un roser florit.

S'hi acosta pantejant, mira i remira;
mes, ai!, lo promontori que hi obira
sembla un penyal per l'ona descalçat;
recula esfereït, com qui entre molsa
d'un fresquívol verger, rosada i dolça,
ha vist un escurçó mig amagat.

Desviant-se amb molt greu de l'aspra serra,
cerca amb deler més planejanta terra,
mes son cor jovenívol no pot més;
en ses venes la sang s'atura i glaça,
i, l'esma ja perduda, al pal s'abraça,
sentint-se caure de la mort al bes.

Mes alça al llantió l'ullada trista,
i a sa claror verda planícia ha vista,
per rebre'l, sos domassos desplegar;
rema d'aire i, de sobte, amorosides,
fins l'ajuden les ones, enternides
de veure'l tan hermós agonitzar.

Gronxant-lo, com en braços de sirenes,
lo posen en blaníssimes arenes,
de joncs i coral·lines en coixí;
quan, com ull amorós en gelosia,
d'entre els cingles de Bètica sortia,
per veure el món, l'estrella del matí.

En lo sorral ou remoreig de passos,
i, oh santa Providència!, obrint-li els braços,
lo venerable vell se li apareix.
—Vine —li diu—; al primer raig de l'alba,

Mary! she is the stripling's comfort too,   85
Who, life enkindled in his heart anew,
    Strikes out with greater power, no more afraid,
And 'neath the starry sign dilating bland,
Sees closer still the unawoken land,
    Like slumbering virgin in a rose-tree's shade.   90

He nears it panting, looks and looks again,
But ah! the point at which his eyeballs strain
    A naked cliff before him stands revealed;
He draws back, sore-affrighted, like a wight
Who, midst a clump of odorous lilies white,   95
    Spies a black-viper cunningly concealed.

And pushing from the crag with mighty toil,
He gazes round him for some surer soil,
    But now no more the youth has heart or breath;
Within his veins the blood is freezing fast,   100
And, all benumbed, he's clutching at the mast,
    Half-conscious of the clammy kiss of death.

But lifting to the glow his saddened sight,
He sees a verdant level by its light,
    Him to receive, expand its carpets glad;   105
He swims with double force; and, soothed at last,
The waves assist him, suddenly aghast
    To see the death-throes of so fair a lad.

Rocking him gently, as with sea-nymph hands
They lay him down upon the smoothest sands,   110
    Of rush and coralline on cushion soft;
What time the star of morning, earth to spy,
Like to a jealous lover's burning eye,
    Between the Betic valleys gleamed aloft.

He hears of nearing steps the faint alarms,   115
And, sacred Heavens! ope'ing wide his arms
    The venerable sage before him looms.
"Come, come," he cries, "at morning's earliest stir

te vull acompanyar a la que et salva,
per qui la primavera refloreix—.

Un viarany que es clou entre falgueres
los guia a un bosc d'alzines i oliveres,
del munt platxeriós turbant gentil,
on veu entre el brancatge que floria,
sota cortines d'heura i satalia,
d'un altar de la Verge el camaril.

Entra el nàufrag al místic oratori,
i, fent d'un aspre tronc reclinatori,
cau als peus de la Imatge de genolls;
i per ses galtes tendres i colrades
pels besos del mestral i les onades,
corren de goig les llàgrimes a dolls.

Dins un esquei, frontera a la capella,
una celda es desclou, celda d'abella,
entre els braços molsosos d'un penyal;
allà de fruit mengívol lo convida,
sobre jonça apelfada, encara humida
per la pluja batent del temporal.

Vora la mar semblava el cap de serra
lo mirador del cel sobre la terra;
un dia que rodaven pel bell cim,
veent lo vell al mariner pensívol,
lo crida a seure sota un roure altívol,
aon no arriba el salabrós ruixim.

I obrint lo llibre immens de sa memòria,
descabdella el fil d'or d'aquesta història,
de perles d'Occident pur enfilai;
i el jove, per qui Europa era poc ampla,
de l'ànima les ales més eixampla,
com l'àliga marina al prendre espai.

De migdia amb los raigs la terra envolta,
com vella els fets de sa infantesa escolta,

I fain would guide thy rescued feet to her,
  Thro' whom the new-born Spring-time buds and blooms."

Smothered in ferns, a winding pathway rude
Conducts them to an oak and olive wood,
    Which crowned the cape with leafy loveliness;
There nook'd in boughs which to each other close,
'Neath ivy-twine and wreathings of the rose,   125
    The Virgin's altar fills the trim recess.

The sailor enters the mysterious cell,
And 'long a mossy trunk (as it befell),
    Before the Image drops upon his knees;
And tears of joy in happy currents race   130
Adown his tender cheeks and honest face,
    Tann'd by the Mistral and the dashing seas.

Fronting the chapel, in a natural grot,
Snug as a bee's, a cosy little spot
    Nestles between a rock's embraces warm;   135
He brings him there to take of fruits his fill;
On a rough matting, which was dampish still
    After the pelting of the recent storm.

The lofty cape appeared, the sea beside,
The watch-tower of high Heaven o'er Earth so wide . . .   140
    Strolling along its lordly crest one day,
The sage, who marked the seaman's thoughtful fit,
Asked him beneath a spreading oak to sit,
    Out of the showering of the salt-sea spray.

And ope'ing wide his memory's book sublime,   145
He there unwinds this golden roll of time,
    Of Western pearls a peerless treasury;
And he, who felt in Europe cribbed, confined,
Spreads more and more the wings of his great mind,
    Like a sea-eagle mad to cleave the sky.   150

The earth enveloped in the mid-day blaze,
Hears, like a crone, her doings of old days;

i el mar, mig adormit, aixeca el front;
tot barreja sa música al gran càntic;
lo vell semblava el Geni de l'Atlàntic,
mes son gentil oient era Colon.

Somni d'Isabel

Ella es posa la mà als polsos,
com un àngel mig rient;
gira a Ferran sos ulls dolços
i així diu-li gentilment:

—A l'apuntar l'alba clara,
d'un colom he somiat;
ai!, mon cor somia encara
que era eix somni veritat.

Somiava que m'obria
la mora Alhambra son cor,
niu de perles i harmonia
penjat al cel de l'amor.

Part de fora, a voladúries
sospiraven les hurís,
dins l'harem oint cantúries
d'àngels purs del paradís.

Inspirant-me en eixos marbres,
jo et brodava un ric mantell,
quan he vist entre verds arbres
rossejar un bonic aucell.

The drowsy ocean lifts his azure brow;
All mix their music to the discourse grave:
He seemed the Genius o' the Atlantic Wave,   155
And to Columbus speaks his tidings now.

— Translated by William Charles Bonaparte-Wyse
(Waterford, Ireland, 1826–Cannes, France, 1892)

Isabella's Dream

Like an angel softly-smiling,
    Fond she moves her lily hand,
And with looks of sweet beguiling,
    Thus she speaks to Ferdinand:

"At the rosy dawn of morning,   5
    Hear! I've dreamt about a dove;
Ay! my heart is sure a warning
    That my dream was from above.

"Hear! I dreamed th' Alhambra palace
    Bared her Moorish heart to me,   10
Beauty's coffer, splendour's chalice,
    Fount of love and melody!

"Sad, without: in circles winging,
    Sighed the houries dispossest,
In the harem hearing singing   15
    Of the spotless seraphs blest.

"Copying these marbles glowing,
    I was braiding thee a glove,
When among the branches blowing
    I beheld a beauteous dove.   20

Saltant, saltant per la molsa,
me donava el bon matí;
sa veu era dolça, dolça,
com la mel de romaní.

Encisada amb son missatge,
vegí'm prendre el ric anell,
ton anell de prometatge,
d'art moresc florit joiell.

«Aucellet d'aletes blanques»,
li diguí, «per mon amor,
tot saltant per eixes branques,
ai!, no perdes mon tresor.»

I se'n vola per los aires,
i el meu cor se'n vola amb ell;
ai, anellet de cent caires,
mai t'havia vist tan bell!

Terra enfora, terra enfora,
l'he seguit fins a la mar;
quan del mar fui a la vora
m'asseguí trista a plorar.

Puix de veure ja el perdia,
i ai, llavors com rellluí!
Semblà que al nàixer es ponia
l'estel viu del dematí.

Quan en ones ponentines
deixà caure l'anell d'or,
d'on, com sílfides i ondines,
veig sortir-ne illes en flor.

Semblava als raigs del migdia,
d'esmaragdes i robins,
petit cel de poesia
fet per mà de serafins.

"Hopping, hopping faster, fleeter,
	From the spray he greeted me;
And his voice was sweeter, sweeter
	Than the honey of the bee.

"At his carol o'er-delighted,   25
	Suddenly he snatched my ring,
Rich thy ring of promise plighted,
	Of Morisco art the king.

" 'Birdie of the snowy winglet!'
	Spake I, 'by my true-love, pray, 30
Do not lose my precious ringlet,
	Hopping so from spray to spray.'

"But afar he skyward dashes,
	And my heart him follows there;
Ay! my ring of fifty flashes,   35
	Ne'er wert thou before so fair.

"Land around me, land around me,
	Him I followed to the sea;
When beside the sea I found me,
	Down I sat to weep, ah me! 40

"Then, he vanished from my vision,
	Then, once more he shone afar,
Beautiful with tints Elysian,
	Like the rising morning star.

"When above the Western waters,   45
	Down he dropt the golden ring,
Whence I saw, like fairy daughters,
	Bowery islands issuing.

"To the mid-day sunbeams seeming
	Emeralds and rubies bright, 50
Little worlds with beauty beaming
	Fashioned by seraphic sleight.

Ell, cantant himnes de festa,
una garlanda ha teixit;
me'n corona humil la testa,
quan lo goig m'ha deixondit.

Aqueix colom és qui ens parla,
missatger que ens ve de Déu;
car espòs, hem de trobar-la,
l'Índia hermosa del cor meu.

Vet aquí, Colon, mes joies;
compra, compra alades naus;
jo m'ornaré amb bonicoies
violetes i capblaus—.

Diu, i d'anells i arracades
se despulla, amb mans nevades,
com de ses perles un cel;
riu i plora ell d'alegria,
i amb son cor en harmonia,
perles, ai!, de més valia
llisquen dels ulls d'Isabel.

"He, with hymns of exultation,
    Wove for me a garland rare;
When I felt the coronation,   55
    Joy awoke me then and there.

"He who now with us is speaking
    Is that dove, and comes from Heaven;
Let us, love! that land be seeking
    To my heart already given.   60

"Columbus, take my jewels with thee,
    Buy thee, buy thee winged ships;
I will deck myself with pretty
    Violets and blue-bell slips."

Speaking so, of ring and earring   65
She despoils herself, unfearing,
    As tho' pearls from heaven fell:
He, with feelings sweetly mated,
Laughs and weeps for joy elated,
Pearls perceiving higher rated   70
    On the cheeks of Isabelle.

   Translated by William Charles Bonaparte-Wyse

11. Cover of *Canigó*, 2nd edition, designed by A. Solé and
F. Jorba (1901). Courtesy of the Biblioteca de Catalunya.

Canigó: Llegenda pirinaica del temps de la Reconquesta
(Mount Canigó: Pyrenean Legend of the Days of the Reconquista, 1886)

The genesis of *Canigó* lies in Verdaguer's extensive summer travels on foot throughout the Catalan Pyrenees between 1879 (when he accompanied Claudi López, the second marquis of Comillas, to the spa at La Presta at the southwestern foot of the Canigó massif) and 1883, including several ascents to the summit of Canigó (9,133 ft) and various other ascents to the highest peaks in the eastern Pyrenees: Puigmal (9,557 ft), Carlit (9,583 ft), La Pica d'Estats (10,311 ft), La Maladeta (10,853 ft), and Aneto (11,168 ft). During these vigorous travels, many recorded in his *Excursions i viatges* (Excursions and Travels, 1887), Verdaguer gleaned from the landscape and its people the striking wealth of geography and lore that he later wove into the narrative.

In *Canigó*, Verdaguer's foundational epic of Catalonia, the poet draws from eleventh-century historical figures and events, sometimes enlarged by legend, in the context of the Christian reconquest of the Spanish March (Catalonia). The poem opens with the knighting of young Gentil, who loves Griselda, a shepherdess whom his father Tallaferro has forbidden him to see. Commanding a militia against the Saracen advance, Gentil is distracted from his post by Flordeneu, queen of the Pyrenean fairies, who has deceived him by taking on the appearance of Griselda. During Gentil's absence, his father Tallaferro and, separately, Guifre, his uncle, rally local militias in an effort to route the invaders. When Guifre climbs up Mount Canigó to scout the enemy's position, he finds his nephew about to wed the fairy and, in a fit of rage, gives Gentil a powerful shove that sends him over a cliff to his death. By way of penitence, Guifre, once the Saracens have been defeated (and having begged forgiveness—or death—from his brother), swears never to leave the mountain and founds (with the help of another brother, Bishop Oliba) the monastery of Sant Martí del Canigó (Fr. St. Martin du Canigou), not far from the already thriving Benedictine monastery of Sant Miquel de Cuixà (Fr. St. Michel de Cuxa).

Mixed in with the main plot involving tragic love, transgression, loss, reconciliation, and renewal, the historical conflict between Christians and Saracens is paralleled by an ideological conflict between a folk mythology rooted in the natural geography and the widely institutionalized universalism of Christianity. Following Llorenç Soldevila (2002, 19), the poem is Verdaguer's response to the need for reaffirming Christian values, reflecting the moderately pro-Catalan conservative thought later formulated in *La tradició catalana* (1892) by Bishop Josep Torras i Bages, for whom "Catalonia will be Christian or not at all." The order of the day, on this view, was a renewed Christianization of Catalonia—in sharp contrast to the growing secular progressivism and political republicanism articulated in Valentí Almirall's *Lo catalanisme* (1886).

The literary triumph of *Canigó* coincided with the inauguration of the restoring of the monastery of Santa Maria de Ripoll undertaken by Bishop Morgades of Vic, to whom Verdaguer dedicated canto 11 of the poem describing, tangentially, the historic refounding of the Ripoll monastery by Morgades's eleventh-century predecessor Bishop Oliba. During the inauguration the bishop stood up and—much to the poet's surprise—crowned Verdaguer with a laurel wreath, proclaiming, "I crown you in the name of Catalonia." Years later, following the bitter confrontation between Morgades and Verdaguer during the 1890s, Verdaguer would retract the dedication for the second (1901) edition of the poem and add as epilogue the separate poem "Los dos campanars" previously published in his collection *Pàtria* (see introductory endnote to "The Two Bell Towers" in this selection). Following Ricard Torrents (2003b, 244), the inclusion of the epilogue recasts the ending of *Canigó*, changing it from *hymnal* to *elegiac*; the elated description of the planting of the cross on Canigó's summit and driving away of the fairies now gives way to the lamentation personified in the dialogue between the bell towers of the two crumbling monasteries. Perhaps, as Torrents suggests, the poem's final lines reflect a sobering realization that the ingredients of national identity may change with the centuries:

> What one century erects, the next brings low,
> But God's enduring monument stands long:
> Nor raging winds, nor war, nor wrath of men
> Will overturn the peaks of Canigó,
> The soaring Pyrenees will not be bent.

The watchword, Torrents suggests, is no longer "Catalonia will be Christian or not at all" but rather "Catalonia will be—even if not Christian." What, then, might be the determining factors of national identity? Torrents reflects: "The debate over Catalan identity is none other than a particular instance of the general debate over the identities of Europe. . . . . In fact, Europe is a sum of identities where each country participates in the particular and the general debate on two fronts: the historical, weighing in the avatars of identities throughout the existence of the entity Europe; and the up-to-date, putting shifting contemporary identities on the table, antagonistic and assimilative alike, resulting from extra-European immigration, political alliances, cultural interchange and globalizing policies" (2004, 120).

According to Torrents, the poem's final lines posit a "telluric" or geographic identity that is more fundamental than that rooted in Christendom. As the late Arthur Terry remarked, in *Canigó* "the actions of the human characters are interwoven with the processes of an intensely animated landscape," and "in a sense, the Pyrenees themselves are the real protagonists of the poem" (2003, 65). Of course, lending the landscape its symbolic force is the literary work itself, magnified by the circumstance that the nineteenth-century Catalan cultural and literary renewal is both reflected and performed in the poem.

The versification throughout the twelve cantos and epilogue of *Canigó*'s more than forty-three hundred lines varies with the poem's shifting themes and tone. The battle descriptions in cantos 5 and 8, for instance, recall the chanson de geste, while the lyrical depiction of Flordeneu's fairy palace and surroundings in canto 3 and part of canto 6 deploys quatrains evoking the English Romantics; at other times, as with the elegant narrative in cantos 2 and 10, Verdaguer's decasyllables evoke the blank verse of Tennyson's *Idylls of the King*; at still others, Verdaguer uses his masterful rhyming alexandrines, feminine at the caesura, as when the Fairy of Mirmanda describes, in canto 7, the thunderous movement of Hannibal's army through the mountain pass on its way to battle at Cannæ.

Dozens of editions of *Canigó* have appeared in Catalan over the past hundred years, including the 1910 stage adaptation by playwright Josep Carner, on which composer Jaume Pahissa and, subsequently, Antoni Massana based their operas, both titled *Canigó*, the latter first performed at Barcelona's Liceu opera house in 1953. Following the first prose translation of *Canigó* into Spanish by J. Nogués i Taulet, published in 1886, came Maria Licer and Luigi Bussi's partial verse and prose translation into Italian of cantos 2, 4, 6, 10, and 12 in 1888. Josep Tolrà de Bordas's 1889 prose translation into French (republished in 1986) included the epilogue, which was to be omitted from the count of Cedillo's part-verse, part-prose translation into Spanish that appeared in 1898 (see introductory endnote to "The Two Bell Towers"). Today, the most widely available Spanish edition is María Parés's modern verse translation published in 1988.

12. Poster by Adrià Gual for Josep Carner's adaptation of *Canigó* to Jaume Pahissa's score, to be performed in Figueres in 1910.

13. Score for the opera *Canigó*, by Jaume Pahissa (1910).
Courtesy of the Biblioteca de Catalunya.

From Cant IV, La Maleïda (Maladeta)

Veus-e-la aquí; mirau sa gegantina altura:
se queden Vignemale i Ossau a sa cintura,
puig d'Alba i la Forcada li arriben a genoll;
al peu d'aqueix olímpic avet de la muntanya,
són salzes les Alberes, Carlit és una canya,
  lo Canigó un reboll.

Dels rius Garona i Éssera sa gran gelera és mare;
Aran, Lis i Benasca podrien dir-li pare,
Mont Blanc i Dhawalgiri li poden dir germà;
a continents més amples d'ossada serviria,
a l'àngel, per tornar-se'n al cel, de graderia,
  de trono a Jehovà.

Un cedre és lo Pirene de portentosa alçada;
com los aucells, los pobles fan niu en sa brancada,
d'on cap voltor de races desallotjar-los pot;
quiscuna d'eixes serres, d'a on la vida arranca
son vol, d'aqueix superbo colós és una branca,
  ell és lo cap de brot.

Cabdill és d'eix exèrcit en ordre de batalla,
la torre que domina la colossal muralla,
entre eixes mil arestes del temple el campanar,
lo Goliat d'eix rengle de filisteus deforme,
d'aqueixos pits i braços l'altívol front enorme
  que es veu de mar a mar.

Al bes del sol llueixen son elm i sa corassa,
l'un fet de neus eternes, l'altra d'un tros de glaça
de dues hores d'ample, de quatre o cinc de llarg;
los núvols en sa espatlla són papallons que hi volen,

From Canto IV, La Maladeta

Here you have her! Behold her giant stature!
Vignemale and Ossau reach to her waist,
Puig d'Alba and La Forcada to her knee,
While at the foot of this Olympian fir,
The Alberes are but willows, Carlit a reed,   5
    And Canigó a sprout.

Her vast snows mother the Garona and the Éssera,
Aran, Lis, and Benasca call her father,
Mont Blanc and Dhaulagiri call her sister:
For broader continents—a fit backbone,   10
For angels traveling skyward—stepping stone,
    And for Jehovah—throne.

The Pyrenees are a cedar flung high;
Peoples nest, like birds, among its branches,
Whence no race-feeding vulture can remove them;   15
Each and every range where life takes hold
Is but a branch of this superb colossus,
    This mighty trunk of life.

Chief is she of this great army's troops,
Watchtower over this colossal wall,   20
Bell tower of a thousand-steepled temple,
Goliath of these ranks of Philistines
Malformed, great brow of all those breasts and arms
    In view from sea to sea.

For helm, perpetual snows catch the sun's sparkle,   25
For corselet there gleams her sheet of ice
Two hours in width and four or five in length;
Clouds on her back are butterflies in dance:

i eix quadro, on llums, tenebres i tinta i foc rodolen,
    té el firmament per marc.

Que altívola és sa calma!; que esplèndida sa roba!
Perquè sia sa règia corona sempre nova
argent li dóna l'alba, lo sol son or més fi;
besen son front quedant-s'hi per joies, les estrelles,
i a voltes diu que hi para, volant pel cel entre elles,
    son vol lo serafí.

Los catalans que hi munten estimen més llur terra,
veient totes les serres vassalles de llur serra,
veient totes les testes als peus de llur tità;
los estrangers que obiren de lluny eixa muntanya,
—Aquell gegant —exclamen— és un gegant d'Espanya,
    d'Espanya i català—.

Veu l'Ebro i lo Garona, Mediterrà i Atlàntic;
com eternal espectre sentint llur plor o càntic,
los pobles veu que arriben, los pobles que se'n van;
del Cid veu lo teatre darrere el blanc Moncayo,
i ençà dels puigs d'Astúries, alt trono de Pelayo,
    la fossa de Roland.

Les àligues no el poden seguir en sa volada
i a reposar s'aturen, si emprenen la pujada
des de la soca als aspres cimals dels Pirineus;
los núvols, que voldrien volar fins a sa testa,
si no els hi puja l'ala de foc de la tempesta,
    s'ajauen a sos peus.

Mes tot sovint hi munten i torna sa corona
nou Sinaí feréstec a on llampega i trona;
lo torb arramba els còdols que el gel li va partint,
llançant-los a l'abisme com trossos de la terra,
mentres, fuet de flames, lo núvol a la serra
    amb llamps va percudint.

Aucells aquí no crien, ni flors les primaveres,
los torbs són l'aucellada, ses flors són les geleres,

Dark-radiant sweep, this churning canvas claims
    The firmament for frame.   30

How high her plateau! How splendid her robes!
Dawn brings silver, the sun its finest gold
To keep her regal crown forever fresh;
Stars kiss her brow, then linger on as jewels,
And at times, it is said, traveling the stars,   35
    Seraphim stop to rest.

Catalans who reach her peaks esteem
Their land the more to see far-stretching sierras
Vassal to their own: heads bowed low before their
Titan's feet; "That giant," cry strangers sighting   40
Her from far away, "is a giant of Spain,
    Of Spain—and Catalan."

She sees the Ebre and the Garona, from Ocean
To Sea, and like an ageless ghost she hears their
Hymns and dirges, sees peoples come and gone,   45
Behind the white Moncayo, El Cid's stage,
Below Asturia's peaks—Pelayo's high throne—
    The grave where Roland lies.

Eagles cannot span her in one flight
And halt to rest, when bent on the ascent   50
From base to rugged Pyrenean heights;
And clouds, eager to hover round her top,
Unless the stormy wings of fire uplift them,
    Stay instead at her feet.

Often, though, they rise to restore her crown,   55
Wild new Sinai flashing with thunderbolts;
Blizzards sort out boulders cracked under ice,
Tossing them like clods into the abyss;
Meanwhile, the cloud, now a flaming whip,
    Claps lightning at the range.   60

No bird broods here, no flower blooms in spring:
Blizzards serve as bird-throng, icefields as flowers,

ses flors que quan se baden cobreixen lo vessant;
les gotes de rosada que en surten són cascades
que salten per timberes i cingles esverades,
    com feres udolant.

Damunt lo glaç negregen granítiques arestes,
com d'ones formidables esgarrifoses crestes,
illots de roca dreta sortint de mars de gel;
emmerletades torres d'una ciutat penjada,
com son Pont de Mahoma damunt la nuvolada,
    enmig de terra i cel.

Hi pugen los pedraires ací en les hivernades
los penyalars granítics a rompre a barrinades?
Los pedraires que hi pugen o baixen són los llamps,
que els llancen arrancant-los d'arrel i els migparteixen
amb los pregons abismes i rius que los glateixen,
    parlant-se amb trons i brams.

Amb tres d'aqueixes pedres faries, Barcelona,
la cúpula i lo frontis que espera per corona
ta seu, que ella mateixa corona és del teu front;
i amb totes les que en esta pedrera esteses jauen,
podrien d'una peça refer-se, si mai cauen,
    totes les seus del món.

Bocins són de cinglera, són ossos de muntanya,
carreus del mur que allunya la França de l'Espanya,
palets que cercarien los rabassuts gegants
si, envolts en rufagosa, massissa pedregada,
l'Olimp prop de sa cima veiés altra vegada
    lluitar déus i titans.

Per què Déu entre abismes posà tanta grandesa?
Per què velà de núvols la torre que al cel besa?
Perquè al baixar a terra tingués un mirador
on l'home, bo o mal àngel sens ales no hi fes nosa,
quan a sos peus somia la terra, com esposa
    lo somni de l'amor.

Flowers that open out to seal the slopes;
The dewdrops they produce are waterfalls
Which, struck with panic, leap sheer-dropping cliffs,   65
    Like wild and wailing beasts.

Above the ice there rise arêtes of blackened
Granite, like breakneck crests on towering waves,
Frozen seas pierced by isles of rioting rock,
Merlons of a city—poised in midair—   70
Like Mahomet's Bridge, perched above the clouds,
    Between the earth and sky.

Do quarrymen in winter season mount
To blast and break the granite ribs of rock?
The quarriers who climb these slopes are firebolts   75
That fling uprooted rocks and halve them out
To craving deep ravines and streams below,
    In thundering conversation.

With three such rocks you could build, Barcelona,
The dome and the façade your See awaits for   80
Crown, she herself the crown that tops your brow;
And with the sum of stones that quarry holds,
One could, should they fall, rebuild in single pieces
    Cathedrals round the world.

Slabs of broad cliffs, bones of mountains are they,   85
Ashlars in the wall that parts France and Spain,
Pebbles to be snatched by stocky giants
Besieged by rains of massive hailstones, should
Olympian summits witness, ever again,
    Gods and Titans warring.   90

What moved God to bound such beauty by chasms?
To veil in clouds the tower the heavens caress?
Why, so on earth He'd have a lookout far
From man—that lackwing angel, good or bad—
When at His feet the earth is apt to dream,   95
    As spouse a dream of love.

Mes per son Déu té sempre la terra alguna espina;
en hàbit pobre, vesta amb què pel mon camina,
un vespre a la cabanya trucava d'uns pastors;
ni llet, ni pa, ni aigua, ni acolliment li daren,
per traure'l de la pleta los gossos li aquissaren,
     los gossos lladradors.

Un rabadà, tan pobre que dorm a la serena,
se lleva la samarra per abrigar sa esquena;
donant-li pa i llet dolça, li diu: —Menjau, beveu—.
Quan obre a punta d'alba son hoste les parpelles,
diu al pastor: —Tes cabres aclama i tes ovelles,
     i fuig darrere meu—.

Fugí i, veient al pobre davant desaparèixer,
mira la serra, l'altra ramada no hi veu péixer:
penyals són les ovelles, penyals los blancs anyells,
lo cabridet anyívol, lo boc, lo gos d'atura,
i llurs pastors, que encara ne tenen la figura,
     penyals eren com ells.

Des de llavors, a vista de l'espectacle horrible,
girant lo cap se senya lo passatger sensible,
lo quadro a l'ensenyar-li de lluny algun bover;
la flor deixa aquells marges, l'aucell fuig d'aquell aire,
com en les migdiades d'estiu fuig lo dallaire
     de l'ombra del noguer.

Fugiu també vosaltres, pastors i excursionistes;
com les visions i històries, aquí les flors són tristes,
est hort de roses blanques cobreix un gran fossar,
dessota cada llosa de marbre un clot se bada,
la neu és lo sudari amb què traidora fada
     vos vol amortallar.

A voltes dins ses coves de vidre sona i canta;
lo viatger ou música suau sota sa planta;
ai d'ell, si no fa al càntic de la sirena el sord!
Lo pont de neu se trenca que amaga la gelera

But earth still bears some distrust for her God:
Clad in rags (guise He takes to walk the world),
He called one evening at some shepherds' hut;
Nor milk nor bread nor water nor good word—   100
To drive him from their pen they sent their dogs
    Out growling in pursuit.

A shepherd boy, so poor he sleeps in fields,
To warm the stranger offers him his sheepskin,
And bread and fresh milk, and says: "Here, take comfort." 105
When at the peep of day the guest awakes,
He tells the boy: "Go fetch your goats and sheep
    And follow at my heels."

And so he did, but soon the beggar vanished;
Behind, he saw the mountain pastures empty: 110
The cliffs above stood out as sheep and lambs,
Rocks now formed by kids, goats, and shepherd dogs;
And their shepherds, remaining to this day,
    All turned to rock as well.

And since that day, when shown by local cowherds   115
The distant shapes that fill this dreadful scene,
The mindful traveler will cross himself;
Flowers avoid the slopes, birds give a wide berth,
Even as the summer reaper, when napping,
    Shuns the walnut's shade.   120

Steer clear of this place, shepherds and travelers!
Like her tales and visions, her blooms bring sorrow.
This garden of white roses cloaks a graveyard,
Beneath each marble headstone lies a pit,
The snows a sheet with which a treacherous faerie   125
    Designs to make your shroud.

At times in glassy caves below she sings;
Above, the traveler hears her gentle music;
Beware the ear that heeds the siren's song!
The snowbridge hid beneath the glacier cracks: 130

i és la clivella on veure-la somia una rodera
  del carro de la mort.

Mirau la cima excelsa tot allunyant-ne els passos,
mirau sa cara, sense voler dormir en sos braços;
paranys amaga horribles amb plecs del seu vestit.
De Neto, déu celtíber, és filla la deesa;
però fugiu: sa nua bellesa és la bellesa
  de l'àngel maleït.

Mes, com sobre sepulcre desert herba florida,
més alt que el dels abismes un àngel bell vos crida:
és l'àngel de la pàtria, que guarda els Pirineus;
amb ses immenses ales cobreix la cordillera,
amb l'una el promontori tocant de cap d'Higuera
  i amb l'altra el cap de Creus.

Quins crits més horrorosos degué llançar la terra
infantant en sos joves anyades eixa serra!
Que jorns de pernabatre, que nits de gemegar,
per traure a la llum pura del sol eixes muntanyes
del centre de sos cràters, del fons de ses entranyes,
  com ones de la mar!

Un jorn, amb terratrèmol s'esbadellà sa escorça,
resclosa d'on al rompre's brollà amb tota sa força
un riu d'aigües bullentes d'escumes de granit,
que al bes gelat dels aires se fixa en la tempesta,
i el mar llançà, per fer-lo més alt, damunt sa testa
  sos peixos i son llit.

Passaren anys, passaren centúries de centúries
abans que s'abrigassen de terra i de boscúries
aqueixes ossamentes dels primitius gegants,
abans que tingués molsa la penya, flors les prades,
abans que les arbredes tinguessen aucellades,
  les aucellades cants.

Pel gel i rius oberta, prengué la cordillera
agegantada forma de fulla de falguera;

The rock-cleft where he courts her in his dream
    Is now the death-cart's groove.

Behold her sublime summit from afar,
See her face, but sleep not in her embrace;
The folds within her robes hide hideous traps.   135
This goddess is daughter of Neto—god
Of Celto-Iberians; fly! Her naked beauty
    Is the Fallen Angel's.

Yet, like wildflowers sweeping barren tombs,
Above the abyss a wondrous Angel calls: 140
The Angel of the birthland keeping watch
Over the Pyrenees—his vast wings span the range:
One to the headland of Cabo Higuer,
    And one to Cap de Creus.

What wrenching wails must Mother Earth have uttered   145
Giving birth, in younger years, to this range!
Overcome with throes by day, groans by night,
To hoist these mountains from her cratered core
Up to the clear sunlight, like waves that swell
    From deep within the sea!   150

One day, a great quake opened up her crust,
Dam through which, once cracked, burst with all its might
The seething granite's boiling river flow,
Hardening fast, when ice-kissed by the winds,
And the sea, to raise it higher, hurled to its top   155
    Her fish and sandy deep.

Years passed, centuries piled on centuries,
Before this bone-frame of primeval giants
Dressed itself in topsoil and timberland,
Before the crags grew moss, the meadows flowers,   160
Before the forests filled with thronging birds,
    The thronging birds with song.

Chiseled by river and ice, the range
Took on the shape of a gigantic fern;

com solc sota l'arada quan cada vall s'obrí,
quan a l'amor i vida la plana fou desclosa,
Déu coronà la cima més alta i grandiosa
    d'eix guaita gegantí.

I Espanya, que tenia ja un mar en cada espona,
sols per bressar-la i fer-li murmuri al llit de l'ona,
que per barrons té els Picos d'Europa i lo Puigmal,
per cobrecel sens núvol lo cel d'Andalusia,
per fer-li de custodi, tingué des d'aquell dia
    un àngel al capçal.

Mirau-lo allí entre els arbres alçar la noble testa:
apar una boirada sa vagarosa vesta;
de blanques se confonen ses ales amb les neus,
de gel és sa corassa, de llum sa cabellera
que amb la del sol barreja, mentres bramant com fera
    lo torb juga a sos peus.

A sos genolls arrima la formidable llança
que veuen des d'Ibèria, que obiren des de França,
semblant a la capçada d'un pi descomunal;
quan la maneja, fent-la llampeguejar en guerra,
quan bat ponts i muralles, volant de serra en serra,
    s'hi aixeca el temporal.

Mes ara, desarmant-los, d'amor amb llaços dobles
lligant va cada dia més fort eixos dos pobles:
los que veïns són ara, demà seran germans;
i, com una cortina fent córrer eixa muntanya,
la gloriosa França, l'heroica i pia Espanya
    se donaran les mans.

And when her vales lay bare like furrows plowed,   165
When once the flatlands stirred with life and love,
God crowned this great and mighty Sentinel's
    Topmost magnificent peak.

And Spain, long soothed by seas at either bedside
In lulling song and speech, whose headboard boasts   170
The Picos de Europa and Puigmal for balusters,
The Andalusian sky for cloudless canopy,
Has forward from that day for guardian had
    An Angel overhead.

See him lift his noble head through the trees: 175
His flowing robes seem mists; his wings of white
Mingling with the snows; corselet of ice;
His hair a sparkling light that fuses with
The sun's; meanwhile, thundering like a wild beast,
    The storm plays at his feet.   180

By his knee he keeps the marvelous lance
That's seen from both Iberia and France
And seems the top of some outstanding pine;
Flashing, when wielded in war to strike down
Battlements and bridges—sweeping the peaks—   185
    It marks the tempest's hour.

But now, each day he knits the double knot
Of amity, and bids both lands disarm:
Today's neighbors shall be tomorrow's brothers;
And drawing back these mountains like a curtain,   190
Glorious France and heroic, pious Spain
    Will outstretch—and join—hands.

14. Autograph manuscript of opening stanzas of "La Maladeta" with corrections (though not yet definitive) and original spelling (ca. 1884). Courtesy of the Biblioteca de Catalunya.

15. Autograph manuscript of fragments of "Guisla" with corrections and original spelling (ca. 1884). Courtesy of the Biblioteca de Catalunya.

Cant X, Guisla

Camí de Cornellà, lo comte Guifre
va a prendre comiat de la comtessa;
que els en troba de tristos aquells marges
on al sol de l'amor ahir tot reia!
Los arbres que s'inclinen remorosos,
com si parlassen de son crim li sembla,
i els joiosos aucells que hi saltironen
li apar que esquerps eviten sa presència,
un a l'altre contant-se l'homicidi,
mal de contar amb ses arpades llengües.
Lo virolat verdum ja no hi refila,
lo rossinyol no hi canta, que gemega,
arpa d'on, l'alegria escorreguda,
tan sols la corda del neguit hi resta.
Lo vent que sòpit en lo bosc dormia
se remou tot plegat com una fera,
s'ouen lladrucs sinistres dins lo còrrec,
i damunt dels teulats cants de xabeca,
i de núvol en núvol per los aires
rodar lo tro, preludi de tempesta.
Quan de sos avis al palau s'acosta,
veu sa Guisla gentil a la finestra,
entre els dos gerros de clavells que a riure
surten quiscun en sa clavellinera;
endolada la veu com una viuda
i avergonyit abaixa els ulls a terra.
Cada graó que de l'escala puja
lo rega amb una llàgrima coenta;
al capdamunt de tots ella és qui plora,
com un desmai doblant sa hermosa testa.
Les paraules que es diuen són paraules
de punyidora i funeral tristesa:
—Adéu —diu ell—, esposa de ma vida;

Canto X: Guisla

Count Guifre makes his way to Cornellà
To see the countess and tell her good-bye;
How cheerless seems to be the landscape now
Where all in sunny love was once so bright!
The passing trees appear to nod and rumor,   5
As if their parley touched upon his crime,
And gleeful birds that flit and leap about
Appear resolved to keep him at a distance
And tell each other of his murderous act—
No easy tale to tell on tongues of harps.   10
The gaily colored greenfinch trills no more,
The nightingale no longer sings, but moans;
For from these harps the joy has now been drained,
Only the chord of agony remains.
The drowsy wind that dozed within the wood   15
Stirs abruptly, like a wild beast disturbed;
Chilling howls are heard in the ravine,
The screech of barn owls high on roofs, and thunder
Rolling closer, low from cloud to cloud,
The sky's portentous prelude to the tempest.   20
Approaching now the palace of his forebears,
He sees his graceful Guisla at the window,
Framed by matching vases of carnations
Set out to brighten up her windowsill;
He pictures her in mourning like a widow   25
And lowers to the ground his eyes in shame.
Each step upon the stairway he ascends
He waters with a bitter burning tear;
And on the topmost it is she who weeps—
Her head a lovely willow's hanging low.   30
The words that they exchange are laden with
The utmost heartrending, sorrowful grief:
"Farewell," says he, "my wedded spouse in life;

a l'arrancar-me del teu cor, se trenca
mon cor emmalaltit, com una branca
que de son tronc un braç cruel esqueixa.
—No te'n deixaré anar —respon sa esposa—,
no te'n deixaré anar, ta vida és meva.
Davant l'altar lo jorn del desposori
estimació sens fi no m'has promesa?
—T'estimaré com sempre t'he estimada,
mes, ai de mi!, serà des d'una celda
d'un monestir que sobre l'oratori
de Sant Martí de Canigó s'aixeca.
Allí morir devia en una forca,
menjat per corbs enmig de cel i terra;
a Déu, que em torna compassiu la vida,
bé li puc oferir lo que me'n resta!—
Respondre vol sa desolada esposa,
mes està de neguit sa ànima plena,
sos ulls sols tenen llàgrimes amargues,
muda sols troba algun sospir sa llengua.
Ell en son front lo darrer bes estampa,
l'estreny entre sos braços i la deixa,
de llàgrimes humits los ulls girant-hi,
com l'infantó arrancat de la mamella.
Llavors escala avall un plor ressona
i un xisclet en la sala li contesta;
ploren amb ell los cavallers i patges,
les dames del palau ploren amb ella,
que veu entrar per on surt ara Guifre
l'espectre glaçador de la viudesa,
amb son cabell estès sobre la cara
i arrossegant la mantellina negra,
caiguts sos braços d'ufanós magnoli
que en sa florida esbrosta la tempesta,
i sos ulls d'aranyó i son front de lliri
ennuvolats amb boires de tristesa.
Quan se revé son cor i de ses llàgrimes
cau amansida la maror primera,
al monestir que l'enviudà tan jove
vol portar, virtuosa, alguna pedra.
Surt a l'eixida del palau que hi dóna

To tear myself from your heart is to break
My own afflicted heart, as if a limb   35
Some cruel arm has ripped out from its trunk."
"I'll never let you go!" replies his wife.
"I'll never let you leave, your life is mine.
Did you not promise everlasting love
The day we took our vows before the altar?"   40
"And I will always love you, just as ever,
But it must be, alas! from a monk's cell
Inside a cloister to be raised above
The shrine of Sant Martí del Canigó.
There I should have left this life, on the gallows,   45
Between the earth and sky, devoured by crows;
Through God's compassion I am granted life:
To Him I mean to render its remainder!"
His wife, heartbroken, searches for reply,
But with the anguish welling in her soul,   50
Her eyes alone now brim with bitter tears—
Speechless, she finds no utterance but a sigh.
He stamps a final kiss upon her forehead,
Embraces her, and now, about to leave her,
He turns to her with tearful eyes himself,   55
An infant snatched away from mother's breast.
A sob now rises from the bottom stair,
And from the hall above is heard a cry;
Nearby the count there weep the knights and pages,
Nearby the countess, ladies of the palace;   60
With Guifre's exit, she sees the entrance of
The chilling specter of her widowhood,
Her hair drawn low to cover up her face,
A dark mantilla trailing at her back,
Her arms a blossoming magnolia's fallen,   65
Torn by the tempest even as it thrives,
And her sloe-colored eyes and iris forehead
Now clouded over in a haze of sorrow.
When once again her heart comes round to her
And grief's initial tide subsides, she sets   70
Her mind to bringing to the shrine of her
Unwedding, some goodly stone of her own.
Out to the palace yard she makes her way

i amb agulla d'argent i fil de seda
vol brodar una càndida estovalla
de la més fina i preciosa tela.
Les barres catalanes hi dibuixa,
sembrant sos entremigs d'alguna estrella,
com si del cel los somnis li vinguessen
entrellaçats amb somnis de sa terra;
sota l'escut posa sa bella firma
i, damunt, sa corona de comtessa.
A cada punt que dóna sa àurea agulla
al cenobi naixent los ulls aixeca,
deixant caure una llàgrima que en l'obra
se podria encastar per una perla.
Ses donzelles voldrien-la distraure
i a sos dolors son pensament s'aferra
i a sos records més íntims sa memòria,
com a les runes d'un palau una heura.
Tot li parla de Guifre: les muntanyes
a on solia batre's amb les feres,
la font on ella eixia-li a l'encontre,
per vasull oferint-li sa mà tendra,
la verda coromina on flors collien,
lo marge fresc del rieró on s'asseien
mirant les aigües a sos peus escórrer
serenes com sos jorns de fadrinesa,
lo salze que els donà redós ombrívol,
los pins que al cim del comellar gemeguen,
com les vibrantes cordes del salteri
que l'aspre geni del mestral punteja.
I dels aucells les fonedisses notes,
los bruits misteriosos de la selva,
lo rondineig de l'aire entre les fulles,
ones li són d'un pèlag de tristesa.

De prompte s'ou lo cant d'una minyona,
com en la mar lo cant d'una gavina
amorosir ses ones amargantes
amb un raig enganyívol d'alegria.
Escolta Guisla la cançó i la troba
en son enyorament massa escoltívola.

With a needle made of silver, and thread
Of silk, to embroider a simple altar cloth 75
Of richest fabric made of finest weave.
Upon it she depicts the Catalan Stripes
And scatters here and there a star among them,
As if the dreams that came to her from heaven
Were interlaced with dreams of her fair land; 80
She makes her signature below the emblem
And places at its top her countess-crown.
With each and every stitch of her bright needle
She lifts her eyes up to the rising cloister,
Now letting fall a tear to be inset 85
As if a pearl upon her handiwork.
Her maids would gladly give her some diversion,
As soon her thoughts close tight upon her troubles,
Her mind upon her inmost memories,
Like ivy pressing round a ruined palace. 90
Everything speaks to her of Guifre: the mountains
Where he battled wild beasts, the spring where they
Once rendezvoused, and which her palms would cull
And offer him in tender cupping hands,
The verdant landscapes where they gathered flowers, 95
The brook upon whose bank so fresh they sat
And watched the flowing waters at their feet
Serene just like the season of their youth,
The willow where they once found shady rest,
The pine trees whistling up the mountain pass 100
Like shuddering strings upon a psaltery
When strummed on by the rudely bred mistral.
The birdsong now heard faint and far away,
Mysterious sounds that reach her from the trees,
The muttering of the wind among the leaves, 105
Seem mounting waves upon a sea of woe.

All at once she hears a maiden singing,
As if a gull whose song far out at sea
Has come to ease the edges of the waves
With some elusive streak of cheerfulness. 110
As Guisla hears the melody she thinks
Its strains too joyful for her sorry state.

—Qui serà —diu— aqueixa dona o àngel
que alegre canta quan tothom sospira?
Voldria anar a veure-la: tal volta
tindria per mes penes medecina—.
Del porxe a l'hort, de l'hort a la boscúria
passeja el feix de sos dolors sens mida.
Totes les flors capbaixes veu com ella,
que n'era no fa gaire la regina,
i li fan aquells arbres més angoixa
on sent més refilets i cantadissa.
Per enjoiar-lo amb raïms d'or i perles,
a l'arc del porxe la sarment s'enrinxa,
l'arítjol filador a l'olm s'enarbra,
braços d'esposa que a l'espòs se lliguen,
i entre ses branques lo colom dels boscos
parrupejant a sa coloma crida,
que aplega per son niu algun bri d'herba
per sa casa de brossa enorme biga.
Lo rieró festeja la nimfea,
somriu a l'astre d'or la margarida
mostrant sobre son pit sa rossa imatge,
segell diví de son bell cor d'aimia;
mes ella mai ha vist lo cel tan núvol,
jamai la terra li semblà tan trista;
oh terra de Conflent, per ta mestressa
com t'has tornada avui tan enyorívola!

Com viatger que assedegat escolta
lo murmuri de l'aigua cristallina,
se n'entra bosc endins, vers la donzella
que entre ovelles i anyells canta i refila,
tot fent rajar lo fil de la filosa,
asseguda a la soca d'una alzina.
Per regalar-se bé amb sa cantarella
camina suaument quan hi arriba,
tan suaument que no doblega el trèvol,
ni fa colltòrcer l'herba que trepitja.
Ja la sent més a prop, ja allí a la vora,
sols la'n separa una frescal bardissa,
ja decantant los sàlics i vidalbes

"Who can this angel-maiden be," she wonders,
"Whose merry song resounds, while others sob?
I'll pay a visit to this maid: perhaps   115
She has some remedy to soothe my grief."
From porch to garden, from garden to wood,
She shoulders her sheaf of measureless care
And sees how every flower droops like her,
She who was, just yesterday, their queen;   120
And now the more she hears the wondrous song
Pour from the trees, the more distressed she feels.
Up the archway bends the curling vine,
Bejeweling it with golden grapes and pearls,
And up the elm tree climbs the clinging bine,   125
With wifely arms that clasp her wedded spouse,
And close among its branches calls the ringdove,
Softly speaking to his mate while fetching
Blades of grass he gathers for their nest,
Within their wispy hearth enormous rafters.   130
The brook busies itself courting the nymphs,
Marguerites smile up at the golden orb,
Each boasting on her breast its golden double,
Divine seal of hearts ever true in love;
Yet never was the sky so thick with clouds,   135
And never was the earth so steeped in sorrow;
O landscapes of Conflent, how you have changed!
What heartache now you visit on your mistress!

Like a traveler beset with thirst
Who hears the murmur of a limpid brook,   140
Into the wood she ventures, toward the maid
Whose song rings clear among the pasturing flocks
And who upon a stump of oak now sits
And through her distaff draws her woolen thread.
Moved to delight by such richness of song,   145
Once near the spot, she now approaches softly,
So soft her footfall does not crush the clover,
Nor does her passing even bend the grass.
Very close she hears her now, quite nearby,
Between them standing cool and brambly shrubs;   150
Drawing aside the osiers and clematis,

entre vergelles de roser la mira,
com una rosa de pastor que esclata
lluny del verger, al sol i a la celístia.
És són brial de rústega burata
com son caputxo de color d'oliva,
caminadora i blanca sa espardenya
és del cànem més fi, com lo que fila.
La cançó que ella entona és d'esperança
de veure l'aimador per qui sospira;
anà amb los moros a lluitar i prompte
deurà arribar, puix sa bandera arriba.
De la tendra cançó a cada posada
llança un sospir la consirosa Guisla,
assaborint ses notes d'una a una,
per son cor trist rosada d'alegria.
L'angèlica pastora se n'adona
i, estranyada de veure-la i oir-la:
—Què té? —diu condolguda a ses donzelles—.
S'haurà plantada al peu alguna espina?
—Me l'he plantada al cor —diu la comtessa—;
tu cantes dolçament i jo estic trista,
jo, que só la comtessa de Cerdanya,
d'aqueix bocí de Pirineus pubilla.
Hauries tu trobada en eixos boscos
pels afligits la font de l'alegria?
—Un dia la hi trobí de primavera,
dia de cel que l'ànima no oblida;
mes, ai!, l'enyorament abans de gaire
sos puríssims cristalls enterbolia.
—Qui és, doncs, lo teu gojat? —diu la comtessa.
—És la flor dels donzells d'aqueixa riba;
l'àngel hermós dels cavallers del comte.
Sols vós no el coneixeu, que li sou tia?
—Gentil? —diu esglaiada la comtessa.
—Gentil! —respon tot sospirant la nina;
i, com pel llamp corsecador tocada,
cau l'esposa infeliç de l'homicida,
son llavi de carmí tornant-se gebre,
les roses de ses galtes satalies.

She glimpses the maiden through rosebush shoots:
She seems a wild rose, unfolding her petals
Far from gardens, beneath the sun and starlight.
The skirt she wears is woven of coarse fabric   155
And matches in its hue her olive hood,
Her espadrilles are white and well for walking,
Of finest hemp just like the thread she spins.
The song she sings is one that tells of hope
To see once more the one for whom she longs;   160
Away to war against the Moors he went,
Now that his colors come home, so must he.
With each new stanza of her tender song
Guisla lets go a melancholy sigh,
As one by one she relishes each note—   165
Dewdrops sprinkling cheer on her sad heart.
Now looking up, the angelic shepherdess
Wonders at the troubled lady, and moved
To compassion, she calls to her companions:
"What's happened? Can some thorn have pierced her foot?"
"A thorn has pierced my heart," replies the countess;
"You sing so sweet and I am racked with grief,
I, who am the Countess of Cerdanya,
The princess of this Pyrenean precinct.
Can you have come upon within these woods   175
The fount of joy that cures the sad of heart?"
"Indeed, I happened on it one spring day,
A skysome day my soul will not forget;
But alas! it came to pass that soon
My heartache dimmed that sparkle once so pure."   180
"Who is this lad you love?" inquires the countess.
"He is the flower of lads that grace these banks;
Fair angel among knights who serve the count.
Unknown to you alone—who are his aunt?"
"Gentil?" utters the countess, seized with dread.   185
"Gentil!" sighs the maid by way of reply;
And the poor wife of he who bore the blame
Now drops as if struck by a deadly bolt,
Her lips of carmine turned to chilling frost,
Each rosy cheek now blanched a white musk rose.   190

En braços se la'n duen ses donzelles
vers lo palau d'on en mal punt ha eixida,
com cadavre vivent cap a la tomba,
des d'on del seu amor la tomba obira.
Plora el Conflent, sos pagesius i pobles,
plora en son niu la tórtora soliua,
i el cel, a on esclata la tempesta,
és com sos ulls, de llàgrimes font viva.
No pot plorar aixís Griselda hermosa,
que, senzilla com és, tot ho endevina;
no pot plorar aixís, que sempre és seca
la més crua tempesta de la vida;
i, no podent sa pena desfogar-se,
va a enterbolir sa testa jovenívola
fent-li perdre lo seny, hermosa estrella
que s'acluca en la nit de la follia.

Her handmaids carry her off in their arms
Toward the palace she left that erring hour,
Like a living cadaver toward the tomb,
Whence she sees, above, the tomb of her love.
Conflent, her farmsteads and her towns now weep,   195
And lone turtledoves in their nests now weep,
And low skies, where the tempest breaks, are like
The eyes of Guisla, a fountain of grief.
But fair Griselda has no tears to cry
When, simple at heart, it all comes to her;   200
She has no tears to cry because in life
The cruelest storms set in completely dry;
And so, unable to pour out her pain,
She muddies her head of flowering years
And forfeits all sense—so lovely a star   205
That fades into a falling night of madness.

SHORTER NARRATIVE AND LYRIC POEMS

16. Monument to Verdaguer in Vic by Andreu Alfaro (2002)
commemorating the centennial of the poet's death.

Dos màrtirs de ma pàtria

(Two Christian Martyrs of Ausona, 1865)

Schooled at the seminary in Vic since age ten, Verdaguer stayed on to study theology in 1863, which is probably when he began composing *Dos màrtirs de ma pàtria*. Now eighteen, he was living at Can Tona (a farmhouse on the road to Vic from Folgueroles), earning his room and board by tutoring the family's children and helping out on the farm, especially in summer. As the young poet noted in his article entitled "Explicació" (Explanation) published in *Eco de la Muntanya* (1 November 1865), when not working he made every effort to write:

> During the afternoon rest the other young farmhands would be stretched out underneath the shade of an old oak, dreaming the delightful dreams of youth, while I, reclining in the shade of another nearby, struggled to spread my spirit's wings, to ascend to a world of wonder and life that I glimpsed high and far through a cleft between bright clouds, even as my eyelids fell under the leaden weight of the morning's labor. In the evening, as we made our way leisurely back to the house with our tools slung over our shoulders, singing the ageless songs that had nurtured me, I was glad to lag behind in my pleasant fantasy, shaping into a stanza some concept that had dawned on me, or reworking some rhyme that rang dull. And later . . . you would have found me alone in my room, musing and emptying out onto the paper what the day had left sketched in my fantasy.

The legendary events of *Dos màrtirs de ma pàtria* take place in Ausa (Vic) during the persecution of Christians under Decius (r. 249–251). Two unsavory youths, Llucià and Marcià, practice magic with the aid of the goddess Venus to achieve their ends with young women until they meet Aurèlia, who converts them to Christianity. Some time later, meeting them again while hunting in the woods, Aurèlia enjoins them to take up the Christian cause and "wipe idolatry from the plain" of Ausona. In a few days she sees them again in the city on the executioner's pyre. She rushes forth, crying, "I too am Christian, I too renounce your gods," but before she can reach the flames the executioner, "taking her for a madwoman," holds her back; "God did not wish her martyr's death should come so soon."

Ricard Torrents (1995a, 26–29) has examined the possible motives behind the young Verdaguer's choosing the epic form and this particular topic. Examples of both epic and lyric poetry on religious and moral topics were studied and imitated by seminary students, but the epic seemed more suitable to the legend. Not only did its solemnity couple naturally with a heroic tale of martyrdom, its high eloquence was suited to the narration of a foundational story set in Catalonia's Roman origins. As for the topic, raising a legend of local heroes to literary stature would in turn raise the stature of a provincial locale like Vic. Perhaps more significant, though, is the implicit parallel arising between the Christianization of the Roman world and Christianity's reaffirmation in an increasingly faithless modern world. A further consideration involves the question of the martyrs themselves. Early-nineteenth-century scholarship had generated growing skepticism about the historicity of Vic's legendary patrons, Llucià and Marcià, while at the same time the city's rival patron, St. Michael de Sanctis (Sant Miquel dels Sants, 1591–1625), canonized in 1862, was enjoying more and more acceptance. The young seminarian, steeped in classicism, leaned toward the more traditional ancient patrons. A further incentive, of course, is the fact that Barcelona's annual literary competition, the Jocs Florals, had been relaunched in 1859 and served as the ideal springboard for aspiring poets.

Intending to enter *Dos màrtirs de ma pàtria* in the 1865 Jocs Florals, Verdaguer sent the completed manuscript late in 1864 to the renowned author and critic Manuel Milà i Fontanals (1818–84), who advised him *not* to submit the classically versified poem but to write a new version of it in the form of a romance, that is, an unstanzaic historical ballad in which Verdaguer would use shorter, heptasyllabic lines of alternating feminine-masculine rhyme instead of the original decasyllabic lines written in ottava rima stanzas (*abababcc*) of feminine rhyme. The length of the original poem is 848 lines divided into two cantos of fifty stanzas each and a concluding section of six stanzas. The new version entered in the Jocs Florals was only 474 lines long. Still, it was the original version—which Torrents (1995a, 63) points out owes more to Lope de Vega and the Spanish epic than it does to Ariosto or Tasso—that would be published in serial form in the literary supplement of Vic's biweekly newspaper *Eco de la Muntanya* during the summer of 1865.

As for the Jocs Florals, although Verdaguer was awarded two prizes that year for shorter poems, "Els minyons d'En Veciana" (Veciana's Squadron) and "A la mort d'En Rafel de Casanova" (At the Death of Rafel de Casanova), his ballad version of *Dos màrtirs de ma pàtria* won no prize. In any event, despite criticisms of its minor flaws, Verdaguer's first long poem prefigures his future epics *L'Atlàntida* and *Canigó*.

Cant I
[fragment]

. . . .
Del torreó sortia l'encisera
minyona ara i adés una vegada
del Mèder sonso per la torrentera
amb sa sirventa a fer una passejada,
coberta amb vel d'argent sa cabellera
i la pell de son front sobregebrada;
però un vel no fou més que una bambolla
per a estroncar la llum que del sol brolla.

Veeren-la, i s'ompliren ses entranyes
d'un foc que mustigà cors en poncella,
gran com Vulcà lo tinga en ses foganyes,
d'impur semblant al que en Sicília bella
gita l'Etna flamant; totes ses manyes
al sol tragueren, per buidà'l amb ella,
des de llavores rastrejant sos passos,
parant-li a cada pas llaços i llaços.

Cada vespre s'oïen dos serenes
vora el Mèder, que de la lluna el disco
feien sortir, en refilar a penes
encisat en lo cèlic obelisco;
debades de la torre en les almenes
passejant però els ulls de basilisco,
i en va amb cançons volien enardir-les,
que servien sinó per a adormir-les.

Del Mèder per la vora pintoresca
prou varen escometre-la amb audàcia
sovint, en prendre per allà la fresca
de verdós saule o de florida acàcia,

Canto I
[fragment]

. . . .
From time to time Aurèlia,   145
Her handmaid at her side, appeared
Below the turret and would stroll
Along the tranquil riverside:
Her softly tinted veil concealed
Her delicate features and her hair,   150
And yet no veil she wore could stay
The radiant sun that shone within.

Now they saw her, and felt the fire
That burns inside such burgeoning hearts,
Like Vulcan's blazing furnaces,   155
Yet foul as Etna's boiling core
Spewed out on Sicily, and bent
On giving vent to their desire,
They spied her each and every step
And set before her tender snares.   160

Each evening to the Mèder's banks
They came to woo her with their song,
Coaxing the spellbound moon-disk out
Into the heavens' obelisk;
And yet, as she walked behind the merlons,   165
Her eyes kept shining clear and sober;
In vain they sought to spark love's light,
Their singing only brought them sleep.

Often they approached her boldly
Along the scenic riverscape   170
Beneath some greeny willow's shade
Or blossoming acacia tree,

sempre de la parella brivonesca
escabullint-se aquell tresor de gràcia,
a llisquívola anguila pareixent-se
de les espesses malles escorrent-se.

Fins de l'hort que enrotllava el seu palaci
de botar s'arriscaren la muralla,
retuts sortint-ne de mortal cansaci,
sense de son bell cor rompre la malla;
estranyant que com torre de topaci
Aurèlia suportàs tanta metralla,
davant de sa patrona a agenollar-se
varen anar un jorn, i així a queixar-se:

—Oh mare d'amoretes, la més bella
de les filles de Jove, si amb tanta ànsia
en la flor ja de nostra edat novella,
per fer-nos grans en l'art de nigromància,
arrancàrem dels pits, que és meravella,
los somnis i joguines de la infància,
fou perquè trampes i lligams tinguéssem
amb què sovint complàurer-te poguéssem.

Qui, com nosaltres, en ta barca rema
amb tant enardiment, gentil deesa?
Qui ha encensat tant i tant ta ara suprema
i arrossega a tos peus tanta bellesa?
I avui nos deixaràs? avui que ens crema
la flama que per tu tenim encesa,
sens dar-nos encenalls per a atiar-la,
ja que aigua no tens pas per a apagar-la?

Bé hauràs ja tingut noves de que encara
hi ha qui es riu de tu en eixa planícia,
que la més fresca i més xamosa cara
que el sol veu des de Roses a Galícia
contra nostra valença avui s'encara,
i debades per rompre sa durícia
l'arquer més assajat al cor li apunta,
que la sageta rebotint s'hi espunta.

But always she, by gift of grace,
Evaded their unseemly schemes,
And slipped away just like an eel   175
From tight-knit nets that sweep in close.

They even climbed the walls that hemmed
The gardens round her house: rebuffed
And flagging from fatigue, they left
Her fair heart's coat of mail intact;   180
And staggered by her strength of topaz
Tower to thwart their every siege,
They came one day to kneel before
Their patroness and made complaint:

"O fairest among daughters born   185
Of Jove, and mother to all lovers,
We gladly shed in flowering youth
Our childhood dreams and sport, and grew
(Now there's a wondrous thing) to be
Adept in the art of necromancy   190
So we might wield the wiles and snares
Enabling us to do your pleasure.

"Who dips your oars with such resolve
As we, noble goddess? And who
So oft has censed your sovereign altar   195
And laid more beauty at your feet?
And now you leave us, when the flame
We keep inside for you burns on,
With no more brush to feed the fire,
Since water you'll not give to quench it?   200

"We're sure you must have heard about
The one who mocks you on this plain:
The freshest and most gracious face
The sun may ever see from Roses
To Galicia flouts our valor;   205
In vain the foremost archer aims
To pierce the armor round her heart:
Each arrow lies repulsed and broken.

I tu asseguda en escambell de vori,
a tos fills deixes que batuts gemeguin?
Per què dar prometeres adjutori
a quants al teu davant genolls dobleguin?
Com d'eixa plana en l'ample territori
vols que de tu i tes ordres no reneguin,
si ens trenques de pla a pla les prometences
i amb lo que més te lloa menos penses?

Lluny per ço de nosaltres tanta aspresa,
ans la que ens dónes amorosa espurna,
com Roma el foc sagrat de Vesta desa,
del pit nosaltres desarem en l'urna:
no ens facis pus lo sord, de la deesa
gentil lo talisman escalaburna
i si a nostres raons arriba a atendre,
tot un món a tos peus vindrem a encendre—.

Escoltada per Venus sobirana
la preguera a son pler, sempre disposta
a fer-los escalfar, de bona gana
deixà sentir eixa cabal resposta:
—Del cor diamantí de l'ausetana
no es trencarà la ben folrada crosta,
ans que la creu que es gronxa en son coll candi,
davant de tot lo món cremar se mandi—.

Per a deixar l'hermosa en contumèlia
la creu robant-li, no els faltà una manya,
que fou pujar al torreó d'Aurèlia,
post lo sol ja darrere la muntanya;
pel llevant en fer l'ull gelosa Dèlia,
d'un gros eixam d'esteles en companya,
tirant ensems moixells de seda blanca
a nostra plana que sa llum estanca.

Vinguda que va ser-ne la vesprada,
de l'Estígia i del Còcito cridaren
les ombres i a coll seu, d'una volada,
de l'alta cambra al finestró es posaren,

"And will you from your ivory seat
Now suffer us to come to grief?   210
Why mete out pledges of relief
To those who come and bend their knees?
How would you have your bidding done
Throughout this ample plain unless
You hold to promises, and think   215
Not least of those who praise you most?

"Far from harboring bitterness,
We hold inside our bosom's urn
The one who gives the spark of love,
Like Vesta's sacred fire of Rome;   220
Shut not your ear: enervate
That noble goddess' talisman,
And if you will support our cause,
We'll set a world aflame at your feet."

Having listened to their prayer,   225
And pleased to hear it, supreme Venus,
Always eager to fan such fires,
Now gladly gave her full reply:
"The casing that protects the Ausonian's
Heart of diamond will not break   230
Until it be ordained the cross
That swings from her white neck should burn."

They drew upon their devious arts
To thieve the fair Aurèlia's cross,
And once the sun had set below   235
The peaks, and jealous Delia rose
With swarms of stars, together pouring
Silky whites into a lake
Of luminescence on the plain,
Up Aurèlia's stair they crept.   240

As evening fell they summoned shadows
From the Styx and the Cocytus,
Upon which rode the two intruders
Till they reached the chamber where

on per altres esprits jeia enrotllada,
davant dels quals los seus tremolejaren
porucs, i al veure que ésser tals degueren,
fent ais de mort acorreguts caigueren.

D'una llàntia als raigs que feia ploure
volador vidre sobre marbres llisos,
veren-la que acabava els ulls de cloure,
traent de rosa vera rics matisos.
Son llavi amor brollant, feien descloure
de cel en somnis verginals sonrisos,
alenats per son àngel de la guia
que al remor de ses ales l'adormia.

En temps de neu, quan lo més lústic astre
amb cintes grogues i daurats vernissos
pinta els monts que apareixen d'alabastre
i dels valls torna edems i paraïssos,
de segur tornaria opaco llastre
gaire a prop de sos bucles torcedissos;
que baixant rossos com un pols de pebre
anaven a enrotllar son coll de gebre.

Amb serrells i aglans d'or lo seu ropatge
feia més bonicoi aquell retiro,
reflectint pels envans i cortinatge
lo seu vermell de púrpura de Tiro:
del llit la prima tela en dolç onatge
anava, d'ella al verginal respiro;
lo que la feia bella com deguna
de les fadades de Nits mil i una.

De totes flors aquella fresca toia
al veure seva els joves, se somreien,
i a cada girant d'ulls més bonicoia,
més aromosa i més gentil la veien.
Vetllant, vetllant lo somni de la noia,
que per la Venus d'aqueix món la creien,
lo vent entrant per la finestra oberta
ses parpelles fereix i la desperta.

She lay amid a host of spirits,   245
The likes of which set theirs to trembling:
And now they felt the weight of fear
And foundered, victims of their shame.

By lantern light that softly shone
In streams upon the polished marble,   250
Now they saw her: eyes just closed,
Her lids the hue of crimson roses;
Her lips, a fount of love, half-parted,
Smiled a maiden's dreams celestial,
Safeguarded by her guiding angel,   255
Who lulled her with a soothing wing.

Upon the snowy land the lustrous
Orb paints alabaster mountains
With lacquered glow and sheeny strokes,
And turns each valley into Eden,   260
Yet all would pale if set beside
Aurèlia's fall of hair that flowed
In golden tangles, showering down
Around her frosty neck like spices.

Her garment set with beads and fringe   265
Enhanced the beauty of her portrait,
Reflecting on the walls and drapes
Its Tyrian purple tinged with red,
While to the rhythm of her breath
The bedsheet rose in gentle waves;   270
She seemed, in all, to match the grace
Of jinnis from *Arabian Nights*.

And seeing this of all bouquets
Was theirs, the youths exchanged a grin:
The more they looked, the more inviting   275
And desirable she seemed,
And while they stood and watched her dream,
And thought her Venus of this world,
A sudden gust swept through the window—
Struck her lids, and woke her up.   280

No tant encara lo xaió se gela
entre ullals al trobar-se de la lloba,
ni passerell que sus la fontanela
entre els unglots de l'esparver se troba,
com s'esglaià la tendra jovencela,
quan de Morfeu deixant la falda tova,
empaitada se veu per dos vestigles,
los més feréstecs que han parit los sigles.

Aguaita esbalaïda i se veu sola,
soleta amb doble, esgarrifós fantasma:
espeteguen ses dents, tota tremola,
com cendra esblanqueïda per l'espasme;
mes la maneta al pit de cop rossola
i per miracle s'ix i s'entusiasma:
que el bàlsam hi trobà de fortalesa,
la creu, lo talisman de la puresa.

Veent pus ells bolcat son plan maligne
d'endormiscada o somiosa haver-la,
no per això deixaren lo designe
i a la força votaren de desfer-la
i d'arrancar abans son coll de cigne
que sortir sense la brillosa perla,
i Llucià ja amb est intent s'hi atansa
i Marcià al darrere s'hi abalança.

Mes tan bon punt lo vel de verdagaia
van per alçar-ne, que el joiell soterra,
una mà amb una empenta els torna a raia,
los fa tintinejar i los aterra.
No per ço encara son esprit desmaia
ni per més vèurer-se bolcats per terra,
ans voten a tot junt lo paganisme,
de Júpiter als genis de l'abisme.

Se palpen i sens nafres al trobar-se,
al cor tota sa sang acorriolen
i tornant l'un a l'altre a llambregar-se,
més que mai verinosos s'enarbolen;

No sheep that wolves have preyed upon,
Nor linnet, lingering at a fount,
That swooping talons swept away,
Was ever seized with so much dread
As mild Aurèlia felt that hour   285
When from the lap of Morpheus
She woke to find the wicked youths,
Divining their corrupt design.

Alone, afraid, she contemplates
This double specter looming near,   290
The colors draining from her face,
Her body trembling from the fear;
But all at once her fingers find
A source of strength—the cross she wears,
A talisman of rectitude,   295
Its balsam giving fortitude.

Their plan to take her in her sleep
Gone wrong, they vow to hold steadfast,
Unflinching, to their wicked scheme
To work their evil on Aurèlia,   300
Swearing that they'd sooner take
Her life than leave the brilliant pearl;
So with this mark in mind Llucià
Steps forward, followed by Marcià.

But just when they're about to lift   305
The graceful veil that drapes the gem,
They meet a sudden thrusting hand
That sends them reeling to the floor.
This sudden setback leaves them dazed,
Yet still, undaunted, they invoke   310
The whole of pagandom for aid:
From Jupiter to underworld.

Assured their bodies are unbruised,
With hammering in their hearts they shoot
A glance at one another, rising   315
With a venom now more deadly;

mes encara no volen atansar-se,
que ja per terra rebatuts rodolen,
com rodones aglans caent d'un roure,
l'embat sa bessa remorosa al moure.

Entraren allavors en coneixença
de que amb un Déu se les volien haure,
que amb un acte només de sa volença
pot del llibre dels sers la terra raure;
i el cor debategant-los de temença,
d'Aurèlia al davant se deixen caure,
a qui creien Deessa de les faules,
dient-li a genollons eixes paraules:

—Qui ets tu, de nostre pla màgica reina,
que sota els peus a qui un món ferma lligues
de Venus en la falda a trossos l'eina
aprés que al cego a encauar-se obligues?
Qui ets tu, per qui acorregut embeina
lo Tàrtaro ses urpes enemigues,
i a qui avinguts no poden doblegar-te
lo llamp de Jove i lo coltell de Marte?

Si ets tu la flor que eix riberal esmalta,
com és que als aires ton capoll no s'obre?
Com és que sobre esforç on lo temps falta?
que falte amor on boniquesa sobre?
I no hi haurà degú en eixa torre alta
que contra nostres encantàries obre?
Que algun Tità hi faria de conserge?
Que algun Déu vetlla lo teu son de verge?

Digue-ho; que, per quants Déus sobre les bromes
la volta de safir d'estels brodada
sosté, juram d'anyells i de colomes
amb sang deixar adés sa ara rosada—.
Açò digueren i, en son llit de plomes
blanament la minyona recolzada,
aquestos mots rajaren de sa boca
amb què estovaren-se sos cors de roca:

But this will prove their last attempt:
For with a staggering second blow
They drop like acorns from an oak
Beleaguered by hard-blasting winds.   320

And now they grasp within their minds
That they have come before a God,
Who with a simple act of will
Could wipe the book of life from earth;
And so, hearts pounding in their chests,   325
And thinking her some fabled goddess,
They throw themselves before Aurèlia,
Uttering, on their knees, these words:

"O marvelous queen, who can you be?
To you the far-famed Venus bows,   330
Her blinded boy, with broken bow,
You drive to hiding in her lap,
And Tartarus, alarmed, retracts
Its ruthless claws—not even Jove
In league with Mars by dint of bolt   335
And sword could hope to hold you back.

"If you're this river's finest flower,
Why does your bud not open up?
Why so much toil when there's no time?
And why no love when there's such beauty?   340
Is there not someone in this tower
Who works against our magic powers?
Have you a Titan for a doorman?
Have you a God safeguard your sleep?

"Tell us; and by as many Gods   345
The star-stitched sapphire vault sustains
Above the clouds, we swear to douse
His shrine with blood of lambs and doves."
This they said, and as the maiden
Sat up in her feathery bed,   350
These words came flowing from her lips,
Softening their hearts of stone:

—Déu és qui vostres somnis esparvera;
mes no un Déu com los vostres qualsevulla,
que arrancara d'arrel, si li plaguera,
lo ferm Olimp com revellida fulla,
i fóra per son buf tota l'esfera
grapat de plomes que el llevant esbulla;
i eix Déu que em vetlla amb tant i tant empenyo,
lo veeu?, és aqueix que aquí us ensenyo—.

I la creu se deslliga que li penja
dels collarets, la que aguaitar no gosen
los dos donzells, i mentres la despenja,
a humitejar los seus ullets se posen,
i entre el goig i temença de sa venja
de petons i de llàgrimes la rosen,
petons de goig que ja del pit los vessa,
plors de dolença i greu que els atravessa.

—No heu llegit en volums d'endevinaire
del lleó enfurismat de la Judeia,
que a son alè més sòbtil i a sa flaire
l'ídol més tiesso tremolava i queia?
Los blancs estels tot rodolant per l'aire,
d'un Déu i d'un sol Déu no us fan ideia?
No us en parlen les ones juganeres,
los rius, aucells, los monts i les esferes?

Mirau's-el pus aquí i mirau com sua
lo moll dels ossos seus que en terra baixa,
com alça al cel plorant sa testa nua
i sos braços sagnants en terra abaixa,
i no el planyeu? Sereu de roca crua,
que ni amb la sang d'un Déu la llavor hi guaixa?
Oh no, bons joves, que al revés demostra
lo plor en què se fon l'ànima vostra—.

Dites eixes paraules per la noia,
dels esglaiats donzells lo cap descubre,
i el signe de la creu fent amb la joia,
del baptisme els banyà amb l'aigua salubre;

"The One who jars your dream is God,
But not a God the likes of yours,
Whose tall Olympus, if He wished,   355
Would crumble like a dried-up leaf;
The very sphere above He could
Convert into a crumpled wad:
Behold the God of whom I speak—
The One who watches over me."   360

She then removes the cross that hangs
Around her neck; they dare not set
Their eyes upon it: yet they feel
A swelling press inside—and so,
Swept by waves of joy and fear,   365
They shower the gem with kisses and tears:
The kisses welling from their hearts,
The weeping from their pangs of grief.

"Have you not read in prophets' books
About Judea's fearsome lion,   370
Who with the subtlest gest can make
The mightiest of idols quake?
Are not the circling stars above,
And waves that break along the shore,
And rivers, birdthrong, peaks, and sky   375
All signs but there's a single God?

"And see how He who came among us
Suffered to the very marrow,
His teary gaze upraised to heaven,
His beaten body bound to earth.   380
And still your hearts remain unmoved?
Will not Almighty God's own blood
Bear fruit? But yes! it does—the flood
That rushes from your souls gives proof."

And with these words she bares their heads,   385
Then takes the gem and crosses them,
And with a flow of wholesome waters
Bathes them in baptismal rites,

i un raig de lluna per la claraboia
entrant, d'un trèmul resplendor los cubre,
capellina flamant de glassa rica
amb què un cel riallós los embolica.

I a la celístia que en l'espai los frèvols
estels llançaven més llampants i lústics,
deixant enrere el torreó, placèvols
botaven del jardí pels cercles rústics.
I l'endemà damunt d'un feix de grèvols,
de romegueres i d'arboços místics,
on lo Làbaro sant cremar devien,
tots sos volums de màgica encenien.

While moonbeams pouring through the skylight
Swathe them in a glimmering shine,   390
In glassy wraps of gossamer
Provided by the spangled sky.

And by the glow the brightest stars
Send softly out through space, they left
The turret; then, while passing through   395
The circling gardens, leapt for joy.
Next day, on bundles of dry holly
And kindling of bramble and arbutus,
Where many a labarum once fed flames,
They set their magic books ablaze.   400

FROM

Idil·lis i cants místics
(Idylls and Mystic Songs, 1879)

After the success of *L'Atlàntida*, Verdaguer, advised by a close friend, fel-
low priest and writer Jaume Collell, turned his attention to publishing a
number of poems of Christian inspiration previously written while study-
ing at the seminary, or subsequently as a young priest, or during his voy-
ages across the Atlantic as ship's chaplain. As he later explains in *Records
de ma Missa nova* (Memories of My First Mass), published in the literary
review *L'Atlàntida* (1 October 1896), Verdaguer's religious poetry counter-
points his literary production, striking a balance with classical and mythic
influences to reveal the Christian–non-Christian dualism inherent in his
native geographic and cultural landscape. The chapel of Sant Jordi de
Puigseslloses, where Verdaguer said his first Mass, stands on a hill above
his birthplace: "The name of this hill is both Sant Jordi and Puigseslloses
[hill of the great stone slabs], that is to say, on its summit there live in in-
timate wedlock patriotic Christian legend along with Cyclopean legend,
from whose two poetic founts I have drunk most eagerly. When I brought
to light my *Mystic Idylls*, to those who reproached me for having written
Atlantis I replied it was not for nothing that I'd said my first Mass between
a dolmen and an altar."
    The first edition (1879) of *Idil·lis i cants místics* contained seventy-two
poems, prologued by historian and critic Marcelino Menéndez Pelayo, who
praised the book and its author before fellow members of the Real Academia
Española, considering the poems superior to *L'Atlàntida* because of the
"Christian fervor and delicacy of form and concepts that shines from them."
Joaquim Molas (2005a, 27–28) has noted that the omission of certain poems
in subsequent editions (1882, 1885, 1891)—the definitive version contains

17. Church of Sant Jordi Puigseslloses, where Verdaguer said his first Mass.

sixty-two—gives the volume greater consistency of genre, better complying with Menéndez's distinction between "mystic" and "devotional" poetry:

> [Mystic poetry] requires a special psychological state, an effervescence of will and thought, a passionate and profound contemplation of things divine and a primary metaphysics or philosophy that seeks a path different from—but not contrary to—that of dogmatic theology. . . . [It] accepts this theology . . . but goes beyond it. . . . [with] the translation into art form of all these theologies and philosophies, driven by the personal, intense feeling of the poet singing his or her spiritual love; . . . the excellence of mystic poetry lies in giving us a vague taste of the infinite, even if enveloped in earthly forms and allegories.

In his prologue to the second edition Verdaguer acknowledges his debt to St. John of the Cross, St. Teresa, Ramon Llull, and the Song of Solomon. Further, he outlines the poems' essential features: (1) they are divinely inspired, (2) they pass along messages of Christian love, and (3) they serve as "balsam" or solace to afflicted hearts. This holds for both the mystic songs and the idylls. Verdaguer's idylls, as Molas notes, tend to be "short narrative plots in romance form, popular in tone, evoking the relationship between various saints and God, or unfolding simple local legends" (2005a, 29).

Marina

Avui, desvetllador, un toc de salva
    ressona dins la nau.
Tal volta hi ha caigut l'estel de l'alba,
    dormint en lo cel blau?

Matinera com ell nasqué una noia
    més rossa que un fil d'or;
enveja el sol sa cara bonicoia,
    la lluna sa blancor.

Benhaja qui et parí! Vine a mos braços,
    colom del paradís,
tu guiaràs volant los nostres passos
    vers l'enyorat país.

Ta mare cantarà perquè no plores
    en ton llitet daurat,
te somriuran sos ulls perquè no enyores
    lo cel d'on has baixat.

Farem-te un bressolet de mareperla
    que el pèlag ha brunyit,
la més gentil que el bes del sol esberla,
    dins son verger florit.

Estels del mar darem-te per joguina,
    i una arpa de coral
que done a nostres penes medecina
    i adorme el temporal.

—Als arbres, mariners, amb les banderes
    del més llampant color,

Marina

Today aboard the ship we wake
    to a salvo of thundering guns.
Can the star of dawn have nodded off
    and fallen from the heavens?

The newborn, fair as skeins of gold,   5
    was fond of daybreak too;
her radiant face eclipsed the sun's,
    her luster dimmed the moon's.

O happy mother! Come, dear child
    —dove of paradise—   10
the land we long to see awaits,
    your flight will be our guide.

In your gilded crib your mother's song
    will chase away your tears,
her smiling eyes will win you from   15
    the skies that sent you here.

Your cradle, mother-of-pearl, will show
    the polish of the sea,
brightest among sea-garden gems
    that catch the sunlight's gleam.   20

And you'll have starfish for your play,
    and a harp, too, of coral,
whose tune will help to soothe our pain
    and calm the gathering storm.

"Crewmen, hoist a shimmering rainbow!   25
    Raise the fluttering colors,

un iris feu de flàmores lleugeres
i gallarets en flor—.

Lo navili com cisne bat ses ales
amb tirs i campaneig,
i s'omple el cel de músiques i gales
a l'hora del bateig.

L'oceà, mut com un anyell, escolta
del sacerdot la veu,
i apar que als mots sagrats la blava volta
vol fer de tornaveu.

Al caure-li del clot d'una petxina
la celestial regó
lo nom escaigudíssim de Marina
li posa el vell patró.

* * *

En desvari sa mare sent cantúries,
i es posa a sospirar.
Si serà que angelets a voladúries
l'hi vénen a buscar?

Sí, que son ull tot just badat s'enllora,
del cel com mirall viu,
i enmig d'un món que l'afalaga i plora
joiosa ella somriu.

I amb llavis freds encara, sembla dir-nos:
—No ploreu pas ma mort;
per què en tan curt viatge despedir-nos,
si jo us espero a port?—

Mes ai!, amb capellina amortallada
lo teu amor te vol?
I ha de servir-te una mateixa onada
de fossa i de bressol?

and streamers flanked by brilliant pennants
    high among the spars!"

The vessel's swan wings wave and crack,
    shots and ship's bells ring,   30
the sky replete with overtures,
    ready the child's christening.

A still and silent ocean hears
    the chaplain's holy words—
returned, it seems, by azure vaults   35
    echoing their accord.

And seeing how a hollow seashell
    collects celestial rain,
the wise old captain gives the child
    Marina for a name.   40

* * *

The mother, hearing marvelous song
    all round, lets go a sigh.
Could it be now hosts of angels
    are coming for her child?

Her eyes, just opened, start to cloud,   45
    the sky's living mirrors;
she smiles with joy out at a world
    that cherishes and mourns her.

She seems to say with lips now cold,
    "Don't cry because of me;   50
our journey's end will once again
    unite this company!"

But must your loved one take you back
    shrouded in this swathe?
And must a single sea swell be   55
    your cradle and your grave?

Per àngel seu la terra te volia,
  per sirena la mar;
més Déu ha dit: —Aqueixa flor és mia,
  la vull pel meu altar—.

I sens veure la terra, amb Déu que et crida,
  te'n voles cap al cel,
ai!, d'eixa mar amarga com la vida,
  a mar d'ones de mel.

Oh!, qui tingués tes blanquinoses ales,
  gavina del cel blau,
a mar i terra amb sos tresors i gales
  per dir adéu-siau!

L'Arpa sagrada

Stabat Mater dolorosa
juxta Crucem lacrimosa
dum pendebat Filius.

  A l'Arbre diví
  penjada n'és l'Arpa,
  l'Arpa de David,
  en Sion aimada.
  Son clavier és d'or,
  ses cordes de plata,
  mes, com algun temps,
  ja l'amor no hi canta,
  que hi fa set gemecs
  de dol i enyorança.
  S'obrien los cels,
  l'infern se tancava,
  i al Cor de son Déu
  la terra és lligada.

The sea would have you for its siren,
    the land for earthly angel,
but God sent word: "This flower is mine,
    I want it for my altar."   60

So called by God, not having seen
    the land, you fly to heaven,
from seas as bitter as this life
    to seas of sweetest honey!

If I but only had your wings,   65
    seagull of skysome romp,
I'd bid farewell to sea and land,
    and all their wealth and pomp.

The Sacred Harp

The sorrowful Mother stood
weeping beside
her Son hanging on the Cross.

    Divine is the Tree
    where hangs the Harp,
    Harp of David,
    beloved of Sion,
    of golden pegs   5
    and silver strings.
    But no more song
    of love is heard,
    only seven cries
    of mourning and heartache.   10
    The heavens opened,
    Hell shrank back,
    and the earth embraced
    God's Heart.

A l'últim gemec
lo dia s'apaga,
i es trenquen los rocs
topant l'un amb l'altre.
També es trenca el cor
d'una Verge Mare
que, escoltant los sons,
a l'ombra plorava:
—Angelets del cel,
despenjau-me l'Arpa,
que de tan amunt
no puc abastar-la:
baixau-la, si us plau,
mes de branca en branca,
no s'esfloren pas
ses cordes ni caixa.
Posau-la en mon pit,
que puga tocar-la;
si ha perdut lo so,
l'hi tornaré encara;
si no l'ha perdut,
moriré abraçant-la,
la meva Arpa d'or
que el món alegrava!—

Rosalia

Fulcite me floribus, stipate
me malis: quia amore langueo.
CÀNTIC DELS CÀNTICS 2, 5

De matí se'n baixa a l'hort
Na Rosalia,
a collir los clavellets
i satalies;

With the last cry   15
the day grew dark,
and mighty rocks
collided and broke.
A Virgin Mother's
heart broke too,   20
and amid the din
she cried in the gloom:
"Angels of Heaven,
take down the Harp,
I cannot reach   25
so high up—
please bring it down,
branch by branch,
the strings and frame
bring no blooms.   30
Put it to my breast,
that I might play it;
if the song has gone,
I'll bring it back;
if it remains,   35
I'll die holding it,
my golden Harp
that brought the world joy!"

Rosalia

Sustain me with raisins, refresh me
with apples; for I am faint with love.
    SONG OF SOLOMON 2:5

        Rosalia goes out to the garden
            early one morning
        to gather a spray of musk roses
            and clove carnations.

n'ensopega un ros Infant
  que ja en collia:
—Infantó, bell infantó,
  les flors són mies.
—Què en faríeu de les flors,
  Na Rosalia?
—Les volia per Jesús,
  que tant m'estima.
—Si les volíeu per Ell,
  jo per l'aimia.
—Si per l'aimia és lo ram,
  dau-li d'ortigues,
que si no me'l dau a mi
  jo us el prendria—.
Tot prenent-li el ramellet
  lo veu somriure;
bon Jesús, prou les entén
  vostres joguines;
amb les joguines d'amor
  vos coneixia.
—Donau-me les flors, si us plau,
  preneu les mies.
—La flor que volia Jo,
  ton cor de nina.
—Si em dau lo vostre d'infant,
  bé us lo daria—.
Mentre es canvien los cors,
  s'és desfallida,
que ja no pot obeir
  tanta delícia.
Lo traïdor del rossinyol
  canta i refila,
amb cançons i refilets
  tot ho espia.
La mareta, que entra a l'hort,
  plora i sospira
quan la veu entre els rosers
  tan esllanguida.
—Filleta, qui t'ha fet mal,
  ma dolça filla?

There she meets a child,   5
    already gathering:
"Child, beautiful child,
    these flowers are mine."
"What could you want them for,
    Rosalia?"   10
"To give them to the Lord—
    He loves me dearly."
"Yours to give to the Lord,
    mine for my loved one."
"Well, if that's the case,   15
    let her settle for nettles;
these flowers, I must insist,
    are mine."
And taking the spray, she sees
    how he smiles: 20
the Lord understands well enough
    your tokens of play;
by tokens of your love
    He came to know you.
"Give me the flowers, please,   25
    and here, take mine."
"The flower I'm looking for
    is but your heart."
"Then give me your childly heart,
    and I'll give you mine."   30
And while their hearts are given
    in exchange,
overwhelmed by such delight,
    she faints.
The telltale nightingale   35
    sings and trills,
in song and trilling
    nothing escapes him.
In tears, her mother finds
    her lovesick daughter   40
sprawled among the roses
    in the garden.
"Sweet child of mine, what's wrong?
    Are you all right?"

—Collint roses i clavells,
  dolceta espina.
—Una agulla tinc d'or fi,
  que la trauria.
—Ni que fos de diamant
  serà prou fina.
—Filleta, què et gorirà,
  ma dolça filla?
—Mare, eixes roses i flors
  que m'han ferida—.
Tot espargint-les-hi al pit,
  sent que sospira:
—Doncs que et tornen a punyir,
  ma dolça filla?—
Sa filleta no respon,
  embadalida
amb qui fuig entre els clavells
  i satalies.
Tot fugint-li, riallós
  los ulls li gira.
Lo cel se va asserenant,
  l'herba floria.

"It's just a little thorn: 45
      really, I'm fine."
"I've got a golden needle,
      we'll pry it loose."
"I'm sure the finest diamond
      would be no use."   50
"Then tell me, child, what cure
      is to be found?"
"Mother, the very roses
      that made the wound."
And showering the flowers on her breast,   55
      she hears her sigh:
"You mean to say—more thorns,
      sweet child?"
Her daughter makes no answer,
      scampering away   60
with the One who holds her enraptured
      through carnations and roses.
She turns once, her beaming
      face still in view,
the sky's expanse serene,   65
      the fields in bloom.

«Mon cor és un llibre ...»

Mon cor és ta casa d'amors.
RAMON LLULL

Mon cor és un llibre
de pàgines d'or,
en totes les pàgines
paraules d'amor
que amb mística ploma
hi escriu l'Aimador.

Mon cor és una arpa
de cordes d'argent:
com l'amor les polsa,
sols l'amor les sent;
ai que dolços aires!
que amorosament!

Mon cor és un àngel
desterrat al món,
al cant de la Glòria
sospirant respon
cada colp que aguaita
sos amors on són.

"My heart is a book . . ."

My heart is Your house of love.
  RAMON LLULL

My heart is a book
with pages of gold,
and words of love
on every page,
the script of my Loved One's   5
mystical quill.

My heart is a harp
with strings of silver;
plucked by love,
only love hears: 10
what soothing airs!
what lovingness!

My heart is an angel
banished on earth,
sighing to heaven-song   15
each time he looks up,
calling to mind
the place of his loves.

18. Montserrat mountain. Courtesy of Montserrat Abbey.

The Montserrat Cycle: *Llegenda de Montserrat*
(Legend of Montserrat, 1880) and
Montserrat: Llegendari, cançons, odes
(Montserrat: Legendary, Songs, Odes, 1899)

Llegenda de Montserrat

Religious and popular tradition held 1880 to be the one-thousand-year an-
niversary of the discovery of the statue of the Black Madonna (La Moreneta)
on Montserrat mountain northwest of Barcelona. The millenary celebra-
tion was marked by a literary competition awarding a harp of gold and
silver as first prize to the best ode in honor of the Virgin, and a bandore
of gold and silver as second prize for the best "popular narrative" based
on existing traditions arising from the history and lore of the Sanctuary
of Our Lady of Montserrat. Although Verdaguer submitted works in both
genres, first prize went to the well-known Mallorcan poet and grammarian
Tomàs Forteza (1838–98); the bandore went to Verdaguer for his *Llegenda
de Montserrat*. Three tales unfold in the *Llegenda*: the story of Garí and
Riquilda (cantos 1–10 and 12), the discovery of the Holy Image (canto 11),
and finally, the destruction of Montserrat Abbey by Napoleonic troops in
1811–12 (canto 13). The poem originally had twelve cantos; after the prize
was awarded, the tale of the mythic origins of the Catalan flag's four stripes
(lines 1–86, canto 10) was added to canto 9 in the first edition (1880), and
in the second edition (1889) separately as canto 10 (to which was added the
final part of canto 9 for narrative continuity).

Maur M. Boix (1997, 23–30) notes that for his legend of Garí and Riquilda
(not included in this selection) Verdaguer drew from two sources: a medi-
eval retable at Montserrat on which the story was written and illustrated and

a codex known as the Red Book of Montserrat (*Llibre Vermell de Montserrat*). Riquilda, daughter of Count Guifré I of Barcelona (840–97), is entrusted to the care of Fra Joan Garí, an ascetic living in a cave on Montserrat mountain, whose diligent prayer by her side will, it is hoped, free Riquilda of the demon that has possessed her. At last overcome by lust, Garí forces himself on Riquilda. To avoid reprisal, Garí murders Riquilda on the advice of Lucifer, who has appeared to him in the form of an aging hermit. Garí realizes his folly when Lucifer sheds his disguise and St. Michael the Archangel comes down from heaven to drive him back into the abyss, banning him from Montserrat for nine hundred years. In penitence, Garí spends the next seven years scouring the mountainside on all fours ("Since he has sinned like a beast, / like a beast he must walk . . . / not raising his eyes to heaven / and living on roots and grass") until the count's hunting party captures him, mistaking him for a wild boar. In Barcelona, Guifré's newborn son speaks miraculously, announcing that God has forgiven Garí, who now stands erect once more. Guifré instructs Garí to show him where his daughter is buried. Riquilda emerges alive ("When, driven by Lucifer, / Garí took my life, / the Virgin harbored me / in her arms like a daughter") and vows to remain on Montserrat, where she will become abbess of a (legendary) Benedictine convent to be established prior to the actual founding of Montserrat Abbey in 1025.

"Discovery of the Virgin": According to experts, the wooden Romanesque sculpture of La Moreneta (Montserrat's Black Madonna) dates from the late twelfth century, but tradition names 880 as the year of the statue's spectacular descent from the sky and discovery in a grotto. When the image proved too heavy to be lifted (a miraculous sign that the Virgin wished to be moved no farther), a chapel was built around her in the Holy Grotto, not far from the present-day abbey.

"Destruction of Montserrat" (not included in this selection): Boix (1997, 137–38) notes that Napoleonic occupation of Montserrat Abbey culminated in the burning and dynamiting of the building in 1812. The full title of canto 13 is "The Destruction of Montserrat: Nine Hundred Years Later," alluding to the period of Lucifer's banishment mentioned above. The poem's final lines evoke the triumphal return of the Benedictines to Montserrat in 1844 and the reconstruction of the abbey begun in 1858.

The *Llegenda*'s thirteen cantos (1,640 lines) are written mostly in the form of a romance, featuring continuous alternating feminine-masculine heptasyllables with assonant rhyme occurring in masculine lines in cantos 1, 3, 6, 9, and 10 and in feminine lines in cantos 2, 4, 5, 7, 8, and 12. Contrasting with the romance form, canto 11 ("Discovery of the Virgin") features mainly

19. Montserrat Abbey. Courtesy of Montserrat Abbey.

six-line stanzas of decasyllables rhyming *aacbbc* (*a* and *b* lines are feminine, *c* are masculine); however, for the song of the seraphim (stanzas 15–22) Verdaguer uses quatrains (*abab*) with alternating feminine-masculine Castilian decasyllables (5 + 5) that are feminine at the caesura (in other words, with an unstressed, uncounted sixth syllable). The only other variation occurs with four six-line stanzas (*aacbbc*) in canto 7 (at the appearance of St. Michael the Archangel) and throughout canto 13 ("Destruction of Montserrat"), where *a* and *b* lines feature Verdaguer's masterful dodecasyllabic alexandrines—feminine at both the caesura and the end—along with (half-length) masculine hexasyllables at the fourth and sixth lines. Molas observes how Verdaguer adapts poetic form to content in the *Llegenda*: "The temptation, crime and penitence of [Garí], the poem's main plot, are narrated in a popular and legendary meter, the seven-syllable romance. In contrast, the celestial apparitions and ideological reflections . . . interrupting the poem's legendary discourse are narrated in noble and diversified forms" (1988, 31n21). The English translation does not reflect the complexity of the Catalan metrics. Verdaguer's decasyllables are rendered here mainly in iambic tetrameter or pentameter, or in stanzaic blank verse.

* * *

Montserrat: Llegendari, Cançons, Odes

On 25 April 1880, opening day of the celebrations in honor of Our Lady of Montserrat in the year of the millenary of the discovery of the Holy Image, Verdaguer published *Cançons de Montserrat*, literary keystone of the sanctuary's millennial festivities, which ran for two years. Many of these, as well as other of Verdaguer's Montserrat poems, had appeared in the literary section of *La Veu de Montserrat* (The Voice of Montserrat)—founded in 1878 by his close friend and fellow clergyman Jaume Collell—to which well-known contemporaries such as Víctor Balaguer, Marià Aguiló, Manuel Milà, and Frédéric Mistral also contributed. Though a second edition of *Cançons* appeared in 1885, it was not until 1899 that a more complete volume of Verdaguer's shorter Montserrat poems was published under the title *Montserrat: Llegendari, cançons, odes* (Montserrat: Legendary, Songs, Odes), in which his shorter Montserrat legends, poems, and odes were compiled along with the *cançons* (songs). A second edition of *Montserrat* came out that same year, and a third edition before the poet's death in 1902.

The *legendary*, or first section, contains thirteen poems dealing with the history and myth of Montserrat mountain. It includes, for instance, "L'espasa de Sant Ignasi" (The Sword of St. Ignatius), recounting St. Ignatius of Loyola's famed visit to Montserrat Abbey on 25 March 1522, and "Colom" (Columbus), depicting Columbus's fabled visit to the sanctuary on his way to Granada. The present selection features only one, "La mort de l'escolà" ("A Choirboy Died"). It is among the best known—which, as Maur Boix and Ramon Pinyol (2004, 110n1) have noted, poet and playwright Josep M. de Sagarra (1894–1961) considered "perhaps the most pure and celestial" of Verdaguer's poems—and was put to music in 1899 by composer Antoni Nicolau (1858–1933) for a six-part chorus of mixed voices with soprano solo (an English version appeared in Boston in 1918; see endnotes). "A Choirboy Died" evokes the burial of a young boy enrolled in the Escolania, Montserrat's renowned school of music and boys' choir. The poem is composed in romance form in stanzas of various length featuring alternating feminine-masculine heptasyllables with assonant rhyme at masculine lines.

The *songs* section, preceding five concluding *odes*, features twenty-one poems including "A Montserrat: Himne del Milenar" (To Montserrat: Millenary Hymn) and "Himne de la coronació" (Coronation Hymn), which accompanied the canonic crowning of La Moreneta and the solemn proclamation of the Virgin of Montserrat as patroness of Catalonia by the Vatican in 1881. Our selection includes only "Virelay," by far the most popular of Verdaguer's songs and the most widely identified with Montserrat. Written

20. Montserrat choirboys. Courtesy of Montserrat Abbey.

21. Image of the Virgin of
Montserrat (twelfth-century
wood carving). Courtesy
of Monserrat Abbey.

especially for the millenary, "Virelay" was published for a competition held in 1880 to select the accompanying music. Among sixty-seven contestants, it was twenty-nine-year-old Josep Rodoreda (1851–1922) whose composition was selected—soon to become part and parcel of "Virelay," devoted to the Virgin of Montserrat, which remains popular to this day. It is written in quatrains (*abab*) with alternating feminine-masculine rhyming decasyllables, featuring a refrain of shorter masculine hexasyllables at the second and fourth lines.

Cant XI. Invenció de la Verge

Era un vespre d'abril. A l'hora bella
en què d'amor la virginal estrella
baixa al tàlem de púrpura del sol,
del Llobregat per la ribera ombrosa
anaven recollint sa vagarosa
ramada uns pastorets de Monistrol.

Com l'aigua que a ses plantes murmurava,
reflectien sos ulls la volta blava,
cercant-hi les petjades del bon Déu;
i amb lo llenguatge pur de la ignocència
retreien son amor i providència,
eix cor que ens ama i aqueix ull que ens veu.

De prompte una llum pura i misteriosa
baixant del cel en la muntanya es posa,
seguida d'altres llums en enfilall;
cadena de meteors lluminosos,
que arrosseguen, al caure tan hermosos,
la llum del cel a nostra fosca vall.

Un regalat perfum de rosa vera
se vessa per los marges i ribera,
com si es tornàs lo riu d'aigua d'olors;
ensems que una dolcíssima harmonia,
com rajolí de mel i d'ambrosia,
per les orelles regalava als cors.

A la volta serena d'on plogueren
tornaren les estrelles i es pongueren,
i els pastors, com si haguessen somiat,
se quedaren tots sols amb ses ovelles

Canto XI, Discovery of the Virgin

It was an April evening. The hour
The star of love was setting low
Upon the purpling solar canopy,
Shepherd boys were bringing in their flocks
That roamed the shady riverbanks   5
Along the Llobregat near Monistrol.

Just like the waters babbling at their feet,
Their eyes contained the azure skies
They scanned to find their Maker's print;
And in a language sprung from innocence   10
They grasped His grace and providence,
And felt His loving heart and watchful eye.

All at once, descending from the heavens,
A pure mysterious light is seen to settle
On the mountain—more lights follow: 15
A string of glowing meteors that carry
Downward all the radiant light
Of skies into the valley's darkness.

Along the sloping riverside there rise
Perfumes of crimson roses—as though   20
The waters suddenly were fragrant,
And in the air the sweetest harmonies,
Like flowing honey and ambrosia,
Delight the ear and heart of all who hear.

Once the shower of lights subsided,   25
The stars returned, then set again,
And shepherds stood beside their flocks
As if it all had been a dream,

i els anyells que jugaven davant elles
entre els saules que abeura el Llobregat.

Quan la pervinca es bada en los herbatges
a la fontana ho diuen los boscatges,
la font ho conta al riu, lo riu al mar;
és que obre els ulls la primavera amb ella
i enamorats lo papalló i l'abella
los hi van tremolosos a besar.

Així de les boscúries al restoble
la nova rodolà, del mas al poble,
del poble riberenc a la ciutat,
i al veure en altre Horeb la mata encesa,
Gotmar, bisbe de Vic, que era a Manresa,
escomet la visió de Montserrat.

Ribera avall les ones acompanya
cap als peus de la històrica muntanya,
on l'enrotllen pagesos i pastors,
i a l'hora en què amb lo cap dessota l'ala
se recull en sa branca la cucala,
se'ls bada el cel en rius de resplendors.

Com rosari d'estrelles de llum pura
que esgranassen los àngels en l'altura,
per aclarir la terra amb raigs divins,
hi baixen d'una a una tremoloses,
pluja suau de lliris i de roses
com no en floreixen pas en los jardins.

Tothom les veu baixar de la serena
volta al serrat, com perles a l'arena,
mes, àngels de la terra, los infants
veuen que són los àngels de la Glòria
los qui en garlanda que els semblà il·lusòria
duen les llums divines en ses mans.

En una cova altíssima que es bada
enmig d'una gran roca acinglerada,

While lambs took up their play beside
The willows watered by the Llobregat.   30

When periwinkles flower in the meadows,
The forests tell it to the brooks,
The brooks to rivers, rivers to the oceans:
The eyes of springtime open as they bloom,
While amorous bees and butterflies   35
Draw near them, trembling, just to steal a kiss.

The tidings flew from wood to fertile field,
From farm to village, from village into town,
And hearing in Manresa there was now
Another Horeb with its burning bush,   40
Gothmar, the bishop there from Vic,
Sets off for Montserrat to see the vision.

He tracks the river's course along the banks
Until he comes before the mountain,
Where peasant-folk and shepherds gather round,   45
And when the raven once again beds down
Among the branches, top tucked under wing,
The skies once more light up with sparkling rivers.

Like rosary beads of shining stars
Unstrung by seraphim on high   50
To bathe the earth in light divine,
One by one the fluttering lights descend,
A gentle rain of lilies and of roses,
With blooms no garden ever saw before.

All watch them showering on the mountain   55
From the skies, like pearls upon the sand;
Only the children—angels of the world—
Can see that these celestial lights
Appearing as a wondrous wreath
Are carried down to earth in angels' hands.   60

Inside a cove that opens high on sheer
Walls of rock, carved out below the cliffs,

l'esbart de serafins para son vol;
i a una claror que en vessa esblanqueïda,
desapareix la seva, avergonyida
com les estrelles al sortir lo sol.

Los uns entre penyals i verdes branques
estenen tot volant ses ales blanques,
dant a la balma celestial dosser;
amb cítares los altres i salteris
umplen lo cel de música i misteris,
la terra d'esperança i de plaer.

Los altres dels turons per les esquerdes
planten llorers i alzines sempre verdes,
festonegen lo llit dels rierons,
cenyeixen amb una heura cada roca,
fan rebrotar la més antiga soca
coronant-la de boixos i timons.

Cantava el rossinyol en la ribera
regalades cançons de primavera,
mes calla al ploure lo primer estel
per escoltar los himnes de la serra:
què valen, ai!, los càntics de la terra
al ressonar la música del cel?

* * *

«Sortiu d'entre núvols, bellíssima Aurora:
d'ençà que us va perdre lo món està trist,
la terra us espera, lo cel vos enyora;
voleu que no us ploren los ulls que us han vist?

»Sortiu, rica Perla, de vostra petxina,
que us vol Catalunya posar en son front;
per gerro preneu-la, roser sens espina,
i s'umplen d'aromes Espanya i lo món.

»Vindran reis i reines a fer-vos visita,
corones i ceptres posant-vos als peus;

The hosts of angels come to rest;
And in the light seen pouring from the cove
Their own light dims and fades—yielding,   65
Like stars that vanish with the light of day.

Some spread their angels' wings in flight
Among the crags and foliage to give
The grotto a celestial baldachin;
Others take up psalteries and zithers   70
And fill the skies with mystery and music,
The earth with pleasure and with hope.

Others set to planting oaks and laurels
In clefts and cracks that open on the slopes,
Adorning with festoons the beds of streams,   75
Circling every rock with clinging vines,
And budding every ancient stump,
Crowning them with holly and with thyme.

The nightingale, in joyful song
Along the riverbank, fell silent   80
With the first of falling stars
To hear the hymns now echoing through
The mountain: how can songs of earth
Compare to music made in heaven?

* * *

"Come out, Aurora, from behind the clouds.   85
Since losing you the world is filled with sorrow,
The earth awaits, and heaven calls to you:
Do tears not fill the eyes of all who see you?

"Come out, precious Pearl, from your shell,
All Catalonia would adorn herself   90
With you—take her, thornless rose, for vase,
And fill with fragrance Spain and all the world.

"Kings and queens will come from near and far,
Laying at your feet their crowns and scepters;

un niu en eix cingle tindreu per ermita,
més pur que ses aigües, més blanc que ses neus.

»Sortiu: per retaule tindreu la muntanya,
per músics los àngels i algun rossinyol,
lo cel per corona, lo món per peanya,
per llànties de plata la lluna i lo sol.

»Tindreu en les boires bonics cortinatges,
de nit les estrelles, de dia la llum,
les ales dels àngels duran-vos missatges,
les ales dels aires cançons i perfum.

»Lo lliri, oferint-vos encens i ambrosia,
aixeca entre jonça son càlzer en flor;
l'aucell per mirar-vos, Estrella del dia,
estira ses ales i canta d'amor.

»Princeses i santes tindreu per servir-vos,
per mossos i patges angèlics infants,
acords i pregàries vindran a oferir-vos
després de les verges los monjos cantants.

»I amb monjos i ascetes serà aqueixa serra
un rusc ple de bresques de mística mel,
de mel que recullen los sants de la terra,
voltant com abelles la Rosa del cel.»

* * *

Aixís, a les angèliques cantúries,
ressonen com un temple les boscúries,
mes prompte els serafins prenen lo vol,
girant a la muntanya els ulls hermosos,
com los gira a la llum que els hi ha desclosos
l'enamorat i tendre rossinyol.

Al perdre's en lo cel la clariana,
s'abaixen tristos a la fosca plana
los ulls que fa plorar l'enyorament,

A nest among these cliffs will be your home,   95
As pure as her waters, white as her snows.

"Come out, you'll have the mountain for retable,
Nightingales and angels for your minstrels,
The sky for crown, the world you take for dais,
And for your lamps there shine the moon and sun.   100

"You'll have for lovely drapes the rolling mists,
You'll have the starlit night, the sunlit day,
Angels' wings will bring you messages,
The breeze will bring you music and perfumes.

"Lilies, with their incense and ambrosia,   105
Raise to you their goblets from the reeds;
And birds, eager to catch a glimpse of you,
Bright Daystar, spread their wings and sing of love.

"Princesses and saints will be your servants,
Your pages and your squires angelic children;   110
Your sisters, after them your monks, will lift
Their voices up in harmony and prayer.

"This mount where cenobites and hermits thrive
Will be a hive that brims with mystic honey,
Honey that the saints of earth collect,   115
Circling round like bees the Rose of Heaven."

* * *

The wooded slopes surrounding all resound,
Echoing the angelic chorus like a temple,
But soon the seraphim takes wing,
Turning round for one last look,   120
Like tender loving nightingales,
To see the light that opened up their eyes.

Once the lights have vanished from the sky,
All lower to the darkened valley
Their eyes the longing fills with tears,   125

i el cor se vessa en resos i pregàries,
que roden per les selves solitàries
fins a apuntar l'aurora a sol ixent.

Muntanya dels misteris, quina rosa
en tes castes entranyes s'és desclosa,
que els serafins la baixen a olorar?
Eixa ombrívola selva que els convida,
quina font té de renaixença i vida
que no es veuen ses aigües regalar?

Si són aigües d'amor, deixa'ns-en beure;
si ets estrella caiguda, deixa't veure
i de ton cel ensenya'ns lo camí,
que és aspre i llarg lo terrenal viatge,
i no té el món una ombra de brancatge
on prenga alè lo pobre pelegrí.

Al raig primer de l'alba matinera,
del bisbe en seguiment, per la drecera
lo poble es va enfilant muntanya amunt:
quatre homes amb destrals obren la via,
i com l'hisop l'alzina s'humilia
perquè els romeus li passen per damunt.

Entre ginebres, pinetells i arboços
onegen cabells blancs i cabells rossos,
com vora el gessamí ginesta en flor;
i es veuen entre cotes de burgesos
les túniques de llana dels pagesos,
la rústega pellissa del pastor.

Suau olor de paradís los guia
vers les timbes altíssimes on nia
de Catalunya l'Àliga gentil;
una heurera li fa de cortinatge,
los ulls no veren més serena imatge
ni més reclòs i místic camaril.

And prayer pours out from their hearts,
Rising in the lonely woods
Till dawn lights up the sky once more.

Mountain of mystery, what rose
Is this now blossomed in your purest core   130
Whose fragrance seraphim draw near to catch?
What fount is this where new life streams
In shady woods that draw such hosts—
And yet no one has ever seen before?

If fount of love, then let us drink;   135
If fallen star, then show yourself
And lead us on your skysome path—
Our journey here on earth is long and bitter:
There are no branches giving shade
To pilgrims seeking rest along the way.   140

With dawn's first early morning ray,
The bishop and his following take
The steepest path straight to the spot:
Four men with axes clear the way
As shrubs and sturdy oaks fall back   145
To let the reverent company pass.

Among the juniper, pine, and arbutus
Move heads of hair now white, now gold,
Like jasmines next to broom in blossom,
And mixed among the townsfolks' coats   150
Show peasants' tunics all of wool
And roughish hides that shepherds wear.

With subtle scents of paradise for guide,
They reach the lofty cliffs that Catalonia's
Graceful Eagle chose to make her nest;   155
Framed on either side by drapes of ivy,
And in the mystic recess of this niche,
She is the picture of serenity.

Tal del Tabor en la sagrada cima
als tres deixebles seus que tant estima
se mostraria un jorn lo Redemptor;
com neu sa vestidura blanquejara,
seria com un sol la seva cara
dins una alba de cèlica claror.

Com los raïms de l'heura que volteja
la cova, al sol sa cara moreneja,
en sa mà dreta un petit món floreix,
que ella mostra a son Fill perquè l'empare,
i assegut a la falda de la Mare,
Ell somrient l'empara i beneeix.

Bisbe i pastors de genollons la miren,
i extàtics oren, canten i sospiren;
tanta hermosura els ha robat lo cor:
Gotmar la pren en sos ditxosos braços,
i ressona per timbes i ribassos
la lletania que inventà l'amor.

«Estrella del matí, Mística Rosa,
on com abella tot un Déu se posa»,
diuen los uns en cor acompassat;
«Causa de nostre goig», diuen los altres,
«pregau, Mare de Déu, per tots nosaltres,
en vostra Casa d'or de Montserrat».

I el nom sempre dolcíssim de Maria
umple el cel i la terra d'harmonia.
Nota robada als cants del serafí,
entrena't en mos himnes amorosos,
que fins los cards se tornen olorosos
si els acompanya un brot de romaní.

Del Llobregat s'aturen les onades
tot parlant-ne a les flors enamorades;
tot escoltant eix càntic de dolçor,
volant s'aturen los aucells en l'aire;

As on the holy summit of Mount Tabor
The Redeemer showed Himself one day   160
To three disciples whom He loved,
With robes that shone as white as snow,
Her face seemed like the very sun
When daybreak comes to light the skies.

Just like the berries of the ivy round   165
Her cove, her face was darkened by the sun;
Her right hand held a tiny world
To show her Son that He might shelter it—
And shelter it He does, and blesses it,
While smiling on His Mother's lap.   170

Bishop and shepherds fall to their knees
And pray and sing and sigh in ecstasy;
Their hearts are taken with her beauty:
Gothmar lifts the image in his arms
And on the slopes and summits rings   175
The litany that love brought forth:

"Morning Star, Mystical Rose,
The Almighty is your honeybee,"
Rise voices now in rhythmic chorus;
"Cause of our joy," others intone,   180
"Pray for us, Holy Mother of God,
In your House of Gold on Montserrat."

And the sweet, sweet name of Mary
Fills sky and earth with harmony.
Notes that come from songs of seraphim,   185
Make my loving hymns the richer,
For even thistles may turn fragrant
If gathered together with rosemary sprigs.

The waters of the Llobregat stand still,
Conferring with the amorous flowers;   190
Birds come to a halt in the air
To listen to the soothing song;

llencen vinyes i boscos més aflaire
i el cel asserenat més resplendor.

I serra enllà la professó anguileja;
com un colom Maria al mig blanqueja,
colom del cel que vol niar aquí:
prop d'on l'esperen ja Aciscle i Victòria,
com heralds de la Reina de la Glòria,
se fa immovible en lo verdós camí.

La portaven gojosos a Manresa,
però de Catalunya la Princesa
vol veure son realme d'aquí estant;
estrella d'Orient de tota Espanya,
vol guiar, des del cim d'eixa muntanya,
als que el sol del Messies cercaran.

—Miracle! —el bisbe crida—, gran miracle!—
Entre boixos li fan un tabernacle
de sos mantells i brostes i verdor;
per sa Regina aquell verger l'adora,
los passerells la prenen per l'aurora,
les donzelles per l'astre de l'amor.

Com la conquilla que en la mar s'esberla
per rebre i estojar la rica perla,
la serra és migpartida a sol ixent;
Déu amb ses mans mateixes l'ha desclosa
per estojar la Perla més hermosa
que li han ofert les platges d'Orient.

De son retaule engarlandat de fulles
ell aixecà les gòtiques agulles,
on l'àliga se cansa de pujar;
féu ses columnes de turons de marbre,
on com aucells al cimeral de l'arbre,
pujaran los ascetes a niar.

I la Reina del cel i de la terra
per trono pren la catalana serra,

Vineyards and woodlands give lovelier scent,
The tranquil sky a purer shine.

The procession winds along the slopes,   195
Mary in its midst, bright shining dove
From heaven come to make her nest: near where,
Like heralds to the Queen of Glory, wait
Aciscle and Victòria along the verdant
Path—she proves impossible to move.   200

They thought to take her to Manresa,
But Catalonia's Princess chooses this
To be her kingdom's belvedere:
To all of Spain the Eastern Star,
Guiding from the summit of this sierra   205
All who seek the sun of the Messiah.

"It is a miracle!" cries the Bishop.
They raise a tabernacle by the box trees
Using cloaks and twigs and foliage,
While orchards hail her as Regina,   210
Linnets take her for the dawn,
And maidens for celestial orb of love.

Like the shell that opens in the sea
To lodge the precious pearl inside,
The mountain was divided facing east: 215
Opened by the hand of God
To lodge the Pearl most beautiful
Of all that shine on eastern shores.

Above the greenery framing her retable,
God raised these jagged Gothic needles   220
Fit to challenge even eagles,
Shaping them in lofty marble columns
Where, like birds that take to tops of trees,
Ascetics will come up to make their nests.

And so the Queen of earth and heaven   225
Takes this Catalan mountain for throne,

sos penyals gegantins per respatller;
los núvols per cortina de sa alcova,
lo Llobregat per franja de sa roba,
i el cor dels catalans per encenser.

For backrest its towering pinnacles—
The clouds are curtains gracing her alcove,
The Llobregat the border of her robe,
And the heart of every Catalan her censer. 230

La mort de l'escolà

Al P. Ramir Rodamilans

A Montserrat tot plora,
tot plora d'ahir ençà,
que allí a l'Escolania
s'és mort un escolà.
L'Escolania, oh Verge,
n'és vostre colomar:
a aquell que ahir us cantava
qui avui no el plorarà?

En caixa blanquinosa
mirau que hermós està,
n'apar un lliri d'aigua
que acaben de trencar.
Té el violí a l'esquerra
que solia tocar,
lo violí a l'esquerra,
l'arquet a l'altra mà.

Sos companyons de cobla
lo duen a enterrar.
Lo rossinyol salmeja,
salmeja més enllà;
quan veu l'Escolania,
calla per escoltar.
Lo cant de les absoltes
comencen d'entonar;
lo primer vers que entonen
del cel sembla baixar,
lo segon vers que canten
se posen a plorar.
Lo mestre de la cobla

A Choirboy Died

To Br. Ramir Rodamilans

All Montserrat cries,
cries since yesterday,
when at her school of choir
a choirboy died.
Your School of Song,   5
O Virgin, is your dovecote:
and who, today, wouldn't cry
for the boy who yesterday sang your songs?

See how handsome he looks
in his white casket,   10
resembling a calla lily
that's only just been broken.
In his left hand he holds
the violin,
the violin he used to play,   15
and in his right the bow.

His companions in song
carry him to the grave.
In the distance psalms
a psalming nightingale;   20
seeing the choir,
he stops to listen.
Now they start to chant
the Requiescat;
the first verse chanted   25
seems to fall from heaven,
and with the second
the tears stream.
The preceptor, to no avail,

los aconhorta en va,
les fonts ja són rieres,
i les rieres mar.

Oh patges de la Verge,
bé teniu de plorar,
al que millor cantava
venint de soterrar.
Los monjos també ploren,
sols canta un ermità,
sentint cantar los àngels
i amb ells lo nou germà,
aucell d'ales obertes
que cap al cel se'n va.

Mentre ell canta pels aires,
lo violí sonà.

Virolai

Rosa d'abril, Morena de la serra,
de Montserrat Estel:
il·luminau la catalana terra,
guiau-nos cap al cel.

Amb serra d'or los angelets serraren
eixos turons per fer-vos un palau;
Reina del cel que els serafins baixaren,
dau-nos abric dins vostre mantell blau.

Alba naixent d'estrelles coronada,
Ciutat de Déu que somià David,
a vostres peus la lluna s'és posada,
lo sol sos raigs vos dóna per vestit.

tries to console them,   30
as streams turn to rivers
and rivers to seas.

O pages of the Virgin,
cry you must,
having just buried   35
the one whose song was best.
The monks, too, cry;
only a hermit lifts his voice,
hearing angels singing—
and with them their new brother,   40
bird with wings spread wide
now rising in the sky.

And while he sings and soars away,
the violin plays.

Virelay

Rose of April, Morena of the mountain,
    Star of Montserrat:
Light up the Catalan homeland,
    Guide us into Heaven.

The angels used a golden saw   5
To notch these peaks and shape your palace:
Queen of heaven whom seraphim sent,
May your blue mantle shelter us.

Breaking dawnlight crowned by stars,
City of God that David dreamed,   10
At your feet the moon bows down,
The sun lays out your gown of beams.

Dels catalans sempre sereu Princesa,
dels espanyols Estrella d'Orient;
siau pels bons pilar de fortalesa,
pels pecadors lo port de salvament.

Donau consol a qui la pàtria enyora
sens veure mai los cims de Montserrat;
en terra i mar oïu a qui us implora,
tornau a Déu los cors que l'han deixat.

Mística Font de l'aigua de la vida,
rajau del cel al cor de mon país;
dons i virtuts deixau-li per florida;
feu-ne, si us plau, lo vostre paradís.

Ditxosos ulls, Maria, los que us vegen,
ditxós lo cor que s'obre a vostra llum;
Rosa del cel que els serafins voltegen,
a ma oració donau vostre perfum.

Cedre gentil del Líbano corona,
Arbre d'encens, Palmera de Sion,
lo fruit sagrat que vostra amor nos dóna
és Jesucrist, lo Redemptor del món.

Amb vostre nom comença nostra història,
i és Montserrat lo nostre Sinaí;
sien per tots l'escala de la Glòria
eixos penyals coberts de romaní.

Rosa d'abril, Morena de la serra,
de Montserrat Estel:
il·luminau la catalana terra,
guiau-nos cap al cel.

Of Catalonia ever Princess,
To Spain you are the Eastern Star;
To virtuous be a pilar of strength,   15
To sinners be safe haven and harbor.

Comfort those who long to see
Your summits, exiled far away;
Hear every prayer on land and sea,
Bring back to God all hearts that stray.   20

Into my homeland's heart pour down,
Mystical Fount, your waters of life;
Let grace and virtue be its blossoms;
Make of it your paradise.

Happy the eyes that see you, Mary,   25
Happy the heart that your light bathes;
Rose of Heaven that seraphim circle,
Enrich my prayer with your bouquet.

Tree of incense, Palm of Sion,
Crown to Lebanon's noble cedar,   30
The blessed fruit your love brought forth
Is Jesus Christ, the world's Redeemer.

Beloved Montserrat, our Sinai,
With your name starts our history:
Let these cliffs clad in rosemary   35
Be for all the stair to Glory.

Rose of April, Morena of the mountain,
   Star of Montserrat:
Light up the Catalan homeland,
   Guide us into Heaven.   40

FROM

Caritat

(Charity, 1885)

When Verdaguer published *Caritat* in January 1885, he was, at age thirty-nine, at the height of his literary career, and his stature was about to soar with the triumph of his second major epic, *Canigó*, to appear later that same year. Moved by the devastating effects of the earthquake that struck Andalusia on 25 December 1884, the poet compiled the thirty poems in the volume as an act of solidarity, as proceeds from it would be added to the relief funds being collected by the bishoprics. In his prologue, an open letter to the bishop of Barcelona, he described the poems he dedicated to "our brothers in Andalusia" as "alms from the heart." The book was a success. Isidor Cònsul (2005a, 289) notes that the funds raised by the first edition surpassed the amount collected by the entire diocese of Vic. A second edition followed in May, and a third in 1893. Ricard Torrents (2002a, 43–44) has pointed out the added significance of the fact that among Verdaguer's duties as chaplain in the service of the marquis of Comillas was that of almoner; in other words, he managed the family's charitable donations. With *Caritat*, the economic gesture carries over into Verdaguer's literary production.

In the opening stanzas of the book's first poem, "La caritat," the cedar of Lebanon symbolizes charity—understood as universal love—the greatest expression of which is God's own love for humankind. The poem is written in five-line stanzas rhyming *abaab* (*a* lines are feminine, *b* are masculine) and feature Verdaguer's masterful alexandrines, feminine at the caesura (seventh syllable unstressed) with (half-length) hexasyllables at the fourth line.

Given the prevalence and symbolic weight of the nightingale throughout Verdaguer's works (see, for instance, "Què és la poesia?" ["What Is

Poetry?"] and "A un rossinyol de Vallvidrera" ["To a Nightingale in Vall-vidrera"]), the regret over the loss of the "broken lyre" in "La mort del rossinyol" ("A Nightingale's Death") is especially poignant. As in canto 1 of *Canigó*, Verdaguer alludes here to the nightingale's place of privilege in Milton's depiction of the earthly paradise (see *Paradise Lost* 4.602–3). The poem is written in quatrains of alternating feminine-masculine deca-syllables rhyming *abab*.

Carola Duran (2003) has traced the genesis of the hard-hitting poem "Amor de mare" ("A Mother's Love") that appeared in English transla-tion by Antoinette Ogden in the May issue of *The International* (Chicago, 1897). Verdaguer wrote it at the request of a dying friend, poet Joaquim Maria Bartrina (1850–80), who showed him an item from a French news-paper with the song it was based on, "Chanson de Marie-des-Anges," to be included in French writer Jean Richepin's novel *La Glu* (published in 1881 and adapted for the stage in 1883). Verdaguer's poem appeared as part of a homage to the late Bartrina in the 1881 edition of the *Calendari Català*; be-cause Bartrina's ideas conflicted with conservative elements in the Church, Verdaguer prefaced the poem with a lengthy caveat (omitted from *Cari-tat*) lamenting his friend's departure from religious observance. As for the French song, following Duran, in Richepin it is "presented as a folk ballad from Brittany, but is in fact a literary creation of . . . Richepin . . . though probably inspired in Scandinavian legend." Duran continues: in response to an article by E. Boix, J. Vic of the Bibliothèque Nationale de París cites J. Bonafont, who in turn cites J. H. Patterson, who "reproduces an Arab legend corresponding exactly to the 'Chanson de Marie-des-Anges.'" To this I would add that "Amor de mare" also bears a striking resemblance to "A Mother's Heart" by Armenian poet Avetik Isahakyan (1875–1957), more recently popularized by its appearance in the opening scenes of the film *Ararat* (directed by Atom Egoyan, 2002).

"Amor de mare" was published in numerous magazines and newspapers during Verdaguer's lifetime. A reading of the poem by the author was re-corded on wax in 1897, later transferred to record and cassette. The above-mentioned 1897 translation by Ogden is reprinted in the endnotes.

La caritat

Heu vist lo cedre altívol, del Líban en la serra,
alçar-se com de fulles i troncs altra Babel?
Ses branques, on la volva de neu jamai s'aferra,
     s'abaixen a la terra,
mentres son front de fletxa s'enfonsa dins lo cel.

Haver podria d'astres del cel una corona,
i se la fa de fulles i un cap de brot humil,
tot lo que rep la branca més alta a la segona,
     aqueixa a terra ho dóna,
a gotes la roinada, la pluja fil a fil.

De la virtut més alta lo cedre és una imatge:
los núvols atravessa cercant lo Criador,
los dons que li demana i aplega amb son brancatge
     són perles per l'herbatge,
són manna per l'abella, rosada per la flor.

Són goig per los que penen, conhort per los que ploren,
per la ferida bàlsam, per la tristor somrís,
lo preu són de la glòria per los que allí atresoren,
     pels cors que a Déu enyoren
són raigs de llum que envia lo sol del Paradís.

Quan amb Jesús baixava del cel, ha vint centúries,
los àngels de la Glòria ploraven de dolçor,
ploraven a la terra, venint a voladúries,
     i al so de ses cantúries,
s'inaugurà entre els homes lo regne de l'amor.

Los homes respongueren, al so de les cadenes
rompudes, amb un himne d'amor i agraïment;
les flors de fel i llàgrimes fins aquell dia plenes,

Charity

Have you seen the cedar of Lebanon
Rising like a Babel in the range?
Its needled branch, where snowflakes cannot cling,
    Stoops to touch the earth,
While with its lofty top it spears the sky.   5

It might collect celestial orbs for crown,
But takes instead a humble top and leaves,
Its higher limbs share downward with the next,
    And those the farthest down
Sprinkle mist and raindrops on the ground.   10

The cedar is the stamp of highest virtue,
It climbs the clouds in search of the Creator;
The gifts it asks Him, culled with boughs spread out
    Are pearls passed on to grass,
Manna to bees, drops of dew to flowers.   15

They soothe the pain and woe of the afflicted,
Balsam to the wound, and cheer to soften grief;
For those who gather them, the price of glory;
    To hearts that yearn for God,
Streams of sunlight sent from Paradise.   20

When twenty centuries past it came from heaven
With Jesus, angels of Glory wept for joy;
They wept on earth in hosts from high above,
    And with their angel song
Began, among mankind, a reign of love.   25

And with the bursting of the chains mankind
Sang out a hymn of love and gratitude;
And flowers that once were filled with bitterness

        tingueren les serenes
estrelles per germanes, a dalt del firmament.

Betlem veia, entre palles, Déu als pastors somriure;
de bat a bat ses portes obriren les presons;
lo monstre de la guerra deixà estimar i viure;
        deixant l'oasi lliure,
de la maisó dels homes fugiren los lleons.

Pel pobre que no sembra los rics llur camp sembraren
i pels aucells que canten d'amor en sos teulats;
per l'orfenet les mares lo velló d'or filaren
        que les ovelles daren,
i la misericòrdia vestí los despullats.

Flor que del cel adolles en terra les aromes,
oh Caritat!, cadena de flors que l'amor féu,
en terra, tu, agermanes los homes amb los homes,
        i atravessant les bromes,
amb anells d'or enllaces los homes amb son Déu.

Were sisters, now, of stars
That shone serene upon the firmament.   30

In Bethlehem God smiled from straw at shepherds,
And prisons everywhere flung back their gates,
And monstrous war gave way to love and life,
    And freeing the oases,
The lions fled the hospice of mankind.   35

Those with fields sowed seeds for those with none,
And for birds with songs of love on rooftops;
For orphans, mothers spun the golden fleece
    That sheep had given them,
And those whose backs were bare, compassion clothed.   40

Flower pouring heaven's fragrance onto earth,
O Charity! love's chain of linking blossoms,
You join, on earth, all men in brotherhood
    And, passing through the clouds,
With rings of gold unite them with their God.   45

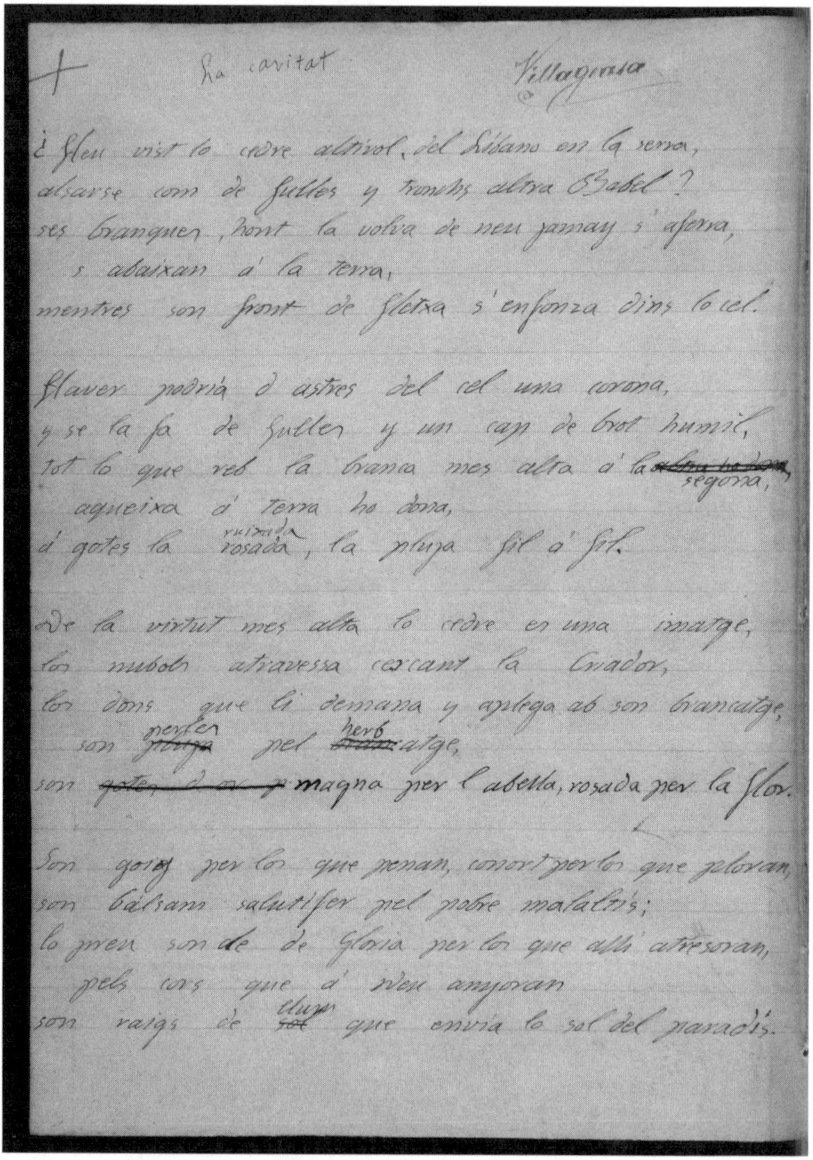

23. Autograph manuscript of opening stanzas of "La mort del rossinyol" (ca. 1885). Courtesy of the Biblioteca de Catalunya.

La mort del rossinyol

Per l'eixerit infant de la masia
la mare avui no troba cap consol;
tirant pedres enlaire aquest migdia
vegé caure a sos peus un rossinyol.

Lo vegé tremolar sobre les fulles
i estendre ses aletes expirant,
i gelar-se, esllanguides, ses despulles,
lira trencada aprés son últim cant.

Ajagut a prop seu sobre l'herbatge
plorà tota la tarda sobre d'ell,
i apetonant-lo, li parlà eix llenguatge,
propi d'un nin parlant amb un aucell:

—Rossinyolet, dels boscos alegria,
per què jo he hagut de ser lo teu botxí,
ja que a ton cant al vespre m'adormia,
i em desvetllava amb ell cada matí?

Mes germanes petites, d'escarnir-te
provaven amagant-se en la verdor;
les grans l'alè aturaven per oir-te,
recordant, somioses, son amor.

Ma bona mare, en èxtasi tranquil·la,
bevia el cant, com rajolí de mel,
dient: «Si en terra així un aucell refila,
com cantaran los angelets al cel!»

Si són ullets dels àngels les estrelles,
del cel al vespre en lo balcó blavís,

A Nightingale's Death

Today the mother finds no way
To set her good child's heart at ease;
Tossing rocks by the farmhouse at noon,
He saw a nightingale fall at his feet.

He saw how it trembled on the leaves   5
And spread its wings as life expired,
Then saw its languid body freeze,
Its last note sung, a broken lyre.

Lying beside it on the grass,
Long through the afternoon he cried,   10
And then, giving the bird a kiss,
He spoke these words, like any child:

"Tiny nightingale, joy of the woods,
Why was it I who brought this on,
The one you lulled to sleep each night,   15
Who woke each morning to your song?

"My younger sisters would mimic your music,
Hiding themselves among the shrubs;
Others, breathless, took pause to hear you,
Calling to mind, dreamful, their loves.   20

"My dear mother, in quiet rapture,
Would drink your song like trickling honey,
And say: 'If birds sing thus on earth,
Imagine the singing of angels in heaven!'

"If high on azure balconies   25
The evening stars are angels' eyes,

n'eixien a escoltar tes cantarelles,
ai!, ressó dels concerts del Paradís.

I eix salari et doní per tes albades,
de la boscúria angèlic trobador!
Arpa del cel, tes cordes he trencades
quan vessaves més himnes en mon cor!

Quin mal m'has fet, perquè et llevàs la vida?
Te podria amb sang meva retornar?
Ai no!, que al cor t'arriba la ferida;
mai més, mai més te sentiré cantar!—

I plora l'infantó tot aquell dia,
ni es vol aconhortar de sa dissort;
plora també a la nit, i si somnia,
gemegant anomena l'aucell mort.

Cosit a les faldilles de sa mare,
l'endemà, que és diumenge, a missa va,
i agenollat, com fill als peus del pare,
son delicte al vicari confessà.

Aliviant sa pura consciència,
plora l'hermós i tendre pecador,
i al perfum de sa angèlica innocència,
lo capellà barreja al seu son plor.

—Torna a ta casa, fillet meu, no plores
—li diu—. Jesús perdona el pecat teu,
del Paradís al músic no l'enyores;
te'l tornarà la gran bondat de Déu—.

L'infantó amb sa mareta se'n tornava,
son cor ple d'esperança i de consol,
i, al ser a casa seva, refilava,
com ahir, en la bardissa el rossinyol.

They just came out to hear you give
Your concerts echoing Paradise.

"Angelic woodland troubadour,
So this is how I've paid your pittance!   30
Heaven's harp, I broke your strings
When best you filled my heart with hymns!

"How did you ever do me wrong?
Might my blood stay your requiem?
No. I've struck you to the heart—   35
I'll never hear you sing again!"

Nothing will console the child,
Who keeps on crying all that day
And night, and if he dreams at all,
It's just to call to the nightingale.   40

He goes to church at his mother's skirts
Next day, Sunday, and come the time,
He kneels like son before a father
And tells the curate of his crime.

Unburdening his conscience brings relief,   45
And the tender child cries for his sins,
While, moved by such pureness of heart,
The curate mixes his own tears with his.

"Now go back home, my son—don't cry.
Jesus will forgive your sin.   50
Your songs of Paradise aren't lost;
God's goodness will bring them back again."

So off went the child beside his mother,
And in his heart fresh hope prevailed,
And when they reached home, like yesterday,   55
In the bramble sang the nightingale.

Amor de mare

. . . lo demés és ayre.

Lo dolent fill a la dolenta filla
    digué un matí:
—Tu ets de mon cel l'estela que més brilla,
    què vols de mi?

Te portaré de casa del meu pare . . .
    tot un tresor;
te portaré les joies de ma mare.
    —Porta'm son cor—.

Lo dolent fill la troba que dormia
    tot somiant:
lo somni dolç que dia i nit somia
    n'és son infant.

Obre son pit i amb un coltell arranca
    son pobre cor,
son cor que viu, com colometa blanca,
    del seu amor!

Com llàntia d'or portant-lo en sa mà dreta,
    batre lo sent.
—Oh qui et sentís, oh cor de ma mareta,
    d'amor batent!—

Tot caminant, de sa estimada queia
    prop del portal,
i amb dolça veu lo cor hermós li deia:
    —Fill, t'has fet mal?

A Mother's Love

. . . the rest is air.

A wicked son remarked to his wicked
  Love one morning:
"Your star lights up my sky the brightest,
  Ask of me anything.

"I'll fetch you piles of treasure from   5
  My father's hearth;
I'll bring you all my mother's gems."
  "Get me her heart!"

He finds his mother fast asleep,
  Dreaming the one   10
Sweet dream she only ever dreams:
  Her beloved son.

Deep in her breast he plunges the knife—
  As though a dove,
He now removes the heart that thrives   15
  On this, her love!

His hand warms to its lamplike pulse,
  Its wealth revealed.
"O mother's heart, your love is such
  A thing to feel!"   20

Just as he reaches the doorway of
  His star most bright,
He stumbles—the heart now asks her son,
  "Are you all right?"

24. The Chapel of La Damunt, scene of the early remembrance evoked in "L'arpa."

FROM

Pàtria

(Country, 1888)

Ramon Pinyol (2002, 24–26) notes that Verdaguer wrote of his projected volume of "patriotic poems" as early as 1881 (by then more than a dozen had been published separately), but not until 1886, following the publication of *Canigó*, could he devote the needed time to the project, and even then he divided his energies between this and two others, completing first *Lo somni de sant Joan: Llegenda del Sagrat Cor de Jesús* (The Dream of Saint John: Legend of the Sacred Heart of Jesus, 1887) and *Excursions i viatges* (Excursions and Travels, 1887). By June 1888, however, the manuscript of *Pàtria* was in the hands of proofreader Josep Balari i Jovany, who had revised *Canigó* and other Verdaguerian works, and the first edition of *Pàtria* (the only one in the poet's lifetime) came out in October. The title, *Pàtria*, alludes to the motto of Barcelona's Jocs Florals, "Patria, Fides, Amor" (Country, Faith, Love); in Verdaguer, *pàtria* takes on a broad sweeping sense to convey not just the notion of "fatherland" but a sense of vital attachment to one's heritage at all levels: cultural, religious, geographic, and historical. To critics who found fault with the book's mixing the religious and the patriotic, the divine and the secular, Verdaguer responded with delight in his prologue to *Dietari d'un pelegrí a Terra Santa* (Diary of a Pilgrim in the Holy Land, 1889): "How thankful I am for this accusation! How even more grateful I'd be if in my heart I knew it to be true! If only I could smoothe the bitter edge of my verses with the honey-sweet, loving name of God!" For Verdaguer, country and faith are inseparable; in his prologue to *Pàtria*, Jaume Collell wrote of his fellow priest and friend that he had "the good fortune of knowing how to fuse within his poet-priest's heart the two greatest of sentiments, the two highest of man's loves: love of God and love of Country."

Of the volume's originally projected sixty-seven poems, Verdaguer pulled twenty-one for publication in subsequent works such as *Flors del Calvari* (Flowers of Calvary,1895) and *Aires del Montseny* (Airs of Montseny, 1901), probably because, as Pinyol suggests, they were too conspicuously inconsistent with the bulk of the poems in *Pàtria*. Although the forty-six poems in the book cover a wide range of topics, a significant number of them deal with either history or *enyorança*, that is, the Catalan version of nostalgia, the longing to return to where one belongs. Pinyol elaborates: "The sentiment of *enyorança* is intimately bound with memory and dream, projecting itself over Catalonia's historic past (the medieval golden age) or over that of the poet (childhood and youth), over the landscape (whether Osona or the whole of Catalonia) or, in mystical tones, over the *celestial paradise*; all of which frequently blend together, the divisions between them blurring as one after another are evinced in his poems." According to Pinyol, "To Barcelona" evokes nineteenth-century progress while highlighting and seeking to secure the city's ties with its past, and "The Two Bell Towers" bears witness to Catalonia's crumbling Romanesque churches and monasteries while urging their restoration, with re-Christianization and cultural renaissance—medieval and modern—fusing in both. "The Harp" evokes a personal memory—the landscape of the poet's childhood, recalling and mythifying the decisive moment of poetic discovery, again inseparable from sentiments both patriotic and religious. In "The Emigrant" (the most widely sung of Verdaguer's poems after "Virelay"), the feeling of *enyorança* comes through as the characteristic longing for one's native soil, a powerful paradigm for nostalgia of all types.

Perhaps the most "patriotic" of poems in *Pàtria* is "Lo Farell" (not included in this selection), whose title refers to a sort of Catalan Paul Bunyan. Verdaguer had been part of a delegation that submitted the Memorial de Greuges (Statement of Grievances) to King Alfonso XII of Spain early in 1885. The main issues were the impending repeal of Catalan civil law under the "unification" of Spanish law and a commercial agreement with England that undermined Catalan industry. The poem is Verdaguer's response to the failure of this initiative. The following lines reflect popular sentiment in the wake of the event:

> Would they have you bow your giant's head,
> Montseny, and yours, divine Montserrat,
> Because Castile is flat?
> . . . .
> Should I straighten my sickle into a saber?
> Forge my plowshare into a cannon?

But the poem's final lines reaffirm Verdaguer's commitment to peaceful process where conflicting interests are aggravated by polarizing ideologies:

> Never! As a son of Spain I'll work for her,
> And wait, and hope the sleeping lion wakes.

The political and cultural issues surrounding the question of peripheral identities versus central hegemony have continued to shape attitudes and policies in Spain throughout the twentieth and into the twenty-first centuries and are woven into the fabric of debate in all spheres whether political, social, or religious. To his credit, Verdaguer, in reflecting ideological sentiments bound up with cultural and geographic heritage, tempers antagonisms by tapping the underlying sense of humanity common to all.

A Barcelona

Barcelona, archivo de la cortesía, albergue
de los extranjeros, hospital de los pobres,
patria de los valientes, venganza de los
ofendidos, y correspondencia grata de firmes
amistades y en sitio y en belleza única.

Cervantes

Quan a la falda et miro de Montjuïc seguda,
m'apar veure't als braços d'Alcides gegantí,
que per guardar sa filla del seu costat nascuda
en serra transformant-se s'hagués quedat aquí.

I al veure que traus sempre rocam de ses entranyes
per tos casals, que creixen com arbres amb saó,
apar que diga a l'ona i al cel i a les muntanyes:
Mirau-la: os de mos ossos, s'és feta gran com jo!

Perquè tes naus, que tornen amb ales d'oreneta,
vers Cap del Riu, en l'ombra no es vagen a estellar,
ell alça tots los vespres un far amb sa mà dreta
i per guiar-les entra de peus dintre la mar.

La mar dorm a tes plantes besant-les com vassalla
que escolta de tos llavis lo *còdic* de ses lleis,
i si li dius «arrere!» fa lloc a ta muralla
com si Marquets i Llanzes encara en fossen reis.

Al nàixer amazona, de mur te coronares,
mes prompte ta creixença rompé l'estret cordó;
tres voltes te'l cenyires, tres voltes lo trencares,
per sobre el clos de pedra saltant com un lleó.

To Barcelona

Barcelona, safehold of courtesy, hospice
to outsiders, ward to the poor, home
to the valiant, vengeance of the affronted,
warm reciprocity in steadfast friendship,
and unique in setting and in beauty.
    CERVANTES

    I watch you lying here on Montjuïc's lap,
    Held fast, it seems, in huge Alcides' wide
    Embrace: to guard the daughter born of his stamp,
    He settled on this spot as mountainside.

    And seeing you take rocks from his entrails   5
    To raise your halls that grow and thrive like trees,
    He seems to say to sky and sea and hills:
    Bone of my bones, she's grown as big as me!

    Each night to warn your homebound ships he lifts
    By Cap del Riu a lantern beaming bright;   10
    Swift-sailing ships come in on swallows' wings,
    He guides them as he wades into the tide.

    The vassal sea sleeps humbly at your feet
    And hears the law proclaimed throughout your shores,
    And when you say: "Step back!" her waves recede,   15
    As though Marquets and Llanzas reigned once more.

    Born Amazon, you took a wall for crown,
    But soon you broke beyond that narrow bind,
    Three times erected, then three times pulled down:
    You leapt the stabling stonework like a lion.   20

Per què lligar-te els braços amb eix cinyell de torres?
No escau a una matrona la faixa dels infants;
més val que l'enderroques d'un colp de mà i esborres;
muralles vols ciclòpees? Déu te les da més grans.

Déu te les da d'un rengle de cimes que et coronen,
gegants de la marina dels de muntanya al peu,
que ferms de l'un a l'altre les aspres mans se donen,
formant a tes espatlles un altre Pirineu.

Amb Montalegre encaixa Noupins; amb Finestrelles,
Olorda; amb Collserola, Carmel i Guinardons;
los llits dels rius que seguen eix mur són les portelles;
Garraf, Sant Pere Martri i Montgat, los torreons.

L'alt Tibidabo, roure que sos plançons domina,
és la superba acròpolis que vetlla la ciutat;
l'agut Montcada, un ferro de llança gegantina
que una nissaga d'hèroes clavada allí ha deixat.

Ells sien, ells, los termes eterns de tos eixamples;
dels rònecs murs a trossos fes-ne present al mar,
a on d'un port sens mida seran los braços amples
que el puguen amb sos boscos de naus empresonar.

Com tu devoren marges i camps, i es tornen pobles
los masos que et rodegen, ciutats los pagesius,
com nines vers sa mare corrent a passos dobles;
a qui duran llurs aigües sinó a la mar, los rius?

I creixes i t'escampes: quan la planícia et manca
t'enfiles a les costes doblant-te a llur jaient;
en totes les que et volten un barri teu s'embranca
que, onada sobre onada, tu amunt vas empenyent.

Geganta que tos braços avui cap a les serres
estens, quan hi arribes demà, doncs, què faràs?
Faràs com heura immensa que, ja abrigant les terres,
puja a cenyir un arbre del bosc amb cada braç.

Why tie your arms with binding towers at all?
An infant's sash ill suits a full-grown woman;
Better to reduce this belt to rubble:
God gives you greater walls, should you want them.

Your God-sent crown's a row of marching peaks   25
(Below them more giants surface from the seas),
Each thrusting out a rugged arm to each,
Your backdrop is a second Pyrenees.

Finestrelles joins Olorda; Montalegre,
Noupins; Carmel and Guinardons are met   30
By Collserola—rivers carved your gates;
Your towers: Garraf, Montgat, Sant Pere Màrtir.

High Tibidabo, oak commanding saplings,
Stands guard, acropolis atop this city;
Montcada's crest: a giant's iron lance,   35
What's left of some unfabled victory.

The timeless bounds of your expanse are these;
So cast into the sea your crumbling walls
That their embrace may catch your harbor's sweep,
And so enclose her woods of masts and hulls.   40

Like you, your far-off farmsteads break beyond
Field and fence, as hamlets turn to towns,
And race like children to their mother's arms:
Where else but to the sea might rivers run?

You grow and spread, and where the flats abide   45
You take the incline, bending to its tilt:
Your quarters swell on hillsides like the tide,
And branching out, you lift them further still.

A giant reaching out to nearby mountains,
Once you get there, how will you go on?   50
Like ivy into trees from off the ground,
You'll wind your upward way with every arm.

Veus a ponent estendre's un prat com d'esmeralda?
Un altre Nil lo forma de ses arenes d'or,
a on, si t'estreteja de Montjuïc la falda,
podrien eixamplar-se tes tendes i ton cor.

Aquelles verdes ribes florides que el sol daura,
Sant Just Desvern que ombregen los tarongers i pins,
de Valldoreix los boscos, d'Hebron i de Valldaura,
teixeixen ta futura corona de jardins.

I aqueix esbart de pobles que viuen en la costa?
Són nimfes catalanes que et vénen a abraçar,
gavines blanquinoses que el vent del segle acosta
perquè amb tes ales d'àliga les portes a volar.

La Murtra, un jorn, la Verge del Port, la Bonanova
seran tos temples, si ara lo niu de tos amors;
los Agudells, en blanca mudant sa verda roba,
abaixaran ses testes per ser tos miradors.

Junyits besar voldrien tos peus amb ses onades,
esclaus de ta grandesa, Besòs i Llobregat,
i ser de tos reductes troneres avançades
los pits de Catalunya, Montseny i Montserrat.

Llavors, llavors al témer que el vols per capçalera,
girant los ulls als Alpes, lo Pirineu veí
demanarà, eixugant-se la blanca cabellera,
si la París del Sena s'és trasplantada aquí.

—No —respondrà ma pàtria—, de mi i la mar és filla;
d'un bes de ses onades, com Venus, m'ha nascut;
per ço totes les aigües digueren-li pubilla,
per ço totes les terres pagaren-li tribut.

Per ço da ducs a Atenes i comtes a Provença,
i per bandera a Espanya un tros del seu penó;
per ço *ni un peix se veia dintre la mar immensa*
que no dugués gravades les barres d'Aragó.

You see that emerald meadow to the west?
A new Nile spawned it from her sands of gold:
Should Montjuïc's lap confine you in your spread,   55
Your tents may there be pitched, your heart unfold.

Those verdant sun-kissed riverbanks in bloom,
Sant Just Desvern, her orange groves and pines,
Timbered Valldoreix, Valldaura, Hebron—
Your future crown of gardens intertwines.   60

Those villages that flock along the coast?
Catalan nymphs, straight to your arms they fly;
This century's winds fetch these blanched seabirds close:
With you, on eagle's wings, they'll sail the sky.

Temples, now cradles of your love, will rise: 65
Murtra, the Harbor Virgin, Bonanova;
The Agudells, whose green robes turn to white,
Will bow their heads to be your belvedere.

Flowing down to kiss your feet before
Your majesty, the Besòs and Llobregat   70
Would serve as forward crenels to your wards
And heartland's breasts: Montseny and Montserrat.

The nearby Pyrenees, afraid you'll take
Them for your headboard, look to the Alps with a start
And ask, giving their snowy tops a shake,   75
If Paris and her Seine now drift apart.

My fatherland replies: "She is my daughter,
Born, like Venus, of waves that kissed my shore,
And so, proclaimed an heiress by the waters,
From all the lands surrounding tributes poured.   80

"Her dukes and counts ruled Athens and Provence;
To Spain she gave for flag a cut of standard:
And *not a fish there was that swam upon*
The sea unstamped by Aragon's bright banner.

Per ço fou sempre l'astre d'Orient per les Espanyes:
amb una mà hi posava de Gutenberg lo flam,
carrils de ferro amb l'altra; i un fill de ses entranyes
fou qui primer va prendre per missatger lo llamp—.

Sos peus dintre l'escuma, son front en ple migdia,
mirau-la allà jaienta si n'és d'hermosa i gran;
apar, oh Catalunya, ton geni que somia
les glòries que passaren, les glòries que vindran.

Mirau-la: santa Eulària l'abriga amb sa bandera,
sant Jordi la defensa de l'infernal dragó,
i guia, quan rescata catius, sa nau velera,
apareixent pels aires, l'Estel de Cervelló.

La volten de sos hèroes les bèl·liques imatges,
los Ataülfos, Jofres, Borrells i Berenguers,
Ramon lo de l'espasa, Ramon lo dels *Usatges*,
i arrossegant sa túnica de dol los Fivellers.

Per Barcelona Balmes deixà del Ter les ribes
com àliga novella quan aixecava el vol;
en ella trau del marbre Campeny imatges vives,
i pasta en sa paleta Fortuny la llum del sol.

D'ací Roger de Llúria sortia, al vent de glòria
movent ses naus les ales com un esbart d'aucells;
jamai, jamai lluitaren sense cantar victòria;
sovint dugueren presos rosaris de vaixells.

Aquí Don Joan d'Àustria les àncores aferra,
duent-li de Lepanto llorers; allí Colon,
tornant d'aquell viatge que duplicà la terra,
als peus dels Reis Catòlics féu rodolar un món.

De Bellesguard li resten perfums; de les despulles
del rusc de Valldonzella, perfums i dolça mel;
entre tallers i fàbriques té campanars i agulles,
com dits que entre boirades de fum signen lo cel.

"She shone on Spanish lands as eastern star,   85
In one hand held the light of Gutenberg,
In one the iron horse; a son of hers
First took the lightning's lance for messenger."

Stretched out magnificent and bright, she seems—
Her head high in the noon, her feet in the foam—   90
O Catalonia, your genius that dreams
Your glories past, your glories yet to come.

See Saint Eulària shield her with her pennon,
Saint George defend her from the dragon's wrath,
And in the skies above her rescue missions,   95
The Star of Cervelló to guide them back.

Her heroes everywhere are seen depicted:
Ataülfs, Jofres, Borrells and Berenguers,
Ramon of the sword, Ramon the law-giver,
And trailing mourning tunics, the Fivellers.   100

For Barcelona Balmes left the Ter,
Just like a fledgling eagle taking flight;
Campeny sculpts life into the marble there,
And on his palette, Fortuny fuses sunlight.

From here Roger de Llúria set out,   105
His fleet's wings fluttering on the winds of glory.
Not once were they in warfare ever routed;
They led their captive ships in tow like rosaries.

Bearing laurels from Lepanto, here
Don John of Austria put in, sails furled;   110
And here Columbus, the earth become a sphere,
Brought back the Catholic Sovereigns a world.

Perfumes of Bellesguard and sweetest honey
From Valldonzella's hive in ruins linger;
Spires and belfries rise by factories,   115
Pointing through the smoke to heaven like fingers.

Com dos soldats que hi resten d'una legió romana,
té dues torres, guaites del seu mural antic;
i, gos de presa vora son amo, la Drassana
que per lladrar s'aixeca quan trona Montjuïc.

Pla amunt se veu Pedralbes, on s'ou la canticela
dels àngels de la terra pel cel aletejant;
i de Marvella vora l'espill, la Ciutadela,
per fer de jardinera ses armes trossejant.

Té a un cap Sant Pau, a l'altre Sant Pere de les Puelles,
Santa Maria, estrella del mar, i la del Pi;
i entre eixes flors li naixen de l'art gentils poncelles:
jamai tanta florida s'és vista en son jardí!

Mes, ai!, com entre els arbres del bosc la fulla d'heura,
lo cor s'aferra als temples i monuments més vells,
i, en hores de misteri, d'amants records s'hi abeura,
sentint-los com conversen i conversant amb ells.

De Sant Miquel, oh temple que els àngels construïren,
anys ha que jaus en terra dels homes oblidat,
i encara apar que et cerquen i de dolor sospiren
les gòtiques imatges de Casa la Ciutat!

Ja que han perdut per sempre tan dolça companyia,
vegessen cara a cara Sant Just i Sant Pastor;
Santa Àgata en sa hermosa capella somriuria;
en cel i en terra els àngels se tenen tant amor!

Sant Jordi de l'Audiència vol veure Santa Clara;
l'antic Palau dels Comtes enyora el del Consell.
Oh!, aterra eixa cortina de cases que separa
l'estàtua de Don Jaume del seu real Tinell.

Enmig d'aqueixa plaça, que no tindrà segona,
les tres columnes d'Hèrcules quan mire el viatger,
creurà veure les Gràcies, per fer-te de corona,
de braços enllaçades, dansant en ton verger.

Two towers, sentries of her ancient wall,
Stand like soldiers left by Roman legions;
The dockyard, field dog at his master's call,
Gives answer to the blast of Montjuïc's cannons.   120

Higher, from Pedralbes, one can hear her
Earthly angels' skysome serenade;
While Ciutadella, near Marvella's mirror,
Has turned her arms to trowels and garden spades.

Saint Paul at one end, Saint Peter the other,   125
Saint Mary of the Pine and of the Sea;
Fine art sprouts graceful buds among such flowers:
Her garden never saw such blooms as these.

Alas! the heart like vines among the trees
Holds fast to age-old monuments and shrines,   130
And drinks the mystery of love's memories
And listens, joining in their talk at times.

Saint Michael's, temple that the angels raised,
By men long years forgotten, here you lie,
And still they seem to search for you, dismayed,   135
While in the Hall the Gothic icons sigh.

Saints Justus and Pastor look face to face,
Their dear companion evermore interred;
Saint Agatha would surely smile: an angel's
Love is measureless in heaven and on earth.   140

Saint George of the Courthouse longs to see Saint Clare;
The Counts' palace misses the Council hall.
Pull down the wall of buildings that now bar
Don Jaume's statue from his royal Tinell!

And Hercules' three columns rising on   145
That unmatched square will seem to travelers now
The very Graces dancing arm in arm,
Descending on your garden as your crown.

Aplica a tos nous barris aqueix immens escaire,
vestigi de l'acròpolis que Roma te deixà;
per eix gran pòrtic deixa passar la llum i l'aire,
la Creu res ha de témer d'un trípode pagà.

La Creu que allí sant Jaume plantava ha vint centúries,
domina com un cedre los arbres del país,
té nius i fruits de vida, murmuris i cantúries,
més pur tornant al Tàber son *Hort del Paradís.*

Amb son mantell de pedra nuat amb gòtics llaços
l'abriga, alçant als núvols sos campanars, la Seu,
i com si fos Don Jaume que aixeca al cel los braços
apar que se n'esbombe sa tronadora veu:

—Avant, ciutat dels comtes, de riu a riu ja estesa,
avant, fins on empenga ta nau l'Omnipotent:
t'han presa la corona, la mar no te l'han presa;
del mar ets reina encara, ton ceptre és lo trident.

La mar, un dia esclava del teu poder, te crida,
com dos portells obrint-te Suez i Panamà:
quiscun amb tota una Índia rienta te convida,
amb l'Àsia, les Amèriques, la terra i l'oceà.

La mar no te l'han presa, ni el pla, ni la muntanya
que s'alça a tes espatlles per fer-te de mantell,
ni eix cel que fóra un dia ma tenda de campanya,
ni eix sol que fóra un dia faró del meu vaixell;

ni el geni, aqueixa estrella que et guia, ni eixes ales
la indústria i l'art, penyores d'un bell esdevenir,
ni aqueixa dolça flaire de caritat que exhales,
ni aqueixa fe . . . , i un poble que creu no pot morir.

Ton cel té encara totes ses flors diamantines;
la pàtria té sos hèroes, ses lires los amors;
Clemència Isaura encara de roses i englantines
fa cada primavera present als trobadors.

Lay out your future quarters to this huge
Angle iron, acropolis of your Roman times,   150
A gate where light and air come streaming through,
The Cross need have no fear of pagan trines.

Like a cedar above the trees of the land there stands,
Brimming with song and nests and fruits of life,
The Cross James raised a score of centuries past,   155
Returning tenfold Tabor's Paradise.

Your See, her stone cloak trimmed with Gothic ties,
Shelters it, raising bell towers to the clouds,
And seems Don Jaume lifting to the skies
His arms and voice of thunder ringing out: 160

"Onward, City of Counts, spread between rivers,
Onward, ship, as far as the Almighty leads—
Queen of the sea, the trident is your scepter:
They've seized your crown, but you hold fast your sea.

"The sea, your servant once, calls out to you,   165
The gates of Panama and Suez open—
Each one extends a sparkling India to you:
Asia and the Americas, earth and oceans.

"For you hold fast your sea, and plains and mountains
Rising up behind you as your cloak,   170
And sky that stretched above me as my tent,
And sun whose rays once lit my ocean road;

"Your spirit, guiding star; and industry
And art, your wings and promise for your future,
And the sweet fragrance of your charity,   175
And faith: a people that believes endures.

"Your sky still shines with all her diamond flowers;
The homeland has its heroes, love its lyres;
And still each spring Clemència Isaura
Gives troubadours her roses and sweetbriers.   180

Lo teu present esplèndid és de nous temps aurora;
tot somiant fulleja lo llibre del passat;
treballa, pensa, lluita; mes creu, espera i ora.
Qui enfonsa o alça els pobles, és Déu que els ha creat—.

"In your excellent present dawns a new day;
Dip into the pages of your past—dreamful;
Work, think, struggle; yet believe, hope, pray.
For God alone brings down or lifts up peoples."

25. Autograph manuscript of opening stanzas of "A Barcelona"
(ca. 1880). Courtesy of the Biblioteca de Catalunya.

26. Autograph manuscript of opening stanzas of "Los dos campanars"
(ca. 1880). Courtesy of the Biblioteca de Catalunya.

Los dos campanars

Doncs, què us heu fet, superbes abadies,
Marcèvol, Serrabona i Sant Miquel,
i tu, decrèpit Sant Martí, que omplies
aqueixes valls de salms i melodies
la terra d'àngels i de sants lo cel?

Doncs, què n'heu fet, oh valls!, de l'asceteri,
escola de l'amor de Jesucrist?
On és, oh soledat!, lo teu salteri?
On tos rengles de monjos, presbiteri,
que, com un cos sens ànima, estàs trist?

D'Ursèolo a on és lo dormitori?
La celda abacial del gran Garí?
On és de Romualdo l'oratori,
los pal·lis i retaules, l'or i evori
que entretallà ha mil anys cisell diví?

Los càntics i les llums s'esmortuïren;
la rosa s'esfullà com lo roser;
los himnes sants en l'arpa s'adormiren,
com verderoles que en llur niu moriren
quan lo bosc les oïa més a pler.

Dels romànics altars no en queda rastre,
del claustre bizantí no en queda res;
caigueren les imatges d'alabastre
i s'apagà sa llàntia, com un astre
que en Canigó no s'encendrà mai més.

Com dos gegants d'una legió sagrada
sols encara hi ha drets dos campanars:
són los monjos darrers de l'encontrada,

The Two Bell Towers

Superb abbeys, what has come of you all?
Marcèvol, Serrabona, Sant Miquel,
And crumbling Sant Martí, who with your strains
Of psalm and melody once filled the vale,
Seeding earth with angels, and sky with saints?   5

What has become of all your cloisters, O dales,
That served so long the love of Christ for school?
Where, O solitude, is your psalter now?
Where, sanctuary, do your monks now file,
As body without soul you lie in sorrow?   10

What of the room where Orseolo slept?
And what of great Garí's abbatial cell?
And what of Romualdo's oratory,
And palliums and retables richly set
A thousand years ago in gold and ivory?   15

Your canticles now silent, your lights extinguished,
The petals of your shining rose are shed,
Your harps and holy hymns all sleeping long,
Like yellowhammers, lifeless in their nest,
Just when the wood rang clear in sparkling song.   20

Of altars Romanesque lie no remains,
Your cloister, Byzantine, has left no trace;
Bright alabaster fallen long ago,
The lamp that shone is but an orb effaced
That nevermore will grace Mount Canigó.   25

Just like two giants from some saintly army,
Alone upon the land there rise two belfries:
Last among the monks to make their departure,

que ans de partir, per última vegada,
contemplen l'enderroc de sos altars.

Són dues formidables sentinelles
que en lo Conflent posà l'eternitat:
semblen garrics los roures al peu d'elles;
les masies del pla semblen ovelles
al peu de llur pastor agegantat.

Una nit fosca al seu germà parlava
lo de Cuixà: —Doncs, que has perdut la veu?
Alguna hora a ton cant me desvetllava
i ma veu a la teva entrelligava
cada matí per beneir a Déu.

—Campanes ja no tinc —li responia
lo ferreny campanar de Sant Martí—.
Oh!, qui pogués tornar-me-les un dia!
Per tocar a morts pels monjos les voldria;
per tocar a morts pels monjos i per mi.

Que tristos, ai, que tristos me deixaren!
Tota un tarda los vegí plorar;
set vegades per veure'm se giraren;
jo aguaito fa cent anys per on baixaren:
tu que vius més avall, no els veus tornar?

—No. Pel camí de Codalet i Prada
sols minaires obiro i llauradors;
diu que torna a son arbre la niuada,
més, ai!, la que deixà nostra brancada
no hi cantarà mai més dolços amors.

Mai més! Mai més! Ells jauen sota terra;
nosaltres damunt seu anam caient;
lo segle que ens deu tant ara ens aterra,
en son oblit nostra grandor enterra
i ossos i glòries i records se'ns ven.

They turn their gaze again, before the leaving,
Upon the ruins of what were once their altars.   30

Two stalwart sentinels is what they are,
Now posted in Conflent, eternal guards:
Tall oak trees seem like bramble at their feet,
And stone-built dwellings rising on the swards
Below these bulking herdsmen seem like sheep.   35

One pitch-dark night the tower of Cuixà hailed
His brother: "Could it be your voice has failed?
Each hour your song would rouse me with its ringing;
Our voices as they blended through the vale
Would lift our praise and thanks to God each morning."   40

"I have no more bells," came down the reply
From sturdy Sant Martí high on the rise.
"But were one day my bells restored to me,
They'd toll for all my monks gone off to die:
For all my monks gone off to die, and me.   45

"How heavy were their hearts the day they left!
All afternoon I watched them as they wept,
And seven times looked back from down the path;
A hundred years this vigil now I've kept:
Might you, below, have seen them coming back?"   50

"No, the miners only, and plowmen take
The Codalet and Prada roads: they say
That every clutch one day returns to tree,
But those who from our branches went their way
Will lift no more their song of love so sweet.   55

"No more! for now they lie within the earth,
While we too, above them, tumble downward;
Abandoned by the century we upraised,
Our fame in its oblivion interred,
Our bones, our glory, our memory betrayed."   60

—Ai!, ell ventà les cendres venerables
del comte de Rià, mon fundador;
convertí mes capelles en estables,
i desniats los àngels pels diables
en eixos cims ploraren de tristor.

I jo plorava amb ells i encara ploro,
mes, ai!, sens esperança de conhort,
puix tot se'n va, i no torna lo que enyoro,
i de pressa, de pressa, jo m'esfloro,
rusc on l'abell murmuriós s'és mort.

—Caurem plegats —lo de Cuixà contesta—.
Jo altre cloquer tenia al meu costat;
rival dels puigs, alçava l'ampla testa,
i amb sa sonora veu, dolça o feresta,
estrafeia el clarí o la tempestat.

Com jo, tenia nou-cents anys de vida,
mes, nou Matusalem, també morí;
com Goliat al rebre la ferida,
caigué tot llarg, i ara a son llit me crida
son insepult cadavre gegantí.

Abans de gaire ma deforme ossada
blanquejarà en la vall de Codalet;
lo front me pesa més, i la vesprada,
quan visita la lluna l'encontrada,
tota s'estranya de trobar-m'hi dret.

Vaig a ajaure'm també; d'eixes altures
tu baixaràs a reposar amb mi,
i, ai!, qui llaure les nostres sepultures
no sabrà dir a les edats futures
on foren Sant Miquel i Sant Martí—.

Aixís un vespre els dos cloquers parlaven;
mes, l'endemà al matí, al sortir lo sol,
recomençant los càntics que ells acaben,

"Alas! my chapels it has turned to stables,
And cast to shifting winds the venerable
Ashes of the Count of Rià, my founder;
Devils have dislodged the work of angels,
Who flew to weep in sorrow on the mountain.   65

"And I wept with them, and I sorrow still,
Alas! all hope of solace lost with all
That was: and gone now all that I desired,
I stand and watch my petals as they fall,
A beeless hive, the stir within has died."   70

"We'll fall together," Cuixà's tower replies.
"Long stood another belfry by my side;
Lifting his broad head, he rivaled the summits,
Sounding wide his voice: now bold, now mild,
Now a crashing tempest, now shrilling trumpets.   75

"Like mine, his life had spanned nine hundred years,
Yet like Methuselah's, his death drew near,
And like Goliath struck upright full force,
He fell headlong, and now upon his bier
Calls out to me, a vast unburied corpse.   80

"And soon my skeleton, deformed and wrecked,
Will lie undone and bleached in Codalet;
My head weighs heavy, and with night advancing,
When rising up to make her vesper visit,
The moon marvels to find me here still standing.   85

"I too will go and rest, and from your hilltop
You too one day will join me on this spot,
And those whose plows above our graves make good
Will never say, nor guess, what was our lot,
Where Sant Miquel and Sant Martí once stood."   90

So spoke the pair of belfries there that night;
But next day, at dawn, in the morning sunlight,
Taking up the strains left off in the vale,

los tudons amb l'heurera conversaven,
amb l'estrella del dia el rossinyol.

Somrigué la muntanya engallardida
com si estrenàs son verdejant mantell;
mostrà's com núvia de joiells guarnida;
i de ses mil congestes la florida
blanca esbandí com taronger novell.

Lo que un segle bastí l'altre ho aterra,
mes resta sempre el monument de Déu;
i la tempesta, el torb, l'odi i la guerra
al Canigó no el tiraran a terra,
no esbrancaran per ara el Pirineu.

L'arpa

Damunt de mon poblet hi ha una capella
d'una roureda secular voltada,
és son altar lo trono d'una Verge
d'aquella rodalia sobirana.
Era ma pobra mare, que al cel sia,
sa més fidel i més humil vassalla,
i sent jo petitó, cada diumenge
a dur-li alguna toia me portava,
a son Fill oferint-me que em somreia,
com jo, assegut en la materna falda.
Un cap al tard, tindria alguna pena,
puix ella féu l'oració més llarga
i esgranà lo rosari més calmosa
barrejant amb sos grans alguna llàgrima,
i lo tornà a resar; li recaria
sola deixar l'amor de la seva ànima.
A l'empènyer la porta de l'església,
un fill de Nàpols eixerit passava,

The ringdove stopped to converse with the ivy,
The daystar to chat with the nightingale. 95

Heartened, the mountain smiled down on the scene,
And boasting a burgeoning cloak of green,
Shone like a bride well decked with jewels and gems,
Then doffed a thousand snowdrifts from its mien
Just like an orange sapling snowy blossoms. 100

What one century erects, the next brings low,
But God's enduring monument stands long:
Nor raging winds, nor war, nor wrath of men
Will overturn the peaks of Canigó:
The Pyrenees, for now, will not be bent. 105

The Harp

There's a chapel that overlooks my village,
hundred-year oaks rising all round it;
its altar serves as throne to a Virgin,
the sovereign of neighboring farms and hamlets.
Of all her servants, the most faithful and humble 5
was my own dear mother, surely in heaven,
who every Sunday when I was a toddler
took me to bring her some flowers we'd gathered,
offering me to her Son, who smiled at me,
He, too, in the arms of His mother. 10
One day she lingered long in prayer
beneath the weight of some sorrow or other,
quietly passing the beads through her fingers,
a tear now and then mixed in, and starting
the rosary again, regretting the moment 15
of taking her leave of her soul's most beloved.
Just as she opened the door to the temple,
there passed a sprightly son of Naples,

duent al coll una arpa tota plena
d'harmoniosa música d'Itàlia.
Ella, escorrent sa bossa escanyolida,
un rajolí de notes li demana
per la Verge Santíssima que es queda
sola i de nit en la boscúria isarda.
A un caire del portal lo jove es posa
i passa els dits per los bordons de l'arpa:
quiscun llança una nota, melodia
que amb melodies cèliques s'enllaça,
murmurioses urnes que s'aboquen
barrejant sa corrent immaculada
de gemecs de neguit, himnes de festa,
defalliments d'amor i crits d'*hosanna*.
Lo temple escolta i, amb la boca oberta,
apar que a la boscúria li demana
si són los passerells que a voladúries
hi solen refilar al trenc de l'alba,
amb aleteigs i música divina
desvetllant la natura endormiscada.
La mare seia al marxapeu del temple,
i jo, mig recolzat sobre sa falda,
i a tres dits de mos ulls l'instrument músic
omplia la rodona portalada.
Jo, mentres l'ona cèlica bevia,
primerenca regor de la meva ànima,
a través de les cordes, fonts perennes
per on lo paradís se m'hi vessava,
a aquell bocí de món que coneixia,
a la terra i al cel doní una ullada.
Que hermosos los trobí! Per la finestra
de reixa d'or si jo els vegés encara!
Vegí el Montseny engarlandat de boscos,
vegí el Puigmal de cabellera blanca
damunt la serra del Pirene altívol
com un gegant al cim d'una muralla,
i entre ells, estesa en son conreu, Ausona
a prop del Gurri de lluentes aigües,
com gentil segadora muntanyesa
que dorm al peu de son falçó de plata.

who bore, strapped to his neck, a harp that
brimmed with the music and melody of Italy.   20
My mother, scraping her paltry handbag,
asks him to pluck out a trickle of harpsong
for the Blessed Virgin she leaves behind her,
alone in the night on the desolate hillside.
The young man stands to one side of the entrance   25
and moves his fingers over the bourdons:
each one launches a note, mingling
its own melody with more, celestial,
a host of urns pouring and murmuring,
mixing their purest of waters, babbling   30
with moans of disquiet, hymns of feastdays,
swoons of the lovesick and cries of *hosanna*.
The temple, its mouth agape, listens
and seems to ask the woods surrounding
if this might be a throng of linnets   35
singing their song that greets the daybreak
with stirring of wings and heavenly music
to waken nature from her slumber.
My mother sat on the chapel threshold,
and I, beside her, leaned on her lap, while   40
before my eyes, at three fingers' distance,
the instrument filled the great round entrance.
Then, as I drank in the skysome billows,
this my soul's first of waterings,
out through the strings, perennial fountains,   45
springs from which paradise poured itself out to me,
I now caught a glimpse of the earth and heavens,
that parcel of world to me familiar.
What a beautiful sight! If only that very
golden-grated vision shone always!   50
I saw Montseny decked out with wooded
garlands, Puigmal with snowy tresses
commanding the towering Pyrenees,
like a giant posted high on the ramparts,
and between them, below, Ausona's farmlands   55
stretched out by the Gurri's glimmering waters,
like, after the harvest, a graceful peasant
sleeping beside her silvery sickle.

Més humil i més pròxima, l'església
vegí de mon poblet, ramat de cases
que com pollets esveradissos viuen
a l'aixopluc de les maternes ales.
Entre elles una n'obirí més xica
que les seves veïnes i més blanca;
lo fum sortia de la llar fumosa,
plena per mi de resplendors de l'alba.
Mos companyons i companyones tendres
feien a dalt del porxe la sardana
i baixaven a l'hort, a rua feta,
papallons joguinosos d'horabaixa;
elles envers les roses que florien,
ells vers on lo cirer vermellejava,
no tant com les enceses barretines
que s'hi veien pujar com una parra.
Feien jocs d'ignocència i de platxeri,
i corrien i reien i cantaven,
i sa dolça cridòria me venia
amb lo melós arpegi barrejada.
Vegí el camp de mon pare, ros de xeixa
crescuda amb son suor. Vegí l'aubaga,
los boscos i solells, nius de mos somnis
d'on lo més primerenc prengué volada.
I vegí vostres peus i vostres cingles
i vostres fronts, oh serres de la pàtria!,
i al pondre's damunt seu l'astre del dia,
corona d'or irradiant de flama,
engolir-se'l vegí l'alt Pedraforca
fet un Vesuvi atapeït de lava;
i entre el floreig d'estrelles que naixien
del vespre hermós entre les fosques ales,
com aurora divina que em somreia,
vegí en lo cel la Musa catalana.

Closer and humbler, the church of my village
stood out above its flock of houses,   60
a scampering of chicks that live together
beneath the sheltering wings of their mother.
Among them I spotted one that was smaller
and whiter, too, than the rest of its neighbors,
with smoke trailing up from out its chimney,   65
from the hearth that held the daybreak's radiance.
There, my tender companions in childhood
joined hands in play up on the terrace,
then down to the garden they went together,
butterflies dancing in the angling sunshine,   70
the girls going straight to the blossoming roses,
the boys to the cherry tree glowing with cherries,
their color no match for the bright *barretinas*
now clinging and climbing like vine up its branches.
The games they played were of joy and innocence,   75
and the songs they sang, and their running and laughing,
and sweet-sounding shouts—now all of it came to me
mingled and mixed with the honeyed arpeggios.
I saw my father's field, now golden
with wheat from his sweat. I saw the woodlands   80
and hillsides, shady and sunlit, nests of my
dreams, where the earliest first lifted upward.
And I saw your feet and your cliffs and your faces,
O mountain ranges that rise on my homeland!
And when upon it there set the daystar,   85
golden crown of flaming brilliance,
I saw high Pedraforca devour it,
a new Vesuvius bursting with lava;
and there in the flowering of stars, born amid
shadowing wings of the lovely evening,   90
smiling at me, divine aurora,
I saw the Catalan Muse in the heavens.

L'emigrant

Dolça Catalunya,
pàtria del meu cor,
quan de tu s'allunya
d'enyorança es mor.

I

Hermosa vall, bressol de ma infantesa,
    blanc Pirineu,
marges i rius, ermita al cel suspesa,
    per sempre adéu!
Arpes del bosc, pinsans i caderneres,
    cantau, cantau,
jo dic plorant a boscos i riberes:
    adéu-siau!

II

On trobaré tos sanitosos climes,
    ton cel daurat?
Mes ai, mes ai!, on trobaré tes cimes
    bell Montserrat?
Enlloc veuré, ciutat de Barcelona,
    ta hermosa Seu,
ni eixos turons, joiells de la corona
    que et posà Déu.

III

Adéu, germans; adéu-siau, mon pare,
    no us veuré més!
Oh! si al fossar on jau ma dolça mare,
    jo el llit tingués!

The Emigrant

Sweet Catalonia,
Land of my heart,
To be far from you
Is to die of longing.

I

Fair valley, cradle of my childhood,   5
    Snowy Pyrenees,
Hedge and brook, grotto in the sky,
    Farewell for evermore!
Harps of the wood, chaffinch and goldfinch,
    Sing out, sing out,   10
I say with tears to rivers and trees
    Farewell to all!

II

Where will I find your healthy climes,
    Your gilded skies?
And where will I find your sculpted summits,   15
    Beautiful Montserrat?
Nowhere will I see, O Barcelona,
    Your tall cathedral,
Nor your mountains, jewels in the crown
    that God set on your brow.   20

III

Farewell, brother and sister, farewell, father,
    I'll never see you again.
I wish I could rest beside the grave
    Where my good mother lies!

Oh mariners, lo vent que me'n desterra
    que em fa sofrir!
Estic malalt, mes ai!, tornau-me a terra,
    que hi vull morir!

O mariners, the winds that banished me   25
    Have brought me only sorrow.
My heart grieves—take me back again
    That I might die on the land.

.

FROM

Jesús Infant

(The Child Jesus, 1890, 1891, 1893)

The *Jesús Infant* trilogy appeared first as three separate books: *Natzaret* (Nazareth, 1890), *Betlem* (Bethlehem, 1891), and *La fugida a Egipte* (Flight to Egypt, 1893). With minor revisions, these were published in a single volume in 1896 featuring the books in their natural order: *Betlem*, *La fugida a Egipte*, and *Natzaret*. Along with *Dietari d'un pelegrí a Terra Santa* (Diary of a Pilgrim in the Holy Land, 1886), it is the direct result of Verdaguer's pilgrimage to Palestine and Egypt in the spring of 1886 and reveals the spiritual transformation and personal crisis the poet-priest underwent during these years (see introduction).

Torrents (2006, 306–16) and Molas (2003a, 567–69) have shown that underlying the *Jesús Infant* trilogy is devotion to the Holy Family, which—given impetus by early- and mid-nineteenth-century Catholic associations founded in France and Belgium with a view to holding up a model for working-class families amid the social and moral crises concomitant to the Industrial Revolution (Hector Berlioz's *The Infant Christ* was first performed in 1864)—had become firmly rooted in Catalonia. Following Torrents, the devotion to the Holy Family finds parallel expression—architectural and poetic—through Antoni Gaudí, who in 1883 at age thirty-one took over the design and construction of what was to become Barcelona's Holy Family Expiatory Temple, and Verdaguer (whose patron Claudi López i Bru, the second marquis of Comillas, was, by his sister Isabel López's marriage, brother-in-law to industrialist Eusebi Güell i Bacigalupi, future count of Güell—and patron to Antoni Gaudí). Of modest provincial origins, both Gaudí and Verdaguer would triumph in Barcelona under the patronage of the most powerful financial and industrial dynasty of their day. Verdaguer writes of Gaudí's project and the spiritual significance of its theme in his *Dietari*'s final entry (Ascension Day 1886):

> When we set out from Suez we saw in the ship's chapel the painting of the Holy Family we'd seen everywhere in Egypt, and we said Mass before it every day until we reached Barcelona, where the Trinity of the earth would have, perhaps within a few years, the greatest and most beautiful temple in the world. May we cross the seas of life in such fine company and under such good guidance as that with which, today, we enter our homeland's harbor, that free from storms and reefs, we might also enter our heavenly homeland's harbor.

Molas has noted how *Natzaret* and *Betlem* draw largely from Verdaguer's travels in the Holy Land, whereas the *Fugida* is connected more closely with his own "exile" at La Gleva, near Vic, the parish to which he was confined after his expulsion from Barcelona. In his prologue to the *Fugida* (the only book of the three for which he wrote one), Verdaguer explains how this final book "translates" three paintings at La Gleva depicting the stages of the Holy Family's exile—flight, sojourn, and return—and we readily grasp through his literary analogy Verdaguer's own feeling of exile. According to Molas, although the entire trilogy was regarded by Verdaguer as a single poem, its narrative unity breaks down into miscellaneous fragments, sometimes akin to popular devotional vignettes. Still, Molas contends that the "poems" can be categorized broadly into three groups: (1) the daily life of a poor family in exile, (2) the ultimate fate of the Child, and (3) the recovery of Christian values. There are seventy-eight such poems in the 1896 edition, featuring a variety of metrical and stanzaic forms including blank verse, which Verdaguer was to use subsequently in "Sum vermis" and (combined with heptasyllables) in "The Milky Way."

Of "The Rose of Jericho," the first poem (after the verse dedicatory) in *Betlem* (evoking the Annunciation and Immaculate Conception), renowned writer, poet, and critic Carles Riba (1893–1959) wrote: "There is no going beyond it in poetry" (quoted in Torrents 2003a, 71). The second poem in this selection, "Thorns," also from *Betlem*, would come under Molas's second category (see above), and the third, "Begging," from *La fugida a Egipte*, might fall under the first or, perhaps more poignantly, the third category for its indictment of unchristian attitudes toward poverty. Torrents has underscored the role of Verdaguer's circumstances at the time and the interests pulling on him from opposite directions: "He felt the contradiction of being on the side of the wealthy and, as almoner, of being on the side of the poor" (2002b, 22–23). Surely in the poverty of the Holy Family in Egypt Verdaguer saw the streets of Barcelona.

La Rosa de Jericó

Verbum caro factum est.

En sa cambreta humil
pregant està Maria,
Maria està pregant
mentres lo món dormia.
Lo sol a l'Orient
per veure-la sortia.
Ella no el mira, no,
sol més bonic somia;
lo sol que està esperant
mai més se li pondria.

En son clavelliner
un roseret tenia,
roser de Jericó
que poncellar volia.
Sola regor que beu
de sos ullets venia,
quan Ella mira el cel
la llum si en baixaria.

Un àngel n'ha baixat
dient-li: —Ave Maria,
lo Senyor és amb vós
i amb tots los homes sia—.
La Verge li respon:
—Sa voluntat és mia;
sa esclava la té ací
que el cor li donaria—.

Sobre Ella un blanc Colom
ses ales estenia,

The Rose of Jericho

And the Word became flesh.

> In her humble room
> Mary is praying,
> the world sleeps
> while Mary is praying.
> The sun in the east   5
> comes out to see her.
> But she doesn't see,
> dreaming another;
> nor will the sun
> she awaits be setting.   10
>
> On her windowsill
> was a rose of Jericho,
> a tiny rose
> ready to blossom.
> From her eyes came   15
> its only water,
> as she looked to the sky
> for light descending.
>
> An angel came down:
> "Ave Maria,   20
> the Lord is with you
> that He might be with all men."
> The Virgin replies:
> "I am His servant,
> His will is mine,   25
> I will give Him my heart."
>
> A bright Dove spreads
> his wings above her,

i amb la claror del Verb
la Verge resplendia.
Lo món s'omple de llum,
lo cel de melodia,
i al test del finestró
la rosa mig s'obria.

Desvetlla't, oh Betlem!,
enrama l'Establia,
guarneix-la com pitxer
amb or i pedreria,
que en tu de Jericó
la Rosa floriria.

Espines

Ella està besant
l'amorós Infant,
i ses galtes mira
que els llavis de Judes
també besaran,
i plora i sospira.

Les flors que somriuen
una a l'altra diuen:
—Per què plora tant?—

Ella està bressant
l'amorós Infant;
tot bressant-lo mira
aquells peus i braços
que en creu clavaran,
i plora i sospira.

and the Virgin shines
in the Word's brightness. 30
The world fills with light,
the heavens with music,
and there on the sill
the rose half opens.

O Bethlehem, wake! 35
Adorn the Stable
with bouquets, like a vase
with gold and jewels—
in you the Rose
of Jericho blossoms. 40

Thorns

She gives the loving
Child a kiss,
and sees the cheek
that Judas, too,
will kiss with his lips, 5
and cries.

The flowers, smiling,
ask each other:
why is she crying?

She rocks the loving 10
Child in the cradle,
and as she does,
sees the feet and arms
to be nailed to a cross,
and cries. 15

L'aucellet que canta,
oint sa complanta,
respon gemegant.

Ella va alletant
l'amorós Infant;
alletant-lo mira
aquells dolços llavis
que amb fel rosaran,
i plora i sospira.

L'ànima que l'ama:
—Pobra Verge! —exclama—,
quin dolor tan gran!—

Se va endormiscant
l'amorós Infant;
difunt Ella mira
lo Fill que cadavre
sos braços rebran,
i plora i sospira.

Un àngel venia
per dar-li alegria;
se'n torna plorant.

Captant

Per amor de Déu.

I

L'infant Jesús demana pa
i sant Josep no li'n pot dar.
Lo Patriarca agafa l'eina
i a la ciutat va a cercar feina;

A tiny songbird,
hearing her sorrow,
laments in reply.

She nurses the loving
Child and sees   20
the tender lips
to be sponged
with bitterness,
and cries.

"Poor Virgin!" starts   25
the soul that loves her,
"What painful suffering!"

The loving Child
now fast asleep,
she sees the Son   30
whose spent body
she'll take in her arms,
and cries.

An Angel come
to bring her joy   35
turns back, crying.

Begging

For the love of God.

I

The Child Jesus asks for some bread,
    Saint Joseph has none in the kitchen.
So the Patriarch packs up his tools and heads
    for the city to seek a position;

de porta en porta va dient:
—Dau-me treball, oh bona gent,
que vinc de fer un llarg viatge,
i no tinc res, ni pa ni hostatge,
per ma Esposa, ai!, i per mon Fill
que de la Glòria és un espill—.

Uns angelets allí a la vora
li van dient amb veu que plora:
    —Per què no ho dieu
que vostre Fill és Fill de Déu?—

Com sant Josep forastereja,
i ja en son cap la neu blanqueja,
no troba un bri de feina enlloc,
i torna a casa sens un broc.
La Verge santa amb ull alegre
surt i asserena son cor negre:
—Aconsoleu-vos, mon Espòs—
diu-li, mostrant-li el Fill hermós;—
tenim un Déu per companyia;
què pot robar-nos l'alegria?
Sentiu com canten los aucells?
Déu nos estima més que a ells;
no ens deixarà sense becada
quan als moixons l'haurà donada!—

II

L'infant Jesús demana pa
i sant Josep no li'n pot dar.
La Verge-Mare al braç se'l posa
sempre serena i amorosa;
posa sos llavis en son front
d'on baixarà la llum al món,
i va trucant de porta en porta
per les cabanyes d'aquella horta:
    —Per amor de Déu,
una almoineta pel Fill meu!—

he calls at door after door and says: 5
        "Kind folk, I'm in need of some earnings,
I have no bread or place to stay,
        and it's been such a very long journey.
It's for my Wife I need your help,
and my Son, who's the mirror of Glory itself."   10

Some onlooking Angels start to worry,
        and think his reluctance odd:
"Why don't you tell them the whole story,
        that your Son is the Son of God?"

Because Saint Joseph is a foreigner   15
        and his hair is turning white,
there isn't a scrap of work anywhere,
        and he goes back home for the night.
The Virgin gives him a loving welcome,
        soothing his grief with joy: 20
"Set your heart at ease, husband,"
        and she shows him their beautiful Boy.
"What could possibly ever go wrong
        in the company of the Creator?
Can you hear the birds singing their songs?   25
        God's love for us is greater;
he wouldn't leave us without a meal
and still give the birds a fair deal."

II

The Child Jesus asks for some bread,
        Saint Joseph sees it's all gone.   30
The Virgin Mother, sure they'll be fed,
        places Him lovingly on
her arm, and putting her lips to His forehead
        where the light of the world will pour,
she calls at the cottages out by the orchards   35
        knocking on door after door:
                        "For the love of God,
                        alms, alms for my Son."

La fruita esbranca la perera;
ningú li diu: «Preneu una pera»;
ningú una engruna li ofereix
del pa que deuen a Ell mateix.
A l'home ingrat i a la font seca
per dar a Déu fins l'aigua els reca.
Si algun ne troba de més bo,
diu a Maria: —Déu n'hi do.

Los angelets allí a la vora
li van dient amb veu que plora:
            —Per què no ho dieu
que vostre Fill és Fill de Déu?

Tot pidolant per les masies
bé sent cantar-ne de follies,
florida almoina que li plou:
«De pobressalla no n'hi ha prou
que de Judea encara en vinga?
Cada cigonya que es mantinga
en son cloquer». Abaixa els ulls
Ella, de llàgrimes remulls,
que amb les de Cristo se barregen
i per les galtes li perlegen:
            —Per amor de Déu,
una almoineta pel Fill meu!—

Pobra Maria! Pobra Mare!
Mes l'ha sentida l'Etern Pare,
i altra pobreta se'n condol
que de la gran Ciutat del Sol
ve de captar més assortada.
Sobre l'herbei taula ha parada:
—Preneu si us plau —li diu,— que més
vos donaria si tingués—.
I amb gran amor parteix amb Ella
lo bé de Déu de sa cistella.

No one tells her: "Take fruit, go ahead!"
    though pear trees sag with yield;   40
no one offers her crumbs from the bread
    that God has put in their fields.
Refusing to God even their water,
    the unhappy are springs that have dried;
while others she meets, less grudging, tell her: 45
    "Surely, God will provide."

The onlooking Angels worry and frown,
    and think her reluctance odd:
"Why don't you give them the full account,
    that your Son is the Son of God?"   50

Begging at houses for alms she hears
    her share of foolishness,
showers of morsels like these in her ears:
    "Don't we already have enough indigents
that Judea must keep on sending us more?   55
    To each belfry its muster of storks."
And so Mary lowers her eyes,
    her eyes that fill with tears,
tears that roll down her cheeks with Christ's,
    rolling down like pearls.   60
                "For the love of God,
                alms, alms for my Son."

Poor Mary! Poor Mother!
    But the Eternal Father has heard,
and another poor woman takes pity on her,   65
    for she has just returned
from the City of the Sun, luckier in alms,
    and spread on the grass is her table:
"Please, take whatever you want;
    I'd give you more, were I able."   70
And she shares with Mary in selfless love
the basket sent from God above.

FROM

Roser de tot l'any: Dietari de pensaments religiosos
(The Rose Almanac: Diary of Religious Thoughts, 1894)

In May 1893 Verdaguer was dismissed from his position as family chaplain and almoner in the Comillas house and, by order of Bishop Morgades, sent—later confined—to the small parish of La Gleva near Vic. The unorthodox channels through which his religious fervor had found expression since his contact with the Duran family and his association with unauthorized spiritual practices proved too extravagant for his high station, as did the debt he incurred with the purchase of Els Penitents, the property on the outskirts of Barcelona connected with exorcisms. Still, as M. Carme Bernal observes, he continued publishing his seven weekly poems in *La Veu de Catalunya* from January through December 1883 "with a clockwork regularity that not even his isolation at La Gleva could break" (1999, 211). These poems (with some minor changes and adapted to the 1894 calendar year) would be published as *Roser de tot l'any*, 365 devotional and intimist poems that, as noted by Molas (2005b, 833), though reminiscent of his earlier *Idil·lis i cants místics*, reflect three decisive new circumstances: the impact on Verdaguer of his pilgrimage to the Holy Land, an aesthetic turn in poetry toward Modernisme under the influence of, especially, Apel·les Mestres (1854–1936), and the growing importance of the press.

Bernal (1999) has examined this last aspect in the context of mounting secularism and the intitiative on the part of leading clerics such as Josep Torras i Bages (1846–1916) to promote renewed devotion and religious practice in a changing society. Though Verdaguer "never wrote a prayer book in the strict sense," Bernal situates *Roser de tot l'any* midway between "a prayer book [for the general public] and a breviary for use by clerics." As for the title, Verdaguer himself was unsure. In a letter to Collell he wrote (see Bernal 1999, 218):

Dear Jaume,

What shall we call my new book? *Flowers of (for) All Year, Mystic Diary (Almanac), Breviary of Love Dedicated to Those Who Love Jesus and Mary, Breviary of the Love of Jesus, Gleams of Light?* Almost all the [poems] are mystic; some dedicated to feasts or saints' days; the month of May to Mary, June to the Sacred Heart. Reply soon . . . they come out this Sunday.

The final title in Catalan, *Roser de tot l'any*, translates literally as "all-year rose" and signifies "evergreen rose" (*Rosa sempervirens*), conveying the figurative sense of "almanac" only in context.

Following Bernal, *Roser de tot l'any* reveals a shift in focus seen also in subsequent works: a tendency "to interiorize, to remove himself further and further away, leading him to create a mystic corpus of tensions and underscoring his growing desire to lift himself skyward" (1999, 221–22). Still, "the ultimate crisis has not yet come, although [we] sense the anguish brought on by his unaccountable removal from Barcelona, his isolation, the uncertainty of his future and his social and economic predicament."

The first poem in this selection, "I found within this Heart . . . ," is a brief mystic song dedicated to the Sacred Heart, blending the spiritual and the natural/sensual in the tradition of St. John of the Cross. The second, "Reception of the Stigmata by Saint Francis," is one of two poems in *Roser de tot l'any* dedicated to Sister Eulària Anzizu, who at age twenty-one entered the Franciscan convent of Pedralbes (see endnote to poem). The third, "Lord, it isn't like You said . . . ," prefigures the *Flors del Calvari* poems in evoking the paradoxical reward that comes with the commitment to suffering. In the final poem, "The day the sun no longer warms . . . ," Verdaguer laments the widespread turning of human hearts from the heavenly to the worldly.

Mes del Sagrat Cor de Jesús

. . . .

Dia 10 [Juny]

«L'he trobada en aqueix Cor . . .»

Quedéme y olvidéme
y el rostro recliné sobre el Amado.
    Sant Joan de la Creu

> L'he trobada en aqueix Cor
> la fontana de l'amor
> d'aigua fresca i regalada;
> aprés que l'aigua beguí,
> fontana endins me n'entrí
> on no té l'Àngel entrada.
>
> En lo bell mig d'aqueix Cor,
> trobí la mar de l'amor,
> i em llancí dintre l'onada.
> Naufraguí o no naufraguí?
> Jesús, Vós sabeu de mi;
> jo per Vós me'n só oblidada.

Month of the Sacred Heart of Jesus

. . . .

Day 10 [June]

"I found within this Heart . . ."

Oblivious, I languished
and reclined my face on my Beloved.
   St. John of the Cross

> I found within this Heart
> the very fount of waters
> —fresh and cool—of love;
> and after drinking of it,
> I made my way in deep,   5
> far from the Angel's reach.
>
> Within this very Heart
> I found the sea of love,
> and flung myself in deep.
> Was I drowned, or not?   10
> Lord, surely you must know;
> Myself, I have forgot.

Setembre

. . . .

Dia 17

Impressió de les Llagues de sant Francesc

In foraminibus petrae.
En los forats de la pedra.
   Càntic dels càntics 2, 14

> *A sor Eulària Anzizu*

—Oh coloma sense fel,
coloma d'aletes blanques,
que et plavies al matí
vora el torrent de les aigües,
com te'n voles tan dejorn
a les celdes solitàries?
Que voldries fer-hi niu
com les tórtores boscanes,
in foraminibus petrae,
de la pedra de Pedralbes?
—Les clivelles on niu faig
de sant Francesc són les Llagues,
roses que el pobre d'Assís
al bon Jesús ha robades—.

September

. . . .

Day 17

Reception of the Stigmata by Saint Francis

In foraminibus petrae.
In the clefts of the rock.
    Song of Solomon 2:14

      To Sister Eulària Anzizu

    "O dove of kindest heart,
    who with your wings of white
    each morning took delight
    beside the streaming waters,
    how can you fly so soon   5
    to cells of solitude?
    Do you mean to make your nest
    like a rock dove in the clefts,
    in foraminibus petrae,
    high on the rock of Pedralbes?"   10
    "The clefts where I make my nest
    are the wounds impressed on Saint Francis,
    roses which, being poor,
    he took from the loving Lord."

Octubre

. . . .

Dia 13

«Senyor, Vós m'heu enganyat . . .»

> Senyor, Vós m'heu enganyat!
> Me prometíeu cadenes
> i em donau la llibertat;
> me parlàveu sols de penes,
> i em donau ja les estrenes
> de vostra felicitat.
> Senyor, Vós m'heu enganyat!

October

. . . .

Day 13

"Lord, it isn't like You said . . ."

> Lord, it isn't like You said.
> You promised there'd be chains,
> and gave me freedom instead;
> You spoke of only pain,
> but now I see the reign
> of happiness You spread.
> Lord, it isn't like You said.

Novembre

. . . .

Dia 18

«Quan deixe el sol d'escalfar . . .»

Miseri, quo itis?
ISAÏES

> Quan deixe el sol d'escalfar,
> Jesús deixarà d'amar.
> Per què tot cor no l'adora?
> Tot en la terra és terrós,
> l'home és un fang amorós
> que sols de fang s'enamora.

November

. . . .

Day 18

"The day the sun no longer warms . . ."

Where are you going, unhappy one?
  ISAIAH

> The day the sun no longer warms
> the Lord above will cease to love.
> Why can't every heart embrace Him?
> All on earth is mixed with earth—
> man is molded clay that loves,
> and falls in love—only with clay.

27. Cover of *Salteri franciscà* (anonymous, 1882), depicting Saint Francis's legendary visit to Vic. Courtesy of the Biblioteca de Catalunya.

FROM

Sant Francesc: Poema

(Saint Francis: Poem, 1895)

Verdaguer spent two years in productive solitude at La Gleva uncertain of his future, his attempts to come to terms with Bishop Morgades and the marquis of Comillas (making unannounced visits to the latter in Barcelona and Madrid) only aggravating the clash. The turning point was the bishop's order of confinement to La Gleva and, soon after, the recommendation that Verdaguer withdraw to a clerical retirement home in Vic. In defiance of the authority that sought to stifle what remained of his restricted freedom, Verdaguer reacted with determination and left for Barcelona in April 1895, taking refuge with the Duran family—from whom he had been expressly barred. The bishop thereupon arranged for his arrest, but Verdaguer was out when the police called at the Duran home, and he later paid a visit to the civil governor, who was an acquaintance of his and intervened in his favor. Responding with renewed determination and vigor, Verdaguer published a statement in the press on 17 July, calling for justice in an appeal to the "up-standing people of Barcelona . . . before God who must judge us all [to pro-test against] the iniquity to which this unfortunate priest is victim, to what end I do not know" (quoted in Torrents 1995c, 109). Hostilities escalated when the bishop announced the suspension of Verdaguer's duties and func-tions as a priest, prompting the counterattack: a series of eleven newspaper articles appearing that summer under the title "A Priest Slandered" and published in the fall as *En defensa pròpia* (In Self-Defense; later expanded to include twenty-six additional articles written in 1897).

Also published in the fall of 1895, *Sant Francesc* reflects in a number of ways Verdaguer's personal struggle and, to some degree, his own iden-tification with the early thirteenth-century ascetic. Isidor Cònsul remarks on the parallel suggested in Verdaguer's prologue to *Sant Francesc*, evoking the saint's tribulations: "'disinherited by his father, betrayed by his own brother, rebuked and derided by his friends and chased through the streets like a madman by children throwing rocks and mud.' The father, brother and friends that abandoned and betrayed [Verdaguer] are Bishop Morgades, [lifelong friend] Jaume Collell, Claudi López and [his cousin] Narcís Verdaguer i Callís" (2003, 783).

As pointed out by Cònsul, the forty-three poems in *Sant Francesc* (construed by Verdaguer as a single poem), written over a span of the previous twenty-six years, reveal a development marked by three salient moments in the poet's life vis-à-vis St. Francis and the Franciscan tradition. The first culminates in the 1874 publication of Verdaguer's first St. Francis poem (not included in this selection), "Sant Francesc s'hi moria" (Saint Francis Almost Died Here), a short romance narrating the saint's alleged visit to Vic in 1212, when, according to local lore, he was revived by a peasant who found him lying exhausted in the countryside; Cònsul (2001, 177–78) observes that the name of the chapel erected on the spot, Sant Francesc s'hi Moria, is no doubt a popularized phonetic departure from Sant Francesc ça Almudia (after the thirteenth-century landowning Almúdia family). The second moment coincides with the celebrations commemorating the seven-hundred-year anniversary of the birth of St. Francis, for which in 1882 Verdaguer published *Salteri franciscà: Romancets sobre la prodigiosa vida del patriarca Sant Francesc* (Franciscan Psaltery: Short Romances on the Prodigious Life of Patriarch Saint Francis). The third and final moment comes with Verdaguer's personal crisis and mounting conflict with Bishop Morgades and the marquis of Comillas during winter and spring 1895, when he composed new poems and revised old ones for the definitive edition of *Sant Francesc*, published that October. Verdaguer drew from a long bibliography of source texts for the poems; the scholarly volumes on St. Francis in his library numbered well over thirty (see Cònsul 2003, 66–77).

Written in the early 1880s, "The Turtledoves" was shortened by four lines for the 1895 edition; Verdaguer alternates unrhymed masculine heptasyllables with shorter feminine tetrasyllables of assonant *o*-sounding rhyme. "Preaching to Birds," one of the five short romances that appeared in the 1882 edition, was very slightly revised; it alternates masculine-feminine heptasyllables featuring assonant *a*-sounding rhyme only at feminine lines. "The Pilgrim" is the last of three poems—preceded by "Greccio" (Greccio) and "Lo violí de sant Francesc" (Saint Francis's Violin), not included in this selection—evoking Christmas in the year 1223, when the saint organized the first living crèche reenacting the birth of Christ outside the Italian village of Greccio, near Rieti. Here the unrhymed masculine heptasyllables alternate with (only slightly shorter) feminine pentasyllables of varying assonant rhyme: *o*-sounding in the first section, *e*-sounding in the second, and *a*-sounding in the third.

Les tórtores

Lo patriarca d'Assís,
    sortint de Roma,
veu venir un infantó
    que hi duia tórtores,
lligadetes amb un fil
    d'ales i potes.
Lligadetes quan les veu,
    tot s'acongoixa:
—Germanetes del meu cor,
    que en sou d'hermoses!
De tudó l'ala teniu,
    peus de coloma.
Infantó, bell infantó,
    doncs on les portes?
—A un aucellaire romà
    que me les compra.
—L'aucellaire què en vol fer,
    tan petitones?
—Les tindrà en un gabial
    si no les ploma.
—Infantó, bell infantó,
    fes-me'n almoina:
jo els daré la llibertat
    que els és tan dolça—.
Lo noiet és compassiu,
    lo niu li dóna,
i les tórtores copsant
    ell les amoixa,
en sa mànega i son pit
    mentres les posa.
—Germanetes —va dient—,
    germanes tórtores,

The Turtledoves

The Patriarch of Assisi,
    setting out from Rome,
sees a child approaching
    carrying turtledoves,
their wings and legs   5
    tied with cord.
It makes him very sad
    to see them tied:
"Little sisters of my heart,
    how lovely you are!   10
You have the wings of wood pigeons
    and delicate feet of doves.
Child, beautiful child,
    where are you taking them?"
"To a Roman fowler,   15
    he'll buy them from me."
"What could he possibly want
    with such tender creatures?"
"He'll put them in a cage,
    or pluck them maybe."   20
"Child, beautiful child,
    give them to me as alms:
I'll give them the freedom
    they hold so dear."
The boy, compassionate,   25
    hands him the nest,
and he takes the turtledoves,
    caressing them,
as he holds them gently
    to his sleeve and chest.   30
"Little sisters," he says,
    "sister turtledoves,

de deixar-vos agafar
    com sou tan totxes?
Mes, veniu al meu convent,
    sereu mes hostes:
quan jo cante cada jorn
    matines i hores,
a mos salms barrejareu
    místiques trobes,
i lloarem tots plegats
    al Déu dels pobres—.
Quan arriben al convent
    la nit s'acosta;
clava en terra son bastó
    prop de la porta.
Lo bastó, que era un vergàs
    pres a una soca,
per miracle en una nit
    alzina es torna:
de la terra fins al cor
    arrels enfonsa,
mentres puja cap al cel
    brancada ombrosa,
de l'alegre monestir
    real corona.
L'endemà, al sortir lo sant
    ans que l'aurora,
a les tórtores per niu
    l'alzina dóna.
Sant Francesc resa davall
    matines i hores,
sant Francesc les resa al peu,
    damunt les tórtores,
i es barreja als refilets
    suau salmòdia,
com a veus de violí,
    veus de viola.
Mig sortint al mirador
    de l'alta Glòria,
entre eixams de serafins
    Déu los escolta.

how could you be so careless
     as to let them catch you?
Come with me to my convent,   35
     you'll be my guests:
Each day when I sing
     the matins and hours,
you'll mix your mystic cansos
     with my psalms,   40
and together we'll praise
     the God of the poor."
As they reach the convent
     night is falling;
into the ground near the door   45
     he drives his staff.
During the night the staff,
     a stout branch cut
from a trunk, turns miraculously
     into an oak: 50
into the heart of the earth
     the roots sink,
while its shady branches
     climb toward the sky,
the bright monastery's   55
     kingly crown.
Next day, the saint comes out
     before daybreak
and gives to the turtledoves
     the oak for nest.   60
Saint Francis, below, prays
     the matins and hours,
Saint Francis on the ground,
     the turtledoves above,
the gentle psalmody mixing   65
     with the trilling,
like the voice of violas
     with violins.
And stepping out on the belvedere
     of Glory on High,   70
among the hosts of seraphim,
     God pauses to listen.

Predicant als aucells

Va l'Apòstol de l'amor
per una selva d'Itàlia:
l'amor que sent per Jesús
ja no cap dins la seva ànima.
Ne parla als rius i a les flors,
i pins i roures abraça.
És desterrat serafí
qui del cel sent enyorança.
D'alegria tot cantant
los aucellets l'acompanyen;
los qui trastegen pel bosc
voleien de branca en branca;
los qui volen per lo cel
paren atents la volada.
Francesc los vol predicar,
sota un roure s'aturava.
Sobre l'herba es posen uns,
los altres sobre les mates,
los més estimats de tots
damunt sos genolls i espatlla;
cada bri d'herba en porta un,
cada arbre una nuvolada.
—Germans aucellets, —los diu—
lo Criador quant vos ama!
Sense sembrar ni segar
teniu sempre en vostra taula
la llavor d'herbeta humil,
de la font la gota d'aigua,
si en lo calze d'una flor
no voleu beure rosada.
Com no fileu ni cosiu,
Déu vos vesteix i vos calça;
vostre vestit i calçat

Preaching to Birds

The Apostle of Love is traveling
through a forest in Italy:
his soul can no longer contain
the love he feels for Jesus.
He tells it to rivers and flowers, 5
takes pines and oaks in his arms.
He is a banished seraph
who longs to return to heaven.
Singing for joy,
his company are birds: 10
the birds of the forest,
flitting from branch to branch,
and birds of the sky,
approaching in expectation.
Stopping beneath an oak tree, 15
Francis means to preach to them.
They take their places, some
on the grass, others on shrubs,
and the dearest of all sit perched
upon his knees and shoulders. 20
Each blade of grass brings a bird,
each tree a congregation.
"Brother birds," he tells them,
"How the Creator loves you!
You neither sow nor reap, 25
yet seeds of the humble grass
are always on your table,
and dewdrops in cups of flowers,
or, if you'd rather,
you can drink from trickling springs. 30
Since you neither spin nor sew,
God takes care that you're clothed;
and these your garments and hose

valen més que d'or i plata.
Vos dóna per llit un brot,
una fulla per teulada,
gentils boscúries per niu,
lo cel i terra per gàbia.
Aucellets, los meus germans,
lo Criador quant vos ama!
Ameu-lo vosaltres, bé,
que amor amb amor se paga;
canteu-li a entrada de fosc,
canteu-li a l'hora de l'alba
d'amor la dolça cançó
que els homes han oblidada!—

Tot predicant als aucells
sant Francesc s'extasiava.
Ells, per fer-li reverència,
sos jolius capets abaixen;
l'oreneta estira el coll,
la perdiu estira l'ala,
alçant los ulls cap al sol
obre son bec la calàndria;
fa l'aleta el passerell,
saltirons la cogullada,
fent pujar i fent baixar
sa cogulla franciscana.
Quan Francesc los beneeix,
un sospir d'amor exhalen
i algun diví rossinyol
preludia amb la seva arpa.
Del signe sagrat que fa
pren la forma l'aucellada,
que cantant se'n vola al cel,
com una creu que s'hi eixampla
de llevant cap a ponent,
de migdia a tramuntana.
Així la Creu de Jesús,
que el Màrtir d'amor abraça,
serà duita a tot lo món
pels fills de l'Ordre Seràfica,

are more precious than silver and gold.
He gives you a bud for your bed,   35
for roof He gives you a leaf,
fine woodlands are your nest,
the sky and earth your cage.
Dear brethren birds,
how the Creator loves you!   40
Love Him well for your part,
for love is repaid with love;
sing to Him when darkness falls,
sing to Him at the hour of dawn—
the soothing song of love   45
that men have forgot."

And preaching to birds,
Saint Francis enters ecstasy.
And they, out of reverence,
bow their graceful heads;   50
the swallow stretches its neck,
the partridge spreads its wings,
the calandra lark opens its beak,
lifting its eyes to the sun;
the linnet struts its wing,   55
and the crested lark hops
all around, his Franciscan hood
bouncing up and down.
When Francis blesses them,
they let go a sigh of love,   60
and a nightingale from above
harps a heavenly prelude.
And the throng of birds now takes
the form of the holy sign he makes,
and they sing as they rise in the skies   65
like a cross growing wider and wider,
stretching from east to west
and far to the north and south.
And so the Cross of Jesus,
embraced by the Martyr of Love,   70
will be carried throughout the world
by the sons of the Seraphic Order,

que, pobres com los aucells,
ja entonen per monts i planes
d'amor la dolça cançó
que els homes han oblidada.

Lo pelegrí

I

La diada de Nadal
    diada és de glòria,
puix la festa de la nit
    al dia es perllonga.
Ja es coneix al refetor
    quan migdia sona:
hi lluenteja el cristall,
    los plats van en doina,
los conills fan bon costat
    a la carn de ploma,
a la bresca el brescalló,
    lo bon vi a les dolces.
Què hi haurà que li desplau,
    puix Francesc és fora?
Al moment de beneir,
    al portal se'ls mostra,
al portal del refetor
    demanant almoina.
Porta barret de romeu,
    barret i valona,
que li deixà un pelegrí
    arribat de Roma.
—Entreu —diu-li el guardià—,
    com a casa vostra.
Pelegrí, bon pelegrí,
    eixa taula és pobra,

who, poor as the birds,
sing on the hilltops and plains
the soothing song of love
that men have forgot.

The Pilgrim

I

The celebration of Christmas
    is a celebration of glory,
festivities of the evening
    continuing through the day.
In the refectory, noontime
    brings the well-known scene:
the hall sparkles with crystal
    and echoes with rattling plates,
and rabbit makes excellent fare
    when served with tasty fowl,
and honeycomb with cracklings,
    good wine with sweet dessert.
What harm is there in this
    while Francis is away?
Just as they say grace
    he appears in the doorway,
the great dining-hall doorway,
    asking for alms.
He wears a hat, a pilgrim's,
    and a short cloak
given to him by a pilgrim
    who just arrived from Rome.
"Come in," says the doorkeeper,
    "make yourself at home.
Pilgrim, good pilgrim,
    our table is sparse,

5

10

15

20

25

mes amb vós compartirem
    lo que Déu hi posa—.

II

Francesc entra al refetor,
    i amb una escudella,
un rosegó pren de l'un,
    de l'altre una ceba,
de l'altre quatre fesols
    a la vinagreta.
Diu a tots: —Déu vos ho pac—
    i s'asseu en terra.
Ja no riuen tant a pler
    los frares que reien,
prenent per suau avís
    la seva ardidesa
d'entrar com a foraster
    dintre casa seva.

III

S'aixeca el bon pelegrí,
    i, aprés de les gràcies,
a sos frares estimats
    dolçament los parla:
—Avui lo bon Jesuset
    està sobre palles,
la pobresa predicant
    com des d'una càtedra.
Nosaltres, que som fills seus,
    seguim ses petjades,
tenint-nos per pelegrins
    que anem a la pàtria.
Lo que guanyàrem al camp
    no perdem a taula,
a la pobresa escarnint,
    nostra sobirana—.

but we'll share with you
    what God imparts."

II

Francis enters the room,
    and with a soup plate takes   30
a scrap of bread from one,
    an onion from another,
and from another some beans
    in a sauce of vinaigrette.
"May God repay you," he says   35
    to all, and sits on the floor.
The merrymaking friars
    make less merry,
taking as gentle reproof
    Francis's uncanny device   40
of entering as a stranger
    under his own roof.

III

The good pilgrim rises,
    and after thanking them
he speaks these gentle words   45
    to his beloved friars:
"Today the Baby Jesus,
    on a bed of straw,
preaches poverty
    as if from hallowed halls.   50
And we, His children,
    follow in his footsteps,
traveling but as pilgrims
    bound for the fatherland.
Let us not lose at table   55
    what we've gained afield,
nor make a mock of poverty,
    our sovereign majesty."

28. Portrait of Verdaguer by Ramon Casas (drawing, 1896–98).

FROM

Flors del Calvari: Llibre de consols
(Flowers of Calvary: Book of Solace, 1896)

Flors del Calvari: Llibre de consols is, following Cònsul, the final of the three books published in the fall of 1895 "that reflect most conclusively the scope of [Verdaguer's personal] drama" (2005b, 1007). Appearing in early December in the wake of *Sant Francesc* and *En defensa pròpia* (In Self-Defense), *Flors del Calvari* (dated 1896) is the crowning work of Verdaguer's four-year struggle to preserve and project his personal, spiritual, and literary integrity in the face of the unrelenting adversity orchestrated by his superiors. If, as Bernal (1999, 221) reminds us, the *Caritat* (Charity) poems were presented as *alms*, the *Calvari* poems aim to provide *solace*. In his prologue Verdaguer tells his readers, "I sought to turn my afflictions into songs," quoting the popular adage *Qui canta, sos mals espanta* (Singing chases one's troubles away). Verdaguer's intent, however, runs deeper than proverbial lore. It is theologically informed. Alluding to the widely read *Imitation of Christ* by fifteenth-century churchman Thomas à Kempis, Verdaguer writes: "So pleasing is it to Our Lord that our souls endure suffering, that according to one pious author, were there no other means, He would dispatch angel[s] to shower [our souls] with tribulations." Elaborating further on the title, he quotes St. Bernard: "The glory of heaven is contained within suffering like the flower within the seed."

In connection with these theological underpinnings, M. Àngels Verdaguer Pajerols (2003) has examined the scholarly buttressing of *Flors del Calvari* in Verdaguer's prolific use of epigraphs preceding the poems. Of its 228 poems, 106 are headed by epigraphs from sources in Latin, Spanish, Catalan, Italian, and French. After the Bible, the most frequently quoted sources are renowned medieval Catalan theologian and mystic Ramon Llull (ca. 1235–1315) and Thomas à Kempis, followed by numerous saints (including St. Teresa and St. John of the Cross), church fathers, doctors, and patriarchs (Saints Augustine, Ambrose, Jerome, Gregory I, Bernard, Francis of Assisi, Bonaventure, and Francis of Sales), and nineteenth-century churchman Father Henri-Dominique Lacordaire.

With the theological foundations of the poetry clearly visible, that is, with the poetic purpose of giving solace in adversity firmly grounded in religious faith, *Flors del Calvari* takes on a twofold significance with respect to Verdaguer's readers and the accusations leveled against him. First, the task of the poet-priest (beyond that of the priest) is unique. As Torrents has observed, Verdaguer, aware of the power of poetry, writes (as if to himself): "[Think of] all the poor souls that carry their crosses—and a good deal heavier than yours—but haven't the joy of turning them into song!" (2002a, 80). Second, backed into a corner by accusations of insanity and incompetence, the poet-priest knows that his reputation and integrity stand or fall with the success of his faith-inspired poetic production. At this crucial moment in his life, more than any other, Verdaguer must prove himself as both priest and poet.

The book is divided into three parts. The first, containing sixty-four poems, is entitled "Crucíferes" (Cruciferae) after the family of plants (also Brassicacerae) with cross-shaped flowers; Verdaguer describes these as "[short] poems or celebrations [*festeigs*] of the Cross ... [composed] somewhat after the current style"; this selection includes "Saint Teresa," "Poverty," "Simile," "Soon," "To a Detractor," and "Shaped like a Cross." The second part, "Esplais" (Departures), contains nineteen longer, wider-ranging poems; this selection includes the two that have drawn the most critical attention: "*Sum vermis*" and "By the Sea." The third part, "Flors de Miracruz" (Flowers of Miracruz), is made up of 145 very short poems, designated by roman numerals, that are often popular aphorisms, most of them quatrains, described by Verdaguer as "simple couplets, spiritual adages or similes of the Cross, comparable to desiccated violets and buttercups placed between the pages of a breviary." They are named after the convent of Miracruz near Donostia (San Sebastián), for it was during a sojourn there with the Comillas family in the summer of 1891 that Verdaguer began composing these for an "ailing person" referred to only as "Matilde" (in a letter to Jaume Collell dated 23 August that year).

Narcís Garolera (2003, 17–21) has summarized the book's major critical reviews. One month after its publication, renowned *modernista* poet Joan Maragall (1860–1911) wrote: "*Flors del Calvari* is one of the most powerful [works] Catalan literature has produced." Some years later, critic Ramon D.

Perés observed that in contrast to Verdaguer's *Idil·lis i cants místics* it is "essentially modern." On the other hand, critic Manuel de Montoliu preferred the earlier mysticism of the *Idil·lis*, *Caritat*, and *Jesús Infant*: "[In *Flors del Calvari*] too much grieving had disastrous consequences for his inspiration . . . [making it more] an autobiographic document than a work of poetry." The book is among the most widely translated of Verdaguer's works, appearing in French (1897), German (1904), Italian (1921), and Spanish (1936), with a subsequent bilingual Catalan-Spanish edition (1954).

Santa Teresa

Ego quos amo, arguo, et castigo.
    APOCALIPSI 3, 19

Quem enim diligit Dominus,
corripit: et quasi pater in filio
complacet sibi.
Lo Senyor castiga a aquell
que ama, com un pare al fill que estima.
    PROVERBIS 3, 12

> Al verger se'n va Teresa,
> al verger a collir flors;
> per Aquell que tant estima
> vol collir-ne un ram o dos.
> Per terra plana no en troba,
> ja n'agafa el camí rost.
> Ja dóna una ensopegada,
> se gira el peu en rodó:
> —Jesús de l'ànima mia,
> de Vós espero el socors—.
> A la veu de sa estimada
> lo bon Jesús no fa el sord;
> rialler se li presenta
> i li torna el peu a lloc.
> —Grans mercès —li diu Teresa—,
> rosamel del meu dolor.
> Mes, per què em deixàveu caure
> quan treballava per Vós?
> —A mos amics així els pago.
> —Per això en teniu tan pocs.

Saint Teresa

I reprove and discipline those whom I love.
REVELATION 3:19

Quem enim diligit Dominus,
corripit: et quasi pater in filio
complacet sibi.
For the Lord reproves the one he loves,
as a father the son in whom he delights.
PROVERBS 3:12

She makes her way to the orchards
to gather flowers,
a spray or two
for the One she loves so much.
Finding none on level ground,   5
she takes the steeper tracts.
All at once she stumbles
and twists her ankle:
"O Lord, my love,
I count on You for help."   10
The Lord's ear is not deaf
to his beloved's call;
smiling, He appears
and puts her ankle back in place.
"Oh thank you! honey julep   15
to my pains," Teresa says.
"But how is it You let me fall?
After all—I was working for You."
"That's how I pay back my friends," says He.
Says she, "That's why You have so few."   20

Pobresa

És la reina de tot.
ST. FRANCESC

> Tot ho he perdut: lo nom i la riquesa,
> les corones de llor que he somiat;
> me diu germà la rònega pobresa,
> s'avergonyeix de mi la vanitat.
>
> Tirí per la finestra ma fortuna
> veient millor fortuna esdevenir;
> quan llançava les coses d'una a una,
> les ales me sentia alleugerir.
>
> Me vingué amb la pobresa la bonança;
> perdent los béns, també en perdia el jou;
> si de res jo sentia la recança,
> me deia Déu: —De mi, no en tindràs prou?—

Poverty

She reigns supreme.
   St. Francis

> I've lost everything: the laurel wreaths
> that filled my dreams, my wealth, my name;
> I'm brother to threadbare poverty,
> and vanity looks away in shame.
>
> I tossed my fortune out the window,   5
> seeing another shining brighter;
> and throwing things out, one by one,
> I felt my wings grow lighter and lighter.
>
> With poverty there came abundance;
> rid of my goods, their yoke went too;   10
> and if I ever felt reluctance,
> God said, "Aren't I enough for you?"

Símil

Beati qui nunc fletis, quia ridebitis.
LLUC 6, 21

Qui hic cruciantur, a te consolantur.
ST. AGUSTÍ

En lo núvol que no plora
no hi riu l'arc de Sant Martí;
quan lo cel blau se'n decora,
llagrimejant se'l teixí.

Aixís en l'ànima nostra
sens les llàgrimes del dol,
somrient-nos, mai s'hi mostra
l'iris hermós del consol.

Simile

Blessed are you who weep now, for you will laugh.
    LUKE 6:21

Those who suffer now will be comforted.
    ST. AUGUSTINE

> In the cloud that doesn't cry
> there is no beaming rainbow;
> gracing the blue sky,
> it was loomed with tears of sorrow.
>
> And if inside our souls
> there come no tears of woe,
> we'll never be consoled
> by comfort's radiant bow.

Aviat

¿Què és amor? . . . És delit i
consolació en la pàtria e
tristícia en peregrinació.
    R. LLULL

I

No les mireu pas, ulls meus,
les vanitats de la terra,
puix veureu a no trigar
del paradís la bellesa.

II

Orelles meves, oïu
amb plaer les contumèlies,
puix aviat sentireu
les harmonies angèliques.

III

Oh, cor meu, vola més alt!
Pels terrenals és la terra;
no és ací on has de fer niu,
sinó damunt les estrelles.

Soon

What is love? It is joy
and comfort in the heavenly home,
and sorrow in pilgrimage.
    R. Llull

I

    Don't look, eyes,
    at the earth's vanities;
    it won't be long before you see
    the wonder of paradise.

II

    Ears, take pleasure   5
    in hearing slurs and smears,
    for soon the time will come to hear
    the melodies of angels.

III

    Fly high, heart!
    The earth is for the earthly;   10
    this is no place to make your nest,
    make it on the stars.

A un detractor

Per crucem ad coronam.

Calúmnia, detractor,
ta llengua de glavi esmola;
los esbroncs són mon plaer,
los penjaments la meva honra.
Si del glavi no en tens prou,
pren al sastre l'estisora;
tu m'has de fer lo vestit
que tinc de dur a la glòria.
L'enclusa pren al ferrer,
a l'argenter la gresola;
no em plangues ni el foc ni el mall,
tu m'has de fer la corona;
una perla és cada insult,
un diamant cada afronta.

To a Detractor

With torments for a crown.

    Slander, detractor,
    sharpens your dagger tongue;
    your tirades are my pleasure,
    your decrial is my honor.
    And if the daggers aren't enough,   5
    take the tailor's scissors;
    you're the one to make the suit
    I'll wear the day I go to glory.
    Take the blacksmith's anvil,
    the silversmith's crucible;   10
    don't spare the fire and hammer,
    you're to fit me out with crown;
    your every insult is a pearl,
    a diamond every injury.

En creu

Aves, quando volant ad aethera,
formam crucis assumunt.
    St. Jeroni

Tenen forma de creu
los aucellets quan volen,
lo gamfaró que oneja,
lo màstil que s'arbora,
los pins i avets que ramen,
los caminals que es troben,
lo remador quan rema,
lo frare que sermona,
lo nin quan veu sa mare,
lo penitent quan ora
amb los braços al cel
com un aucell que hi vola.

— 28 octubre 1895

Shaped like a Cross

Birds, flying up to the sky,
take the shape of a cross.
   ST. JEROME

> Birds, flying,
> are shaped like a cross,
> and so are the masts of tall ships,
> and the crusader's rippling banner,
> and pines and firs that spread their limbs,   5
> and paths that meet,
> the boatman as he rows,
> the friar delivering his sermon,
> the child that runs to mother,
> the repentant sinner, praying,   10
> arms raised to the sky,
> like a bird, flying.

— 28 October 1895

Sum vermis

Non vivificatur nisi
prius moriatur.

    1 Corintis 15, 36

E carcere ad aethera.

Dant vincula pennas.

> Veieu-me aquí, Senyor, a vostres plantes,
> despullat de tot bé, malalt i pobre,
> de mon no-res perdut dintre l'abisme.
> Cuc de la terra vil, per una estona
> he vingut en la cendra a arrossegar-me.
> Fou mon bressol un gra de polsinera,
> i un altre gra serà lo meu sepulcre.
> Voldria ser quelcom per oferir-vos,
> però Vós me voleu petit e inútil,
> de glòria despullat i de prestigi.
> Feu de mi lo que us plàcia, fulla seca
> de les que el vent s'emporta, o gota d'aigua
> de les que el sol sobre l'herbei eixuga,
> o, si ho voleu, baboia de l'escarni.
> Jo só un no-res, més mon no-res és vostre;
> vostre és, Senyor, i us ama i vos estima.
> Feu de mi lo que us plàcia; no en só digne,
> d'anar a vostres peus; com arbre estèril,
> de soca-rel traieu-me de la terra;
> morfoneu-me, atuïu-me, anihilau-me.

> Veniu a mi, congoixes del martiri,
> veniu, oh creus, mon or i ma fortuna:
> ornau mon front, engalonau mos braços.
> Veniu, llorers i palmes del Calvari;

Sum vermis

What you sow does not come to life
unless it dies.
   1 Corinthians 15:36

From prison to sky.

Chains bring wings.

     See me, Lord, here at your feet,
     stripped of everything good, sick and poor,
     lost in the abyss of my own nothingness.
     Worm of the low earth, I've come to crawl
     a brief moment among the ashes.   5
     My cradle was a particle of dust,
     and so will be my grave.
     Would that I were something to offer You,
     but You would have me small, and useless,
     stripped of glory and prestige.   10
     Do with me what pleases You, dry leaf
     swept up by winds, or drop of water
     soaked up by sun on grass,
     or, if You will, a foolish mockery.
     I am nothingness, but my nothingness is Yours;   15
     it is Yours, Lord, and it loves You.
     Do with me what pleases You;
     I am not worthy of your feet; uproot me,
     a sterile tree, from the earth;
     stifle me, vanquish me, annihilate me.   20

     Come to me, agonies of martyrdom,
     come, O crosses, my gold, my fortune,
     adorn my forehead, trim my arms with braids.
     Come, laurels and palms of Calvary,

si em sou aspres avui, abans de gaire
a vostre ombriu me serà dolç l'asseure'm.
Espina del dolor, vine a punyir-me;
cuita a abrigar-me amb ton mantell, oh injúria;
calúmnia, al meu voltant tos llots apila,
misèria, vine'm a portar lo ròssec.

Vull ser volva de pols de la rodera
a on tots los qui passen me trepitgen;
vull ser llençat com una escombraria
del palau al carrer, de la més alta
cima a l'afrau, i de l'afrau al còrrec.
Escombreu mes petjades en l'altura;
ja no hi faré més nosa, la pobresa
serà lo meu tresor, serà l'oprobi
lo meu orgull, les penes ma delícia.
Des d'avui colliré los vilipendis
i llengoteigs com perles i topacis
per la corona que en lo cel espero.
Muira aquest cos insuportable, muira;
cansat estic de tan feixuga càrrega;
devore'l lo fossar, torne a la cendra
d'on ha sortit: *sum vermis et non homo.*
Jo no só pas la industriosa eruga
que entre el fullam de la morera es fila
de finíssima seda lo sudari.
Jo me'l filo del cànem de mes penes;
mes, dintre aqueixa fosca sepultura,
tornat com Vós, Jesús, de mort a vida,
jo hi trobaré unes ales de crisàlide
per volar-me'n amb Vós a vostra glòria.

if today I find you bitter, your shade   25
will soon be sweet to sit beneath.
Thorn of pain, pierce my flesh,
wrap me in your blanket, injury;
slander, your mire and mud surround me,
wretchedness, come drag me away.   30

I want to be the speck of dust in the
wheel-tracks trod by all who pass;
I want to be tossed away like refuse
from the palace into the streets, from the highest
peak to the depths of the yawning ravine.   35
Wipe my footprints from the summits;
I'll not intrude there longer, poverty
will be my treasure, reproach will be
my pride, sorrows my delight.
As of today I'll gather scorn   40
and scoffing as pearls and topaz for
the crown I wait for in the sky.
Let my body die its death;
I weary of its awkward burden;
devour it, grave, turn it once more   45
to ash, *sum vermis et non homo.*
I am not the industrious worm
that spins among the mulberry leaves
a burial shroud of smoothest silk.
Mine I spin from the hemp of my grief;   50
but in this somber sepulchre,
like You, Lord, come from death to life,
I'll find my wings of chrysalis
to fly with You in all Your glory.

Vora la mar

Al cim d'un promontori que domina
    les ones de la mar,
quan l'astre rei cap a ponent declina
    me'n pujo a meditar.

Amb la claror d'aqueixa llàntia encesa
    contemplo mon no-res;
contemplo el mar i el cel, i llur grandesa
    m'aixafa com un pes.

Eixes ones, mirall de les estrelles,
    me guarden tants records,
que em plau reveure tot sovint en elles
    mos somnis que són morts.

Aixequí tants castells en eixes ribes
    que m'ha aterrat lo vent,
amb ses torres i cúpules altives
    de vori, d'or i argent:

poemes, ai!, que foren una estona
    joguina d'infantons,
petxines que un instant surten de l'ona
    per retornar al fons;

vaixells que amb veles i aparell s'ensorren
    en un matí de maig,
illetes d'or que naixen i s'esborren
    del sol al primer raig;

idees que m'acurcen l'existència
    duent-se'n ma escalfor,

By the Sea

Up on a headland that overlooks
    the sea and its waves,
when the king of orbs is westering low,
    I go to meditate.

By the brightness of that burning lamp   5
    I regard my nothingness;
I regard the sea and sky, crushed
    by the weight of their greatness.

Within the waves that mirror stars
    my memories are kept,   10
and often I delight to see
    the dreams of mine now dead.

Many a castle I raised on these shores,
    of ivory, silver and gold,
erected with high-reaching domes and towers   15
    that winds have now laid low:

poems, ay! that were for a while
    only child's play,
shells beached for an instant, then
    swept back to the deep by the waves: 20

ships gone under with sails and rigging
    one morning in May,
golden islets come out, then vanished
    with the sun's first ray:

ideas that cut my existence short,   25
    despoiling the warm essence,

com rufagada que s'endú amb l'essència
l'emmusteïda flor.

A la vida o al cor quelcom li prenen
les ones que se'n van;
si no tinc res, les ones que ara vénen,
digueu-me, què voldran?

Amb les del mar o amb les del temps un dia
tinc de rodar al fons;
per què, per què, enganyosa poesia,
m'ensenyes de fer mons?

Per què escriure més versos en l'arena?
Platja del mar dels cels,
quan serà que en ta pàgina serena
los escriuré amb estels?

— Caldetes, 10 gener 1883

LIV

Sabés on venen calúmnies,
calúmnies i vituperis,
jo n'aniria a comprar;
tot l'or i argent ne daria,
de la terra los imperis
i les illes de la mar.

like gusts of wind that carry off
    the withered flower and its fragrance.

Something is taken from life, or the heart,
    by waves that go their way;   30
but tell me, what, if I have nothing,
    will waves coming in take away?

One day by waves of the sea, or of time,
    I'll be swept to the deep;
so why have me build up worlds at all,   35
    deceitful poetry?

Why write more verses in the sands?
    Heaven's seashore:
when, on your clear and peaceful page,
    will I write them in the stars?   40

— Caldetes, 10 January 1883

LIV

If I knew where slander was sold,
slander and insult,
I'd go out and buy them;
I'd give my silver and gold,
earthly empires,
the ocean's isles.

LXX

Darrere el puig ve la vall,
darrere la nit l'aurora,
després de la pluja el sol,
després de la creu la glòria.

XCVI

Brevis gloria quæ ab hominibus
datur et accipitur.
    Tomàs de Kempis

La vana glòria del món
posa a l'home ales de cera;
al que pugen més amunt
de més amunt lo despenyen.

LXX

After the mountain comes the valley,
after the night the dawn,
after the rain the sun,
and after the cross, glory.

XCVI

Brief is the glory
given and gotten by men.
  THOMAS À KEMPIS

The shallow glory of this world
fits out men in wings of wax;
those they lift the highest
are flung down furthest.

FROM

Santa Eulària
(Saint Eulària, 1899)

Following the second series of articles published in the Barcelona press during the summer and fall of 1897 (later added to the 1895 series under the single title *En defensa pròpia* [In Self-Defense]), with no end in sight to his conflict with Bishop Morgades, Verdaguer was invited to Madrid, where he enjoyed the decisive support of the Augustinian friars at El Escorial. Moreover, thanks to the intervention of Bishop Cos of Madrid-Alcalá, the bishop of Vic, anxious to save face, accepted a letter of apology written by Verdaguer in January 1898, assuring him that he "had no intention of offending His Excellency, nor acting to the detriment of the Holy Church in any way." His priestly capacities fully recovered, Verdaguer soon resumed clerical duties in Barcelona at the parish of Bethlehem, located, ironically enough, on the Rambla just across the street from the Comillas residence he was forced to leave five years earlier.

It was during his three-month stay in Madrid, ending in mid-February 1898, that Verdaguer completed *Santa Eulària*. Abel Beltran (1999, 278–88) has examined the genesis of and possible motives behind the work, which was suggested to Verdaguer by Lluís Carles Viada i Lluch, editor of the weekly paper *El Sarrianés*, who had stood by him during his ordeal. In his preface to the book—a letter to Viada i Lluch—the poet recalls how in the spring of 1897 the two men took walks in Sarrià, Eulària's birthplace, searching the natural landscape for lingering traces of its long-vanished Roman past. Apart from the fact that as patron saint of Barcelona St. Eulàlia (as she is known today) was a popular figure, the recent restoration of her convent in Sarrià made her a current item of interest in the press. Further, according to Beltran, the promotion of religious tradition (e.g., lives of saints and martyrs) strengthened popular acceptance of the Church. Finally, as Beltran observes, "Verdaguer is sure to have seen Eulàlia as a sister in suffering for God. . . . The saint is persecuted and tortured by a pagan world that does not allow her to live her Christian religion, and the poet, too, is persecuted by a hostile world that fails to understand the consistent putting into practice of his Christian [beliefs]."

Because of Verdaguer's financial straits—he was still burdened with debts and feared his creditors would impound the volume as they had others—*Santa Eulària* was not published until 1899, more than a year after its completion. The book, subtitled by Verdaguer as a single *poemet* (short poem), has two parts. The first consists of nine poems sketching the life of St. Eulàlia, including the discovery of her relics in the year 877 by Bishop Frodoí of Barcelona in an earlier Christian church where Santa Maria del Mar now stands; the five poems in the second part deal with other aspects of the St. Eulàlia tradition. Following the poems are seven appendixes (most likely compiled by Viada i Lluch) of historical sources documenting the saint's life and related tradition since the seventh century.

Martiri

Margaritha sub sole rubescit.
    Plini

I

Mes al tigre del tirà
les dents li cruixen de ràbia:
fent-la lligar pels lictors
de colzes a una pilastra,
d'assots descarrega un riu
sobre ses nues espatlles,
fins que brollant-li la sang
damunt sa túnica blanca,
de fil a fil i a serrells
li'n posa una altra de grana.

II

I corre el puríssim doll
i per lo Tàber rodola,
deixant lo seu front vermell
amb la púrpura del Gòlgota.
Amb la sagrada regor
batejada és Barcelona,
batejada és amb la sang
de sa filla més hermosa.
Del grandiós peristil
la columnata ressona,
ressona com los bordons
d'una lira monstruosa,
entre mar i terra i cel
cantant sa immensa victòria.

Martyrdom

The pearl reddens in the sun.
    PLINY

I

But now the tiger tyrant
gnashes his teeth in rage:
and with her elbows tied
by lictors to a pilaster,
he looses on her naked   5
back a stream of lashes
till the blood wells up,
forming on her white
tunic the fabric and fray
of another—scarlet in color.   10

II

The pure stream flows
down the sloping Tabor,
leaving its face red
with the wounds of Golgotha.
And with this sacred watering   15
Barcelona is baptized,
christened in the lifeblood
of its loveliest daughter.
The columns of the great
peristyle ring out,   20
resounding with the bourdons
of a vast lyre that sings
to sea and earth and sky
the immensity of her victory.

III

Lo lliri blanc del Desert
ja és clavellina purpúrea,
mes, ai!, que de tant patir
és tota esfullada i mústia.
Tement que se li morís,
Dacià el martiri muda:
deslligant-la del pilar
dalt de l'ecúleu la puja.
Amb dolorós cruiximent
sos ossos se descoiunten
i s'esgalabra el seu cos
de ferro verge amb les úngules.
Lo que el garfi va unglejant
atxes enceses ho abrusen,
fins que el foc, més compassiu,
per no cremar-la, recula.

IV

Veient acostar les flames,
també recula Dacià:
la tanca dins una tina
que té sagetes per claus,
tota encerclada de glavis
i ganivets de dos talls.
Baixada de Santa Eulària,
tu la veres rodolar
d'un abisme a l'altre abisme
per aquells rostos avall,
deixant per rastre en les herbes
un bell rosari de sang.
—On és Déu que no t'ajuda?—
tot rient diu-li el tirà.
—És en mon cor —respon ella—,
no veus tu que em va ajudant?
—Doncs, perquè el tingues per sempre
a la vora i abraçat,
de Jesús amb la ignomínia

III

The white lily of the Desert   25
is now a crimson carnation,
petals fallen and withered
from all her suffering.
Fearing she may die,
Datian has removed her: 30
untying her from the pillar,
he puts her on the rack.
With sharp cracks of pain
Eulària's bones disjoint,
and ungulae of iron   35
pierce her chaste body.
And where the hooks pierce through
live firebrands scorch,
till the fires, feeling pity,
suddenly retract.   40

IV

Seeing the flames leap close,
Datian, too, jumps back;
he puts her in a barrel
that's nailed together with darts
and fitted all around   45
with knives and daggers.
The street that bears her name
watched her rolling by,
from one abyss into
another, down its grade,   50
leaving behind in the grass
a rosary of blood-red beads.
"Where is your God and help?"
mocks the tyrant.
"He's in my heart," she replies.   55
"Don't you see Him helping me?"
"Fine—and so you'll always
feel his fast embrace,
you'll share upon a cross

tu la creu compartiràs;
mes, com Ell, fora muralla;
no deshonres la ciutat—.
I esglaiada Barcelona,
com un rebuig veu llençar
amb sa joia de més vàlua
lo que el món té de més gran.

this Jesus' own disgrace;   60
like Him, outside the walls,
without dishonor to the city."
And Barcelona, heart-struck,
now sees tossed out like trash,
with its most precious gem,   65
the world's greatest gift.

Aires del Montseny
(Airs of Montseny, 1901)

In March 1896 the Duran family—and Verdaguer—were evicted from their apartment on Carrer Portaferrissa, prompting Verdaguer to move into the small living quarters of Els Penitents (his property in Vallcarca), then on the outskirts of Barcelona. According to Pere Tió (1999), here Verdaguer—still painfully and publicly rebuked by Church authorities—undertook a number of new works: *Perles del Llibre d'Amic e d'Amat* (Pearls of the Book of the Lover and the Beloved, recreative variations on Ramon Llull's mystic poetry published posthumously in 1908), the long autobiographic poem *La pomerola* (The Shadbush), *Aires del Montseny*, and *Al cel* (To Heaven).

Molas (1999), in examining the genesis and significance of *Aires del Montseny*, notes that with this volume devoted to the Montseny massif, the "epopee" of Catalonia's three great mountains—Montserrat, Canigó, and Montseny—is now complete. In his prologue Verdaguer writes that Montseny is Catalonia's *pedró* or great stone landmark complete with cross and cupola: its cross planted on the summits by renowned nineteenth-century missionary St. Antoni Maria Claret i Clarà (the weathered cross was replaced by Bishop Morgades in 1894), its cupola overhead "the gigantic vault of the firmament." Rising some 5,600 feet to the south of his birthplace, Montseny fascinated Verdaguer as a child and later, during the crisis years, became a source of solace:

> Montseny showed me its enormous Cross, as if to say: I, a mountain, and therefore without sin, hold my Cross high, and you, a poor sinner, would throw aside your burden? And so I took it up and carried it willingly, though not so straight and high, following that example; and so well did I remember that Cross, that

I founded a weekly [magazine] with some associates and called it *Creu del Montseny* [Cross of Montseny]. Our enthusiasm grew, until . . . on 3 September 1899, I made a short pilgrimage with co-workers and friends, climbing [to the summit] to see it.

Reflecting in his long prose appendix to the volume on the Christian legacy and its history in Catalonia and throughout Spain, Verdaguer places the cross—the centermost of Christian symbols—at the center of his own reflection: "The Cross is everything for us: it is our staff along the rugged road of existence; it is our anchor throughout the journey on the bitter sea of life; it is the sword of those who battle for God; it is our book of truth while we live in the realm of deceit; it is solace to those who suffer, joy to those who weep, strength to the weak, and banner to the ranks of the chosen." Reaffirming the idea encapsulated in the poem "Shaped like a Cross" (*Flors del Calvari*) that the cross/suffering is the way to heaven/salvation, Verdaguer recalls theologian Jaume Balmes's instructions, on his deathbed in Vic, that his windows facing Montseny be opened wide: "[as he was] about to make the everlasting journey, the Cross of Montseny was perhaps for him the Cross [signaling] the road to heaven."

Molas notes that the thirty-five poems in *Aires del Montseny* can be divided into three broad categories: those written in the 1870s and 1880s in connection with strengthening the moderately pro-Catalan Catholic base, those arising from Verdaguer's spiritual crisis and subsequent confrontation with Bishop Morgades, and finally, those dealing with popular lore and legend. It is, therefore, anthological in character, often veering topically from the title's purported theme, while its poems—some recent, others from youth—vary in form, some unpublished, others published previously in literary magazines, yet all subsumed "by extension" under a locally common human geography of Christian stamp.

Written in 1896, the poem "What Is Poetry?" reformulates the Verdaguerian theme of earthly banishment from the celestial home, the nightingale again representing the poet who "brings delight to banished souls / And gives them mystic wings—his own." The nightingale metaphor is developed further: "He won't be caged in any palace, / Nor lured by riches or their dazzle," spotlighting the poet's solitary calling and the divine nature of his task. This is in contrast to the distracted crowd: "The bubble and boil of things mundane / Turns us from celestial strains." In the final stanza the sentiment of *enyorança*, longing for home, envelops the poet's past as well, calling to mind the "morning in May," alluding, it seems (as proposed by Codina 2003, 85, and Molas 2003b, 23), to the moment of poetic discovery described in "The Harp."

Què és la poesia?

La poesia és un aucell del cel
que fa sovint volades a la terra,
per vessar una gota de consol
en lo cor trist dels desterrats fills d'Eva.

Los fa record del paradís perdut
on jugava l'amor amb la innocència,
i els ne fa somiar un de millor
en lo verger florit de les estrelles.

Ella és lo rossinyol d'aquells jardins,
són llur murmuri bla ses canticeles,
que hi transporten al pobre desterrat
dant-li per ales místiques les seves.

No es deixa engabiar en los palaus,
no es deixa esbalair per la riquesa,
en la masia amb los senzills del cor
ses ales d'or i sa cançó desplega.

Mes per sentir-l'hi modular a pler
la pobra humanitat està distreta;
qui està distret amb lo borboll mundà,
com sentirà la refilada angèlica?

L'aucell del paradís no es fa oir, no,
de qui escolta la veu de la sirena:
lo cel que es mira en la fontana humil
no s'emmiralla en la riuada tèrbola.

De poetes cabdals prou n'hi ha haguts,
cap d'ells la dolça melodia ha apresa;

What Is Poetry?

Poetry's a skysome bird
Whose frequent visits to the earth
Bring trickling drops of ease to saddened
Hearts of Eve's long-banished children.

It brings to mind the paradise   5
Where love once danced with innocence,
And dreams a greater one by far
Where gardens bloom among the stars.

It is those gardens' nightingale,
Their tender murmur is his song   10
That brings delight to banished souls
And gives them mystic wings—his own.

He won't be caged in any palace,
Nor lured by riches or their dazzle;
In the house where simple hearts unite   15
His golden wings and song take flight.

And yet humanity has long
Been heedless to his heaven-song:
The bubble and boil of things mundane
Turn us from celestial strains.   20

Those who serve the siren's voice
Hear not this bird of paradise:
In humble pools the skies find mirrors,
Not in turbid, muddy rivers.

Not one among the masterful many   25
Has learned his gentle melody;

qui n'arribés a aprendre un refilet,
aquell ne fóra l'àliga superba.

Mes l'aucellet refila tot volant,
calàndria de l'empírea primavera,
allí dalt entre els núvols de l'orient
llença un raig d'harmonies i s'encela.

Jo l'he sentida un bell matí de maig,
lo bell matí del maig de ma infantesa;
jo l'he sentida la gentil cançó:
per ço m'és enyorívola la terra.

— 15 maig 1896

Who but a single measure uttered
Would soar like an eagle above the others.

The songbird sings and spreads its wings,
Calandra lark of empyreal spring,   30
And pours down music as he flies,
High through clouds in eastern skies.

I heard the song one morning in May,
Brightest of all my childhood days;
So graceful was the song I heard   35
That longing fills my heart on earth.

— 15 May 1896

29. Monument to Verdaguer at the Willow Fountain.

FROM

Al cel
(To Heaven, posthumous, 1903)

"I want to go to Heaven," Verdaguer begins in his prologue, ". . . [but] I don't want to go alone," which is why, he explains, he wrote for publication these thirty-eight "songs of longing (*enyorança*)," described by him as the sequel to *Flors del Calvari* and "brother to those bitter complaints, child of those pains and sorrows." Verdaguer continues: "Homer tells in the *Odyssey* how Ulysees's companions found the fruit of the lotus so fine they forgot their homeland. . . . Man is a prisoner on earth, as his soul, in origin and end, is entirely celestial; but he is a prisoner so accustomed to chains, suffering and prison that he fears the sound of opening doors." Recalling his notion of poems as alms in *Caritat*, Verdaguer tells his readers that it is "a work of charity, indeed the greatest of all, to speak, write, and sing of Heaven."

As understood by Tió (1999, 296), Verdaguer's poetic production during the years 1896 and 1897 signals a fourfold shift as he (1) sets aside his own bitter experience, (2) reaffirms himself as poet, (3) takes up again the aspirations of his youth, and (4) lifts his gaze to the heavens. *Al cel* was one of the later works that Verdaguer left ready for publication but that did not appear till shortly after his death—perhaps, as Torrents suggests, to rebut accusations that he wrote only to achieve fame for himself. In his prologue, written in 1897 (five years before his death), Verdaguer ends with a remark on the book's title: he changed it from *Celísties* (Celestial Poems, or Poems of the Heavens) to *Al cel* (To Heaven) because the latter, though "perhaps less poetic, [was] more uplifting and, above all, more Christian."

Still, Verdaguer strikes a balance between the spiritual and the material in things celestial. With the composition of *Al cel*, his upward gaze coincides with a new interest—astronomy: references are found in the manuscripts to popular French astronomers Ferdinand Hoefer and Camille Flammarion, and Verdaguer's library came to include more than half a dozen works on the subject. In the poem "The Milky Way," his fascination with the night sky weighs ancient Greek metaphysics against popular Christian legend, while in "The Moon" the poet's imagination is sparked by the popular cosmology of Provençal lore.

La Via Làctea

    Què és aqueix riu d'estrelles
que com anell guarnit de pedres fines
cenyeix la immensitat de l'hemisferi?
    Jo ho preguntí als mitòlegs,
i un respongué: —És un raig de llet de Juno
caigut mentres donava el pit a Hèrcules—.
Altre em digué que Faetó, al caure
de son carro de foc, un astre, eixint-se
    de son camí ordinari,
socarrimà l'espai en sa carrera.

No gaire satisfet de la resposta,
ne demanava als filosops i astrònoms.
Me respongué Aristòtil: —És un núvol
de vapors secs que més amunt de l'èter
cabellera de flames arrossega.
—No! —digué un seu deixeble—. En lo principi,
al començar lo sol los seus viatges
per la volta estel·lífera, son carro
deixà en lo firmament eixa rodera.
    —Jo crec —digué Demòcrit—
que és la claror dels astres que a miríades
en la blavor sidèrea s'acongesten
com sobre el Nil los platejats nenúfars—.
Demaní son parer a Teofrastes,
i: —És això —em respongué— la soldadura
amb què Déu encaixà els dos hemisferis
que formen l'estrellada. Per l'escletxa
que deixa lo cosit, la llum de dintre
del firmament brolla i traspua a fora—.

Demaní el seu a un vell pastor de Núria
i em digué que és la via de Sant Jaume

The Milky Way

What is this river in the stars
girding the celestial sphere,
set, like a ring, with precious gems?
    I put it to the mythologists;
said one, "It's milk that Juno spilled   5
while giving breast to Hercules."
Another held that Phaëthon's fall
from his fiery chariot sent the orb
    swerving off its course,
scorching the trackless space in its path.   10

Not entirely satisfied,
I tried philosophers and astronomers.
Aristotle replied: "It's a cloud
of parched vapors with flaming hair
trailing high above the ether."   15
"No!" said a disciple. "When first
the sun began its travels through
the starry spheres, its chariot left
this imprint on the firmament."
    "I think," said Democritus,   20
"that it's the light of countless stars
all gathering in the sidereal blue
like water lilies bright upon the Nile."
I asked Theophrastus to state his view,
and his reply was this: "That's where   25
God united the halves of the starlit
vault of heaven. You can see in the cleft
at the seam where they once were welded together
the light of the firmament seeping through."

I asked an old shepherd from Núria what he thought,   30
and he told me it was the Way of St. James,

per on, a son exemple,
les ànimes se'n pugen a la Glòria.

No sabia més lletra que ses cabres,
lo vell pastor de Núria,
mes posí sa contesta lluminosa
damunt la d'Aristòtil
i la de tots los savis de la Grècia.

La Lluna

La luno es un soleu
que ha perdù sa perruco.
ADAGI PROVENÇAL

Del cel un dia en la planície blava
se posaren los astres a dansar;
jo no sé pas quin astre se casava
amb no sé quina estrella
del món la primavera a l'apuntar.

L'Estrella del capvespre, somiosa,
dóna la mà a l'Estrella del matí;
l'Orion que floreix com una rosa
s'aparella amb lo Sírius,
lo lliri blanc del sideral jardí.

Amb sos amants satèl·lits giravolta
cada amorós planeta resplendent,
i, arrossegant sa cabellera solta,
lo vagarós cometa
deixa estela de foc pel firmament.

Voltegen la Polar ses companyones,
com busques d'un horari gegantí;

where, following his example,
souls make their ascent to Glory.

He couldn't read or write any more than his goats,
    this old shepherd from Núria,   35
but I put his shining answer above
        that of Aristotle
and all the sages of ancient Greece.

The Moon

The moon is a sun
that has lost her wig.
    PROVENÇAL ADAGE

One day on the blue plains of the sky
the stars and planets began to dance;
what planet had taken which star for bride
    I really don't know,
the world's spring season was not far advanced.   5

The evening star, given to dream,
extends a hand to the star of morning;
Orion, with his roselike gleam,
    pairs with Sirius,
brightest of lilies in heavenly gardens.   10

Each amorous planet spins and shines,
its satellite lovers circling by,
And comets with hair sweeping behind
    wander and roam,
tracing a glimmering wake in the sky.   15

Like pointers on a gigantic dial
the Pole Star's companions revolve around her;

prop del Tauro es rumbegen pariones
les Híades i Plèiades;
lo Cisne s'acomboia amb lo Delfí.

Amb son anell immens Saturno juga,
i amb ses vuit llunes que no minven mai,
com un joglar tirar enlaire puga
sa rutlla i ses pilotes
que pugen i davallen per l'espai.

Vora la Lira d'or fan la sardana
sis atxes resplendents en lo zenit,
brillants de la Corona que Ariana
deixà en lo cel suspesa
perquè en son front la rumbejàs la nit.

Pare del dia, el Sol dansa amb la Lluna,
que era allavors esplèndida com ell;
sa cara, un temps, com ara no era bruna,
sos ulls guspirejaven,
i era de raigs de l'alba son cabell.

Parlaven de son garbo les estrelles,
los meteors retreien sa rossor,
i com eixams de cèliques abelles,
los astres festejaven
de son jardí l'enlluernanta flor.

Al sentir-se lloar de tan hermosa,
esbalaïda deixà caure el vel
amb què fóra llavors poncella closa,
i un crit de meravella
féu ressonar la cúpula del cel.

Lo Sol s'engeloseix, tira a sa cara
de ses antigues cendres un grapat,
que enterboleix sos ulls i l'emmascara:
astre es quedà la Lluna,
mes sense llum, com un carbó apagat.

Hyades and Pleiades, matched in style,
     promenade near Taurus,
and the Swan and the Dolphin escort one another.   20

Like a juggler tossing balls and hoop
up in the air, Saturn plays
with his eight never-waning moons
     and huge ring,
all sailing high and far through space.   25

At the zenith, six candles arrayed in a round
near golden Lyra glimmer bright,
diamonds in Ariadne's crown,
     which she left in the heavens
to preside as crowning jewel in the night.   30

Father of day, the Sun comes to dance
with the Moon—as splendid back then as he;
her face had not yet lost its brilliance,
     and her eyes flashed,
her hair shining bright with daybreak's beams.   35

The stars spoke long about her grace,
meteors remarked on her sparkling color,
and celestial orbs swarming through space
     drew near like honeybees,
courting her garden's dazzling flower.   40

Hearing her beauty bring such praise,
she suddenly dropped her veil—overwhelmed,
revealing her blossom to everyone's gaze,
     and a cry of wonder
resounded throughout the sky's steep realm.   45

The Sun, bitten by jealousy, throws
a handful of ashes into her face,
clouding her eyes and masking her glow:
     the moon still an orb,
but as embers, now dims, her brilliance effaced.   50

Des de llavors, com una flor d'obaga,
rodant per les tenebres de la nit,
sempre la Lluna pàl·lida s'amaga
    de l'astre hermós del dia,
si el troba pels camins de l'infinit.

Since then, like a flower on a shady slope,
as through dark night she makes her way;
if she meets him along infinity's roads,
    the pale Moon
hides from the shining orb of day.   55

FROM

Barcelonines

(Barcelona Poems, posthumous, 1925)

Barcelonines is the title containing twenty-six poems published in 1925 as volume 28 of the *Obres Completes* (Complete Works) of Verdaguer begun in 1914 by publisher Francesc Matheu, nineteen of which (some previously published in magazines, others unpublished) were written between 1896 and 1902, the last six years of Verdaguer's life. According to Verdaguer's wish, an additional eighteen poems and three prose texts connected with Barcelona (not included in *Barcelonines*) were to be combined with the *Barcelonines* and published under the comprehensive title *Barcelona*. The projected volume did not materialize, though the additional works had appeared, most of them in books (*Caritat, Pàtria, Santa Eulària*, and others) published in Verdaguer's lifetime, a few posthumously. More recently, Francesc Codina (2006) has compiled and edited the first book collecting the remaining twenty-five poems and five prose texts that Verdaguer intended to be included under the title *Barcelona*.

In "A un rossinyol de Vallvidrera" ("To a Nightingale from Vallvidrera") Verdaguer evokes, once again, the nightingale (singer of heavenly song in "A Nightingale's Death," "Preaching to Birds," and "What Is Poetry?"), with which the poet identifies. Composed in May 1897, before Verdaguer's confrontation with Church authorities was resolved, the poem conveys his sense of worldly banishment and *enyorança*, longing for the heavenly home, while at the same time it reaffirms his poetic ideal informed by Christian Romanticism.

30. Verdaguer's funeral procession in Barcelona (1902).

A un rossinyol de Vallvidrera

Romancet dedicat a mos amics
D. Antonio Rubió i D. Lluís Carles Viada

Rossinyol, bon rossinyol,
he sentida la teva arpa,
l'he sentida un dematí
de Vallvidrera a Valldaura,
fent rodolar-hi tos cants
com perles dintre de l'aigua:
cantaves l'amor a Déu,
l'enyorament de la pàtria,
los misteris de la nit,
les llums de la matinada,
ton amor entre les flors,
ton niuet entre les branques,
ta mainadeta, que viu
de cançons i de becada.
Trobador del mes de maig,
rossinyol, refila i canta,
mes no deixes eixos cims
per los vergers de la plana:
no hi vingues a la ciutat,
que hi ha una gent molt ingrata.
Diu que estima als aucellets,
diu que en son cor los regala,
mes als que canten millor
los posa dintre la gàbia.

— Vallvidrera, 9 maig 1897

To a Nightingale from Vallvidrera

A short romance dedicated to my friends
Don Antoni Rubió and Don Lluís Carles Viada

Nightingale, fine nightingale,
I've heard your harp: I heard it all
the way to Vallvidrera from
Valldaura on a morning when
you rolled your songs out from its strings   5
like pearls through water.
You sang of love for God,
of longing for the homeland,
of mysteries of the night,
the morning light,   10
your love among the flowers,
your nest among the branches,
your young who thrive
upon your song and beak.
Troubadour of month of May,   15
nightingale, trill your song,
but do not leave these summits
for orchards on the plain:
come not into the city—
the people there are thankless.   20
They say they love you, songbirds,
and that they hold you in their hearts,
but those whose song is loveliest
they only put in cages.

— Vallvidrera, 9 May 1897

NOTES

From L'Atlàntida: *Introduction*

LINE 1: Lusian Sea: the Atlantic Ocean off the coast of Lusitania, the ancient Roman province identified with Portugal.

LINE 6: Near to her cubs: revising Wyse's "Gist with her cubs."

LINE 60: The Ter: river near Vic.

LINES 73–74: Revising Wyse's "From heaven suspended erst a lamp of gold / It dazed him with its beams, but, waxing old" since the "lamp of gold" is the hermit himself, whose wisdom once shed light on the world.

LINE 84: Our Star o' the Sea: *stella maris*, invocation to the Virgin Mary.

LINE 90: Rose-tree: poetic rendering of the Catalan *roser* (rose bush); on the fabled rose-tree, see Hans Christian Andersen's "The Snail and the Rose-Tree."

LINE 114: Betic valleys: Bætica, Roman region in Hispania.

LINE 119: Her: the Virgin Mary.

LINE 132: Mistral: northerly wind.

LINE 135: Nestles: revising Wyse's "nestled."

LINE 152: Hears: revising Wyse's "lists."

LINE 155: Genius o' the Atlantic Wave: angel or guardian spirit of the Atlantic (cf. the Angel of Spain in "La Maladeta" line 174).

LINE 156: Revising Wyse's archaic "But *Colon* was his auditor, I trow!"

From L'Atlàntida: *Isabella's Dream*

In this ballad Isabella tells Ferdinand of her dream and resolves to support Columbus's voyage.

LINE 6: Hear: revising Wyse's "list" (also in line 9). Dove: the Catalan *colom* (dove) is homonymous with *Colom* (Columbus); Verdaguer uses the Hispanicized form *Colon*, also homonymous with the Spanish *colon* (dove).

LINE 9: Alhambra: the Moorish palace in Granada where the Catholic Monarchs, Ferdinand and Isabella, received Columbus before his first voyage.

LINE 20: Dove: the dove is Columbus, both metaphorically and homonymously (see note to line 6).

LINE 61: Columbus: for Verdaguer's "Colon" (see note to line 6).

From Canigó: *La Maladeta*

This central section of canto 4, "The Pyrenees," takes up almost half the canto, which describes the eastern Pyrenees as seen by Gentil and Flordeneu (queen of the Pyrenean fairies) as they fly above the summits in her chariot. In contrast to the decasyllabic eight-line stanzas surrounding it, the ode to La Maladeta—the highest and most rugged massif in the Aragonese Pyrenees—features six-line stanzas of Verdaguer's masterful dodecasyllabic alexandrines rhyming *aabccb* (feminine rhyme in *aa* and *cc* couplets), feminine at the caesura (i.e., with an unstressed, uncounted seventh syllable) in lines 1 through 5 and followed by a final *b*-rhyming (half-length) masculine hexasyllable.

TITLE: The name La Maladeta refers both to the massif (see note above), whose highest peak is Aneto (11,168 ft.) and, farther north in the massif, the peak of La Maladeta (10,853 ft.), both of which Verdaguer ascended in the summer of 1882.

LINES 1–6: Verdaguer contrasts La Maladeta with several other Pyrenean massifs and peaks of lower elevation: Vignemale (or Vinhamala), massif in the west-central Pyrenees bordering France and Spain; Ossau (or Aussau), mountain peak in the Pyrénées-Atlantiques (France) west of Vignemale; Puig d'Alba, mountain peak in southeast Ariège (France); La Forcada (today, La Forcanada or Malh des Pois), mountain peak in Val d'Aran east of Aneto; the Alberes, range running east-west at the eastern end of the Pyrenees along the French-Spanish border; Carlit, massif in the Pyrénées-Orientales west of the Canigó massif.

LINE 7: Garona (Fr. Garonne): river emerging en Val d'Aran, flowing northward, and emptying into the Atlantic at Bordeaux. Éssera: river emerging in the La Maladeta massif, flowing southwesterly through Benasc to join the Cinca and the Segre farther south.

LINE 8: Aran: Val d'Aran, modern county in northwestern Catalonia (east of La Maladeta), where a variety of Languedocian is spoken. Lis: valley north-north-west of La Maladeta in Haute-Garonne (France). Benasca (or Benasc): Pyrenean valley circling north of La Maladeta.

LINE 9: Mont Blanc: western Europe's highest mountain. Dhaulagiri: once thought to be the world's highest mountain.

LINES 13–18: Verdaguer's depiction of the life-giving quality of the landscape resonates with a cultural multiplicity endowed with vigor and thriving as an extension of nature's diversity.

LINE 22: Goliath: cf. Verdaguer's *Excursions i viatges* [22 July 1882], where he describes La Maladeta, seen from Benasc, as "the Goliath of our mountains."

LINE 43: Ebre (Sp. Ebro): major river emerging in the Cantabrian Mountains, flowing southeasterly, gathering waters from the Pyrenees, and emptying into the Mediterranean at the Delta de l'Ebre, southeast of Tortosa.

LINE 46: Moncayo: massif and peak west of Saragossa. El Cid: Rodrigo Díaz de Vivar, *El Cid Campeador*, eleventh-century hero celebrated in the Spanish epic *Cantar de Mio Cid*.

LINE 47: Pelayo: (?-737), Visigothic lord and first king of Asturias, whose victory over the Saracens at Covadonga ushered in the Christian conquest of Muslim Spain.

LINE 48: Roland: (?-778), (from the Germanic *hrod*, "glory," and *land*), hero of Charlemagne's court whose death in battle at Roncevaux is related in the Old French epic *La chanson de Roland* and whose legendary exploits are further related by Ariosto in *Orlando Furioso*; references to Roland, a popular figure in Pyrenean legend, appear elsewhere in *Canigó*.

LINES 71: Mahomet's Bridge: narrow plunging ridge climbers straddle to reach the summit of Aneto from the north.

LINES 73-78: Cf. *Excursions i viatges* [22 July 1882]: "What quarrier comes to blast and break these cliffs?"

LINES 79-80: Construction of Barcelona's present-day cathedral began in 1298, but the façade (completed in 1913) was not undertaken until 1885.

LINES 97-114: On the legend of the beggar and the shepherds, see Garolera and Wittlin 2002, 146.

LINES 127-32: Cf. *Excursions i viatges* [22 July 1882]: "With a great leap, I was able to cross the crevice and resolved . . . not to listen to any more strange noises and sirens' songs . . . [and to avoid] the gaping graves [lying] open to the living, grooves of the death-cart."

LINE 136: Neto: Celto-Iberian god after which is named Aneto, the highest peak in the massif of La Maladeta.

LINES 140-44: Cf. *Excursions i viatges* [22 July 1882]: "The plains of Toulouse and all the south of France were covered in a white mist, as if the Angel of Spain were sheltering it with his wings so that our eyes not rove, and that our Spanish and Catalan hearts might give themselves completely to our beloved homeland."

LINE 143: Cabo Higuer: promontory in the Bay of Biscay north of the town of Hondarribia at the western end of the Pyrenees.

LINE 144: Cap de Creus: Catalonia's easternmost promontory, where the Pyrenean foothills descend to the Mediterranean northeast of Roses.

LINE 171: Picos de Europa: massif along the Asturias-Cantabria border in the Cantabrian range. Puigmal: second-highest peak (after Carlit) in the eastern Pyrenees (see note to lines 51-52 in "The Harp").

LINE 172: Cf. *Excursions i viatges* [22 July 1882]: ". . . a blue sky, like that of Andalusia, thrown into relief by the loftiest of Pyrenean summits."

LINE 174: An Angel overhead: guardian spirits were sometimes attributed by Verdaguer to collective identities or geographic features (cf. *L'Atlàntida*, "Introduction," line 155).

LINES 187-92: In Verdaguer's day the Napoleonic occupation of Catalonia and Spain was relatively recent in historical memory.

From Canigó: *Guisla*

In canto 10 Count Guifre, responsible for the death of his nephew Gentil, pays a visit to his wife Guisla to tell her he has resolved to live a life of solitary penitence at Sant Martí del Canigó, the monastery to be built on the mountain. Later, Guisla comes across Griselda, the shepherdess who loves Gentil and awaits his return. Verdaguer's feminine decasyllables feature assonant rhyme at even-numbered lines, *e*-sounding in the first section and *i*-sounding in the shorter second, third, and final sections.

LINE 1: Count Guifre: Guifre II of Cerdanya (GEE-fruh), (ca. 970–1050), uncle to Gentil, whom he knights and later hurls to his death, after which he resolves to found Sant Martí del Canigó and end his days in reclusion; according to legend, he spent nights in his own tomb that he carved out in the wall of rock next to the bell tower. Cornellà: Cornellà de Conflent (Fr. Corneilla-de-Conflent), village south of the Têt River in the valley northwest of Mount Canigó, where Guifre's palace stood.

LINE 22: Guisla: the countess.

LINE 44: Sant Martí del Canigó (Fr. St. Martin du Canigou), monastery perched on a ridge (3460 ft.), founded ca. 1000 by Guifre and his brother Bishop Oliba; dedicated to St. Martin (ca. 316–97), bishop of Tours and patron of knights.

LINE 77: Catalan Stripes: the Catalan flag has four vertical red stripes on a yellow field.

LINE 137: Conflent: the heart of the historic county of Cerdanya in North (or French) Catalonia (see note below).

LINE 173: Cerdanya: historic county in northern Catalonia held by Muslims until the Carolingian Empire established a foothold in the ninth century. The modern county of Alta (upper) Cerdanya lies west of Conflent, today part of North Catalonia (France); extending southward, Baixa (lower) Cerdanya is today a county in Catalonia (Spain).

LINE 185: Gentil: see introductory note.

LINE 194: The tomb of her love: the monastery.

LINE 199: Griselda: see introductory note.

From Dos màrtirs de ma pàtria

The complete title in Catalan is *Dos màrtirs de ma pàtria, o siga Llucià i Marcià: Poema en dos cants que llegí l'estiu passat en un cèrcol d'aficionats al llenguatge i a les glòries de la pàtria* (Two Martyrs of My Fatherland, or Llucià and Marcià: Poem in Two Cantos That I Read Last Summer in a Circle of Enthusiasts of the Language and Glories of the Fatherland). The long subtitle follows the literary trend of the times. The term *pàtria* (literally "fatherland") is central to the Catalan Renaixença, launched in 1833 with the publication of Bonaventura Carles Aribau's "La pàtria," hailed as the first Romantic poem in Catalan; it linked the term to the cultural, and later political, struggle to preserve Catalonia's language and traditions. In *Dos màrtirs de ma pàtria* the term denotes a more restricted geographic and cultural sphere as well, signifying Ausona (today the county of Osona), of which Vic (Ausa in Roman days) is the capital. Finally, in the context of Verdaguer's Christian Romanticism—Chateaubriand's influence is certain here by way of Vic's native son and theologian Jaume Balmes (1810–48), if not directly—the term *pàtria* takes on a broader sense encompassing Christendom.

LINE 145: Torrents (1995a, 46) notes that Verdaguer "places the feminine figure in the foreground." Aurèlia, of "noble Roman descent," relegates the heroes to a secondary role.

LINE 148: The River Mèder flows eastward through Vic.

LINES 155–57: Torrents (1995a, 146) notes how this mythic depiction of fire underscores the evil intent of the youths and at the same time symbolizes love (see note to line 219); Vulcan was the husband of Venus as well as the god of fire.

LINE 160: Torrents (ibid.) notes the biblical allusion: "We have escaped like a bird from the snare of the fowlers; the snare is broken, and we have escaped" (Psalm 124:7).

LINE 169: See note to line 148.

LINE 184: Their patroness is Venus, goddess of love, associated here with worldly desire.

LINES 204–5: From Roses to Galicia: spanning the entire Iberian Peninsula from northeast to northwest.

LINE 206: The foremost archer: Cupid.

LINES 219–20: The one who gives the spark of love: epithet for Venus. Vesta: goddess of the burning hearth, in whose shrine her priestesses, the Vestal Virgins, kept a sacred fire burning. The epithet and subsequent simile underscore, once again, the metaphoric association of fire with love (see note to lines 155–57).

LINE 222: Here "noble goddess" refers to Aurèlia; cf. line 194, where Llucià and Marcià invoke Venus with the same words; cf. also line 278, where Aurèlia seems to them "Venus of this world." Talisman: the cross Aurèlia wears around her neck.

LINE 236: Jealous Delia: the moon, personified in Diana, goddess of the woods and fertility, also associated with the Greek goddess Selene (later Artemis and Phoebe), jealous in her love for Endymion.

LINE 242: Styx and Cocytus: rivers of the netherworld.

LINE 252: Crimson roses: the French rose or *Rosa gallica* (Cat. *rosa vera*) is frequently found in Verdaguer, associated, for example, with the Blessed Virgin in *Llegenda de Montserrat* or in *Canigó* with the queen of the fairies.

LINE 286: Morpheus: god of dreams and sleep.

LINE 324: Book of life: allusion to Revelation 3:5.

LINE 331: Blinded boy: Cupid.

LINE 333: Tartarus: the underworld.

LINE 334: Jove: Jupiter.

LINES 339–40: Torrents (1995a, 158) notes how the young Verdaguer's use of chiasmus exemplifies his putting into practice the classic precepts of rhetoric learned at the seminary.

LINE 370: Judea's fearsome lion: the Messiah.

LINES 378–80: The scene described is the Crucifixion.

LINE 399: Labarum: the imperial standard of Constantine (r. 306–37) bearing a cross and the chrismon monogram; in other words, the cross (although, as Torrents notes, Verdaguer's use proves anachronistic here since Decius precedes Constantine by more than half a century).

Marina

Verdaguer includes a subhead that reads: "Poem written in the horse latitudes after the Christian burial at sea of a girl by that name, who died just a few hours after birth."

LINE 11: The land we long to see: heaven.

LINE 41: The separation preceding the final seven stanzas marks a thematic shift from the worldly to the heavenly.

LINE 65: Cf. Psalm 55:6.

The Sacred Harp

EPIGRAPH: From the medieval hymn "Stabat Mater."

LINE 1: The Tree: the Cross.

LINES 2–3: The Harp represents Christ, who in messianic tradition was descended from David. The metaphor is strengthened by the literal sense in line 3, recalling that authorship of the Psalms is ascribed to David.

LINE 9: Christ's seven cries from the cross: (1) Father, forgive them; for they know not what they do. (2) Verily I say unto thee, today thou shalt be with me in Paradise. (3) Women, behold thy son! (4) My God, my God, why hast Thou forsaken me? (5) I thirst. (6) It is finished. (7) Father, into Thy hands I commend my spirit.

Rosalia

Verdaguer includes the following note: "The venerable Rosalia Viau, later Mother of the Sacred Heart of Jesus, lived in the Convent of Mercy in Barcelona during the French Revolution; she died in the Casa de la Pietat in Palma, Mallorca, in 1832, and lies interred there near the main altar. She was the daughter of a horticulturist near Avinyó [between Vic and Manresa], and it was in her garden that this tender, affectionate idyll between her and her beloved Jesus took place."

LINE 7: The formulaic use of epanadiplosis renders the verse popular in tone (cf. lines 13 and 21 in "The Turtledoves" and line 1 in "A Nightingale from Vallvidrera").

Discovery of the Virgin

The Virgin: the Black Madonna of Montserrat (La Moreneta); she has been dated from the late twelfth century, but according to tradition she descended from the sky in 880.

LINE 6: Llobregat: major Catalan river flowing southward from the Pyrenees, emptying into the Mediterranean just south of Barcelona. Monistrol: town below Montserrat mountain.

LINE 20: Crimson roses: see note to *Dos màrtirs de ma pàtria*, line 252.

LINE 30: Llobregat: see note to line 6.

LINE 39: Manresa: city near Montserrat.

LINE 40: Horeb: Mount Sinai (cf. Psalm 106:19).

LINE 41: Gothmar: first bishop of Vic (886–901) after the Saracen invasion of 718. M. Boix (1997, 121) notes he may have taken refuge in Manresa.

LINE 85: Aurora: the first of several epithets for the Virgin Mary (cf. Daystar, line 108; Rose of Heaven, line 116).

LINE 89: Pearl: Verdaguerian epithet for the Virgin Mary (cf. line 217; *Canigó* 4.40).

LINE 111: "Your sisters, after them your monks" alludes to Montserrat's legendary convent which preceded the Benedictine abbey.

LINE 155: Graceful Eagle: the Virgin Mary.

LINES 159–61: The transfiguration of Christ on Mount Tabor is described in Matthew 17:1–19, Mark 9:2–8, and Luke 9:28–30.

LINES 177–80: Morning Star (*Stella matutina*), Mystical Rose (*Rosa mistica*), Cause of our joy (*Causa nostræ lætitiæ*): invocations of the Virgin Mary from rosary litany.

LINE 182: House of Gold (*Domus aurea*): invocation from Marian litany.

LINE 199: Boix (1997, 70–71, 127) notes that St. Aciscolo (Cat. Sant Aciscle, dim. Sant Iscle) and his sister Victoria were fourth-century martyrs from Córdoba. St. Aciscolo's, one of five early medieval chapels on Montserrat, is located in the present-day gardens of the abbey.

LINE 204: Montserrat, located in the northeast of the Iberian Peninsula, is Spain's "Eastern Star" (cf. lines 217–18; "Virelay," line 14; *Canigó* 4.40).

LINES 217–18: Pearl . . . on eastern shores: see notes to lines 89 and 204.

A Choirboy Died

The poem appeared in *Caritat* (Charity, 1885) and, with some slight changes, in *Montserrat* (1899). For the musical version, more significant changes were made by Verdaguer together with composer Nicolau: (1) lines 19–22 were omitted, (2) lines 29–32 were thematically modified to invoke the Virgin, and (3) an additional line was added at the end: "I dins lo Cel entrà" (And he entered into Heaven). The freely translated musical version by Deems Taylor and Kurt Schindler that appeared in English under the title *Spanish Choral Ballads: Sacred and Secular Catalonian Folk Music; In the Monastery of Montserrat*, edited by Kurt Schindler (Boston: Oliver Ditson, 1918), seems to be based on the Catalan musical version. It reads: "In Montserrat is mourning; / Great sadness reigneth there, / Where lies within his coffin / A wondrous lad so fair. / Here in Thy haven, O Virgin, / Thine own appointed place, / Lies he who sang Thy glory, / Illumined by Thine own grace. // Around his snow-white coffin / The brothers come to mourn. / He seems a broken lily / That from its stem is torn. / Still within his fingers / The violin he holds. / Its strings his left hand touches, / His right the bow enfolds. // Behold his young companions / That bear him to the tomb. / Now there rises a chanting; / Clear voices pierce the gloom. / Now the first chant is surging / Like angel voices sweet / From heaven's gate descending, / Their brother's soul to greet. // The second verse is chanted, / And all are weeping sore: / "O Virgin, fount of goodness, / Thy mercy we implore! / Thou holy Virgin blessed, / Oh, take him to Thy breast, / Take him who always praised Thee, / And give him rest!" // Now grief has hush'd their chanting: / A voice resounds on high, / Amid the choirs of angels / That seem to fill the sky. / A bird unfolds its pinions; / Its flight to heav'n it wings . . . // What music sounds from yonder / that floats from mystic strings? // Requiescat in pace."

DEDICATION: Boix and Pinyol (2004, 112n10) note that Brother Ramir Rodamilans (Ramon Rodamilans i Sanllehí, 1848–99) was the monk who told Verdaguer about the recent death of a choirboy on one of his visits to the abbey during the millenary celebrations.

LINE 5: School of Song: The Escolania, Montserrat's school of music and boys' choir founded in the sixteenth century.

LINE 6: Virgin: the Virgin of Montserrat.

LINE 38: Montserrat mountain has drawn hermits and ascetics since medieval times.

Virelay

LINE 1: Rose of April: the Virgin of Montserrat, whose feast day is 27 April. She is also referred to as Morena, "dark-colored one" (dim. Moreneta).

LINES 5–6: The highest of Montserrat's jagged peaks rise some 4,000 feet.

LINE 7: The legendary descent of the Holy Image is described in "Discovery of the Virgin."

LINE 10: City of God that David dreamed: J. Vilamala (1999, 224n) points out that "the temple in Jerusalem, dwelling place of the God of Israel, was built by Solomon, but projected by David, his father. Mary, who bore in her womb the Son of God, Jesus Christ, is invoked as the city where God dwells."

LINE 13: The Virgin of Montserrat is Patroness of Catalonia.

LINE 14: Eastern Star: see note to "Discovery of the Virgin," line 204.

LINES 29–30: Sion: Jerusalem. Parallel figures of the palm and cedar of Lebanon in the invocations appear in Psalm 92:12: "The righteous flourish like the palm tree, and grow like a cedar in Lebanon" (cf. also Song of Solomon 5:15; 7:7–8; Isaiah 2:13).

Charity

LINES 1–5: Isaiah 2:12–13 reads: "For the Lord of hosts has a day against all that is proud and lofty, against all that is lifted up and high; against all the cedars of Lebanon, lofty and lifted up." The potential character conflict—haughtiness versus humility—is resolved in stanzas 2 and 3, where humility prevails with the cedar symbolizing charity, the "highest virtue."

LINE 21: It: charity.

A Nightingale's Death

LINE 28: Your concerts echoing Paradise: allusion to Milton's "wakeful nightingale" in *Paradise Lost* (4.602–3); cf. "While, echo of heaven, the nightingale trills / Angelic passages once learned in Paradise" (*Canigó* 1.90).

LINE 29: As troubadour, the nightingale symbolizes the poet.

LINE 31: Heaven's harp: the songs of the nightingale—and the poet—express the glory of the Creator/Creation.

A Mother's Love

Antoinette Ogden's 1897 translation (see headnote to this section) reduces Verdaguer's six quatrains to five. It reads: "A wicked son unto his wicked love / Said once at dawn of day: / 'Of my heaven the brightest star art thou, / Thee will I obey. // 'Shall I bring thee from my father's stores / A world of art? / E'en would I steal for thee my mother's jewels.' / 'Bring me her heart!' // The wicked son finds her sleeping, / Her countenance so mild, / A mirror sweet of thoughts, reflecting / Dreams of her child. // He tears her breast, and with a knife cuts out, / Alive and warm, / Her trusting heart. Poor heart, so weak in love, so strong / To shield from harm! . . . // He hastens, runs unto his paradise / With steps alert, / But at the portal falls; in anxious fear the heart cries out: / 'Son! Art thou hurt?' "

EPIGRAPH: Verdaguer modified the popular adage "Amor de pare, lo demés és ayre" (A father's love, the rest is air) to suit his topic; it was omitted from *Caritat*.

To Barcelona

Begun in 1873–74 in Barcelona prior to Verdaguer's first transatlantic voyage, this ode in its earliest version was twenty stanzas long. The poet revised and expanded it to thirty stanzas in 1882–83, entering it in, and winning, a competition held by the

Revista Literaria for the "best ode to Barcelona." The success of the event, and the poem's topic, drew keen interest from Francesc Rius i Taulet, mayor of Barcelona, who agreed to publish 100,000 copies of the poem. The prospect of such a wide readership (with the city's population at 350,000, distribution amounted to about one copy per family) impelled Verdaguer to further revision and expansion, so when published by city hall in June 1883 the poem was forty-six stanzas long. Concurrently, this longer version won Barcelona's Jocs Florals. Ramon Pinyol reflects on the poem's immense success: "The poem is a song to the city's vitality and is prophetic in vision . . . so it is no wonder it sparked the enthusiasm of the generation of bourgeoisie that was erecting the new Barcelona (rising from the ruins of the old city walls, the Ciutadella [fortress] and numerous medieval buildings), of which Mayor Rius i Taulet . . . was genuinely representative. . . . [Nor] is it any wonder Barcelona's city hall appropriated [the poem] right away since it reflected the city's dynamic present and the conservative, moderately pro-Catalan ideals of its political leadership" (2002, 93).

In a note to the poem, Verdaguer acknowledges his debt not only to the Jocs Florals and Mayor Rius i Taulet but also to "the Catalans of the Philippines," who printed Francesc de Mas i Otzet's Spanish translation of the ode and presented Verdaguer with a silver laurel wreath he offered to the Virgin of Montserrat; "Als catalans de Filipines" (To the Catalans of the Philippines), not included in this selection, was written as a gesture of gratitude. "To Barcelona" features quatrains of alternating feminine-masculine alexandrines, feminine at the caesura (seventh syllable unstressed), particularly suited to conveying the poem's gravity and eloquent flow.

EPIGRAPH: From *Don Quixote de la Mancha* (2:72).

LINE 1: Montjuïc: mountain (567 ft.) at the southern end of Barcelona.

LINE 2: Verdaguer refers here to the myth he revived in *L'Atlàntida* whereby Alcides (Hercules) founded the city of Barcelona, keeping the promise he made to Jupiter at Montjuïc prior to his encounter with Geryon (*L'Atlàntida* 1.269–76; 10.211–14).

LINE 4: Montjuïc is personified as Alcides, the "giant that watches over her always" (ibid., 10.213).

LINE 5: The quarries of Montjuïc provided stones for Barcelona's construction.

LINE 10: Cap del Riu: headland at the mouth of the Llobregat River below Montjuïc, where in 1848 an old watchtower was made into a lighthouse to warn ships away from sandbars.

LINE 14: Catalan maritime law, the Consolat de Mar, was established in 1258.

LINE 15: According to Pinyol (2002, 96), the phrase "fa lloc a ta muralla" refers to the enlargement of the harbor begun in 1870.

LINE 16: Marquets and Llanzas (forming the plural -*as* in English): influential families in maritime affairs during the thirteenth and fourteenth centuries.

LINES 17–20: Daughter of Alcides, Barcelona is personified as an Amazon or powerful woman, enclosed first by Roman walls, which, along with the later medieval and eighteenth-century walls, became obsolete with successive periods of growth.

LINES 21–23: Controversial development of the Eixample District by urban engineer Ildefons Cerdà (1815–76) called for the tearing down of remaining sections of wall. As Vilamala notes, "Verdaguer identified clearly with expansionist politics in Barcelona, so it comes as no surprise that his poem was well received by the town hall" (1999, 152n).

LINES 24–36: Verdaguer enumerates and situates the mountains and peaks encircling the city. Sant Pere Màrtir: modern form of Sant Pere Martri (after St. Peter).

LINES 39–40: See notes to lines 15 and 21–23.

LINES 45–48: The Sant Gervasi and Horta districts developed on the city's hills.

LINES 54–56: "Sands of gold" and "New Nile": the Llobregat delta and river; "your tents" completes the biblical imagery.

LINES 58–59: Verdaguer enumerates surrounding wooded areas.

LINE 64: Verdaguer alludes here to the popular notion that young eagles fly on their mothers' wings (cf. Exodus 19:4; Deuteronomy 32:11). In *Folklore* (posthumous, 1907) he writes: "She carries her young on her shoulders. If unsure whether they're hers . . . she makes them look toward the sun; if they blink it's a sign they aren't, but if they gaze steadily without shame, they're hers."

LINE 66: Murtra: monastery of Sant Jeroni de la Murtra. Harbor Virgin: chapel of La Mare de Déu del Port. Bonanova: church of La Mare de Déu de la Bonanova.

LINE 67: The Agudells: peaks above the district of Sant Genís dels Agudells.

LINE 70: The Besòs and Llobregat: rivers at the northern and southern ends of the city.

LINE 72: Montseny: massif north of Barcelona rising 5,600 feet whose headwaters feed the Besòs. To the west, Montserrat (4,000 ft.) drains into the Llobregat.

LINES 77–89: As noted by Francesc Codina (2003, 107–8) the fatherland's speech (expanded from two to three stanzas for the edition published by city hall) dispels any notion of Barcelona's being a mere imitation of Paris (see line 76); Catalonia's "daughter," she was "born, like Venus, of waves that kissed [his] shore . . . ruled Athens and Provence . . . [and] shone on Spanish lands as eastern star," that is, as Iberia's gateway to progress (echoing Catalan conservative discourse even today); Barcelona's origins and trajectory are original, not modeled on those of Paris.

LINES 79–80: Catalan political and commercial expansion throughout the Mediterranean reached its height in the thirteenth and fourteenth centuries.

LINE 81: The duchy of Athens came under Catalan rule briefly in the fourteenth century, as did Provence from the early twelfth to mid-thirteenth centuries.

LINE 82: Allegedly, the Catalan flag served to inspire the Spanish flag.

LINES 83–84: Verdaguer cites thirteenth-century chronicler Bernat Desclot, who attributes the phrase to Roger de Llúria, admiral who defeated French naval forces off the coast of L'Empordà in 1284.

LINE 85: Barcelona is Spain's "eastern star" because it lies to the east.

LINES 86–88: Light of Gutenberg: books were printed in Barcelona as early as 1475. The iron horse: Spain's first railroad (Barcelona-Mataró) began operating in 1848. Lightning's lance for messenger: Francesc Salvà i Campillo (1751–1828) invented an electric telegraph in 1790.

LINE 93: St. Eulària (or Eulàlia) is Barcelona's patron saint. Her pennon (featuring the St. Andrew's cross on which she was martyred in 304) presided the fall of Barcelona during the Bourbonic siege of 1714.

LINE 94: St. George (Sant Jordi) is Catalonia's patron saint.

LINE 96: Star of Cervelló: Maria de Cervelló (1230–90), or Maria dels Socors, inspired by the Brotherhood of Our Lady of Ransom (Mercedarians) and their pleading on behalf of Christians held captive by the Turks, founded and headed the first feminine order of Mercedarians.

LINES 98–100: Under Ataülf (?–415), Alaric's successor, Barcelona was briefly the seat of the Visigoth kingdom. Verdaguer evokes renowned ninth- through twelfth-century Barcelona counts. The laws (Usatges de Barcelona): basis of Catalan civil law established under Ramon Berenger IV (r. 1131–62). The Fivellers: Ramon and Joan, whose clash with Ferdinand I of Catalonia-Aragon (r. 1412–16) earned them repute as champions of independent municipal government.

LINE 101: Theologian Jaume Balmes (1810–48), born in Vic. Ter: river near Vic.

LINE 103: Damià Campeny (1771–1855), renowned neoclassic sculptor.

LINE 104: Marià Fortuny (1838–74), regarded as the outstanding painter of the Renaixença.

LINE 105: Roger de Llúria (1250?–1305): the most famous of medieval Catalan admirals (see note to lines 83–84).

LINES 109–10: Don John of Austria defeated the Turkish fleet off Lepanto, Greece, in 1571.

LINES 111–12: Columbus is said to have brought news of the New World to Ferdinand and Isabella in Barcelona's Tinell Hall (see note to line 144).

LINES 113–14: Bellesguard: medieval royal residence in today's Sant Gervasi district and site of the wedding celebration of Martin I of Catalonia-Aragon (r. 1396–1410) and Margarida de Prades. Valldonzella: medieval Cistercian convent destroyed during the secessionist uprising (the Reapers' War) of 1640–52.

LINES 115–16: Codina (2003, 109) notes that the industrial progress evoked here, despite its drawbacks, is seen as compatible with Catholic tradition, whose "spires and belfries" rise "pointing through the smoke to heaven."

LINE 117: Two towers: the Episcopal Palace and Casa de l'Ardiaca erected on the Plaça Nova.

LINES 119–20: Pinyol notes that according to A. Esclasans "in Verdaguer's time there were still cannons at the dockyard that, formerly in times of war, would respond to Montjuïc's. [The lines] may also mean there was an echo" (2002, 104).

LINES 121–22: The monastery of Pedralbes has been home to the Franciscan order of nuns since the early fourteenth century.

LINES 123–24: Ciutadella (now spelled with two *l*s): citadel built by absolutist Philip V of Spain (r. 1700–46), who precipitated the War of the Spanish Succession (1701–14); symbol of repression, the citadel was torn down in the 1870s and converted into a park (cf. Isaiah 2:4). Marvella (from *mar bella*, "beautiful sea"): beach area in the Poblenou district.

LINES 125–26: Saint Paul: monastery of Sant Pau del Camp in the Poble Sec District. Saint Peter: monastery of Sant Pere de les Puelles in the Old Quarter near Ciutadella Park. Saint Mary of the Pine and Saint Mary of the Sea: basilicas of Santa Maria del Pi and Santa Maria del Mar in the Old Quarter.

LINES 129–32: The personification of monuments and shrines expresses the sense of vital attachment to the city's historical, religious, and cultural heritage (see headnote to this section).

LINES 133–36: Saint Michael's: erected, according to tradition, by angels, the church of Saint Michael (Sant Miquel) was torn down early in the nineteenth century to expand city hall. The Hall (Casa la Ciutat): city hall.

LINES 137–40: Saints Justus and Pastor: basilica of Sants Just i Pastor behind city hall; Justus and Pastor were brothers martyred near Madrid in 304 at ages thirteen and nine. Their dear companion: Saint Michael's. Saint Agatha: the majestic royal chapel of Santa Àgata dedicated to this third-century martyr on Plaça del Rei, not far from the cathedral.

LINES 141–44: Saint George of the Courthouse: chapel of the Palace of the Generalitat (seat of Catalonia's government), converted into a courthouse by Philip V (see note to lines 123–24). Saint Clare: convent of Santa Clara, formerly located in the Royal Palace on Plaça del Rei. Counts' palace: the Royal Palace. Council hall: city hall. Don Jaume's statue: statue of James I of Catalonia-Aragon (1208–76) on the facade of city hall. Tinell: Tinell Hall (Saló del Tinell), reception room of the Royal Palace.

LINES 145–48: Hercules' three columns: columns of the former Roman temple to Augustus (not Hercules, as thought in the nineteenth century) standing in the courtyard of Number 10 Carrer del Paradís, at the summit of Tabor Hill behind the present-day cathedral, the highest point in the old Roman city. (A fourth column, added later, was constructed from the remains of ruined columns recovered from neighboring buildings.) Graces: daughters of Zeus and Eurynome, goddesses of beauty.

LINES 149–51: Codina (2003, 110–11) notes how Verdaguer reconciles the quadrangular rationality of Barcelona's expansion in the Eixample District (see note to lines 21–23) with its remote past as the columns form a "huge angle iron . . . where light and air come streaming through."

LINE 152: Pagan trines: here, the three columns of Hercules (see note to lines 145–48).

LINES 153–58: Codina (2003, 111) says that according to tradition, when the apostle James brought Christianity to Barcelona he planted a cross next to the pagan temple on Tabor Hill (see note to lines 145–48), and around the cross, "shelter[ing] it" with "her stone cloak," was built the cathedral. According to Vilamala (1999, 158n), it is said that in Roman days Tabor Hill was the site of a beautiful garden, perhaps giving rise to the name Carrer del Paradís (Paradise Street); alternatively, the name may derive from the fact that there was once a cemetery behind the cathedral.

LINE 159: Don Jaume: James I (see note to line 144), evoked here because of his decisive role not only in the Christian conquest of Catalan-speaking territories but in fostering cultural achievement as well.

LINES 161–84: The cathedral's speech was expanded from one to six stanzas for the edition published by city hall.

LINE 161: Barcelona is referred to as the Ciutat dels Comtes (City of the Counts).

LINE 166: The Suez Canal had been completed in 1869; the first attempt to build the Panama Canal began in 1881, preceding the poem by only two years.

LINES 171–72: The cathedral, speaking here, embodies the expansion of Christendom.

LINES 179–80: Clemència Isaura: muse and protectress of Barcelona's Jocs Florals, medieval literary competitions restored in 1859 that came to symbolize the recovery of the Catalan language, and ultimately, Catalan political institutions.

The Two Bell Towers

The earliest version of the poem, begun in 1879–80 (see Torrents 1995b, 219), was thirteen stanzas long, already featuring the full eleven-stanza-long dialogue between the bell towers of the (then) crumbling monasteries of Sant Martí del Canigó and Sant Miquel de Cuixà below Mount Canigó (Fr. Canigou) in the French-Catalan Pyrenees. Torrents explains that Verdaguer first construed the poem, in all likelihood, as a separate elegy, then expanded it (adding in particular the final three stanzas) to serve as epilogue to his yet-to-be-written second major epic, *Canigó*. It was, as Verdaguer explains in a note to the poem in *Pàtria*, "the first part [of *Canigó*] I wrote, [but] afterwards, when the entire poem was completed, [it] had no place in the work." Not that the restoration of the two monasteries was no longer an issue, but their relevance in *Canigó* had been displaced, Torrents argues, by the prominence in the poem of the Santa Maria de Ripoll monastery, whose restoration had recently been undertaken by Bishop Morgades of Vic, to whom Verdaguer dedicated canto 11 of *Canigó*, describing the medieval refounding of Santa Maria de Ripoll by Bishop Oliba (founder of Montserrat) in the early eleventh century. Nevertheless, for the French translation of *Canigó* published in 1889, translator Josep Tolrà de Bordas obtained Verdaguer's permission to include "The Two Bell Towers" as the epilogue, carrying out in the French version Verdaguer's original design (although the Count of Cedillo's 1898 translation of *Canigó* into Spanish did not include it). As it happened, "The Two Bell Towers" had drawn attention in Perpignan when, in 1886, it was awarded an outstanding prize in a competition sponsored by the Société Agricole, Scientifique et Littéraire des Pyrénées-Orientales; Verdaguer's "La corona" (The Wreath, not included in this selection), dedicated to the Société, was also included as an annex to the French translation (it describes the elaborate gold wreath Verdaguer received, which he later offered to the Virgin of Montserrat). Finally, in the second Catalan edition of *Canigó* (1901), "The Two Bell Towers" was reinstated as the epilogue. Now, however, in the wake of Verdaguer's confrontation with Bishop Morgades, the dedication to him was omitted. Moreover, as Pinyol notes: "Verdaguer dedicated ['The Two Bell Towers'] to Bishop Carselade of Perpignan, precisely in recognition of his leading role in the reconstruction of Canigó's two monasteries, and in the context of this undertaking, the elegy to Sant Martí [del Canigó] and [Sant Miquel de] Cuixà takes on an added emblematic value" (2002, 178).

As in "To Barcelona," the symbolic significance in connection with Christian, moderately pro-Catalan, traditional ideals is twofold, poeticizing first the recovery of the monasteries (where spiritual communities will thrive once again) and, second, the foundational history of Catalonia. Regarded as one of Verdaguer's finest poems, the Catalan "Two Bell Towers" is composed in five-line stanzas of decasyllables rhyming *abaab* (*a* lines are feminine, *b* are masculine).

TITLE: See introductory note above.

LINES 2–3: Marcèvol: twelfth-century priory of Santa Maria de Marcèvol near Arboçols (Fr. Arboussols). Serrabona: eleventh-century priory near Bula d'Amunt (Fr. Boule-d'Amont). Sant Miquel: Benedictine monastery of Sant Miquel de Cuixà (Fr. St. Michel de Cuxa) near Codalet, founded in 879, administered today by Montserrat. Sant Martí: monastery of Sant Martí del Canigó (Fr. St. Martin du Canigou) perched on a ridge at 3,460 feet, founded ca. 1000; formerly Benedictine, it is today the home of the Community of the Beatitudes, who manage the abbey with its more than 60,000 visitors each year.

LINES 11–13: Orseolo: St. Peter Orseolo, doge of Venice (976–78); after numerous initiatives in Venice (e.g., beginning the construction of St. Mark's Cathedral), fearing for his safety, he secretly took refuge at Cuixà, where he died in 988. Garí (or Garin): renowned tenth-century abbot of Cuixà who brought Orseolo to the abbey. Romualdo: St. Romualdo (or Romuald), who accompanied Orseolo to Cuixà, returning later to Italy to found the Camaldolese Benedictine monastery (1012) near Arezzo.

LINE 17: Rose: rose window.

LINE 22: Much of the "Byzantine" (i.e., Romanesque) cloister of Cuixà is now at The Cloisters, Metropolitan Museum of Art, New York.

LINE 25: Mount Canigó: massif rising 9134 feet in the French-Catalan Pyrenees.

LINE 32: Conflent: historic county in the Têt river valley north of Mount Canigó in North (or French) Catalonia.

LINE 52: Codalet and Prada: towns north of Cuixà.

LINE 63: Count of Rià: Guifre II of Cerdanya, whose castle was in nearby Rià, founder of Sant Martí del Canigó; alternatively, Sunifred II of Cerdanya, founder of Sant Miquel de Cuixà, in which case the tower of Sant Martí speaks erroneously (on this question see Pinyol 2002, 183, and Torrents 1995b, 220).

LINE 72: One of Cuixà's original two bell towers fell as a result of severe lightning storms in the 1830s.

LINE 77: Methuselah: cf. Genesis 5:27.

LINES 78–80: Goliath: cf. 1 Samuel 17:46–49.

LINE 105: In the epilogue to *Canigó* (second edition, 1901 [see introductory note above]) this line reads: "No esbrancaran l'altívol Pirineu" (The soaring Pyrenees will not be bent).

The Harp

Probably composed in the mid-1880s, "The Harp," as critic Manuel de Montoliu (1877–1961) points out, links the ancient symbol of poetry—the harp—with the poet's own life experience, resulting in a brilliant touch of originality (see Pinyol 2002, 227). Pinyol notes further that "the symbol of the harp [is] what provides the link between the earthly and celestial worlds," as it did in "The Sacred Harp" (from *Idil·lis i cants místics*) as well as in a subsequent poem from *Flors del Calvari* also titled "The Harp" (not included in this selection). In other words, following Jorba, the poet "synthesizes . . . the symbolic relationship among his nearest surrounding landscape, the religion learned in the intimacy of his family environment, and poetry" (Jorba 1995, 6). It is written in *romanç heroic* meter, that is, unstanzaic feminine decasyllables with assonant *a*-sounding rhyme at even-numbered lines.

LINES 1–2: The chapel, Pinyol (2002, 228) notes, is the Capella de la Damunt, near Verdaguer's native Folgueroles, commanding a view of the village, the plain of Vic, the Pyrenees, and Montseny (see note to line 51); the oaks are gone today.

LINE 6: Verdaguer's mother died on 17 January 1871.

LINE 18: Codina (2003, 85) underscores the minstrel's "exotic" origins in the subsequent powerful unveiling of poetry.

LINES 51–52: Montseny: massif north of Barcelona rising 5,600 feet. Puigmal: second-highest peak (after Carlit, in France) rising 9,557 feet in the eastern Pyrenees overlooking the plain of Vic.

LINES 55–56: Ausona: modern county of Osona, of which Vic is the capital. Gurri: river flowing northward from Montseny (see above) and passing near Vic.

LINE 73: *Barretina*: traditional Catalan hat, seen today at folk events and worn frequently in Verdaguer's day, especially in the countryside; popularized more recently by Catalan painter Salvador Dalí (1904–89).

LINES 87–88: Pedraforca: mountain branching from the pre-Pyrenean Cadí range; named "forked rock" after its jutting peaks (8,192 and 7,874 feet) separated by erosion; in the poem the sun sets just between the peaks, suggesting the eruption of Vesuvius and evoking for the second time "exotic" Naples (see note to line 18).

LINE 92: Catalan Muse: Pinyol notes this "allusion to Catalan poetry and conclusion to the various sources and early poetic inspirations to which Verdaguer has made reference throughout the poem" (2002, 231).

The Emigrant

Pinyol (2002, 232) notes the suggestion of Verdaguer biographer Joan Torrent i Fàbregas that underlying "The Emigrant" was a fear that the poet—embarking on his transatlantic voyages (1874–76)—might never again see his native land or family and that, unable to say good-bye in person, he wrote it as a farewell gesture. In any event, with the poem's immense success following the 1890 musical version by composer Amadeu Vives (1871–1932), and as one of Catalonia's most popular and heartfelt songs, it has come to encapsulate the sentiment of *enyorança*, or longing for home, marked even more poignantly by the masses of exiles resulting from twentieth-century dictatorial rule. The poem has three eight-line stanzas (*ababcdcd*)—*a* and *c* are feminine-rhyming decasyllables, *b* and *d* masculine-rhyming tetrasyllables—and a refrain (*abab* quatrain) with alternating feminine-masculine rhyming pentasyllables.

LINE 7: Grotto in the sky: mountain caves inhabited by ascetics (cf. note to line 38 in "A Choirboy Died").

LINES 15–16: Sculpted summits . . . Montserrat: the jagged peaks of Montserrat mountain, home of the Montserrat monastery north of Barcelona (see Montserrat poems in this selection).

LINE 19: Your mountains: Barcelona's surrounding mountains (cf. lines 24–36 in "To Barcelona").

LINES 25–28: Pinyol (2002, 235) notes the parallel with the closing lines of "Lluny de ma terra" (Far from My Land, not included in this selection): "If only to undo those steps / And reach, homeland, your harbor! / If only to sleep in your arms, / Even the sleep of death!" According to Pinyol, Verdaguer may have been influenced by Magí Pers i Ramona (1803–88), whose poem "A Espanya" ends: "My only wish, only desire, / Is to leave the wavy sea: / Return to Spain, see her sky, / Breathe her fine air, and die there."

The Rose of Jericho

The rose of Jericho (*Anastatica hierochuntica*), or resurrection plant, produces small white blooms and is also known in Catalan as *rosa de Nostra Senyora* (rose of Our Lady), as reflected here in Verdaguer's epithet for the Virgin Mary. According to folklore scholar J. Amades, this is the tradition: "When Jesus was born all the

roses of Jericho opened their bright flowers to show that the delivery of the Mother
of God had gone well, and ever since, at the stroke of midnight on Christmas,
each one of them opens its bloom all over the world" (1982–83, 1:103). Separately,
Verdaguer makes reference to the rose of Jericho in *Dietari d'un pelegrí a Terra
Santa* ("Anada al Jordà," 1888), in *Flors de Maria* (Flowers of Mary, 1902), and in
the posthumous *Brins d'Espígol* (Sprigs of Lavender, 1981).

EPIGRAPH: From John 1:14.

LINE 20: *Ave Maria*: Hail, Mary.

LINE 27: Dove: the Holy Spirit.

LINE 30: The Word: Christian revelation; figuratively, Christ.

LINE 36: The Stable: Christ's birthplace in Bethlehem.

Thorns

Vilamala (1999, 205n) cites writer and poet Maurici Serrahima i Bofill (1902–79)
in connection with this poem: "When he spoke of the fatherland, Verdaguer's
inclination was to climb high into the branches of rhetoric. In contrast, when he
spoke of faith, Christ, or the Mother of God, he tended [naturally] toward tender
familiarity."

LINES 21–23: Christ was given a sponge soaked in vinegar to drink on the cross (cf.
Matthew 27:48; Mark 15:36; Luke 23:36; John 19:29).

Begging

Verdaguer's unusual use of irregular stanzas of alternating masculine/feminine octo-
syllabic couplets (*aabbccdd...*) and a refrain (for the chorus of angels) gives this
poem and its "tender familiarity" (see note to "Thorns") a disarmingly humor-
ous touch, throwing into relief the charitable act at the poem's close. It is set in
Egypt during the Holy Family's exile but, as Torrents (2002b) has argued, gives
expression to Verdaguer's personal crisis of the early 1890s (see headnote to this
section).

LINES 23–28: The lines reiterate the lesson of faith in the gospel (Matthew 6:26).

LINE 46: See above note.

LINE 67: City of the Sun: ancient Heliopolis, today Matariya (near Cairo), site of the
Tree of the Holy Virgin, where, according to extracanonical legend, the Holy
Family found shade and the Child Jesus created a well; in his *Dietari* Verdaguer
wrote of his visit there.

"I found within this Heart . . ."

EPIGRAPH: From "Noche oscura del alma" (Dark Night of the Soul).

LINE 6: The Angel: the Fallen Angel.

Reception of the Stigmata by Saint Francis

Mercè Anzizu Vila Girona i Bacigalupi (1868–1916) entered the Franciscan convent of
Pedralbes at age twenty-one. Raised by her maternal grandparents after the death
of her parents (Ignasi Anzizu i Girona and Josefa Vila i Bacigalupi, Eusebi Güell's
cousin), she had been thirteen when she first wrote to Verdaguer, whose poetry

she admired, and later came into further contact with him as a member of the wealthy López-Güell clan. M. Carme Bernal (2003) has examined her relationship with Verdaguer, underscoring her own legacy as a mystic poet, her fervent religious vocation, and her crucial role in restoring the Pedralbes monastery with her personal fortune. Following the breaking off of relations between her spiritual adviser Jaume Collell and Verdaguer in 1895, there is no further evidence of contact between Sister Eulària Anzizu and Verdaguer.

LINE 12: The wounds impressed on Saint Francis: the stigmata, or marks, resembling the wounds inflicted in the hands, feet and side of Christ at the crucifixion.

The Turtledoves

Cònsul (2001, 172) notes the poem is based on an account in *I fioretti di San Francesco*, embellished by seventeenth-century St. Francis biographer Damián Cornejo.

LINE 1: Patriarch: title given St. Francis of Assisi for founding the order of Friars Minor (Franciscans).

LINE 13: See note to line 7 in "Rosalia" on the rhetorical figure of epanadiplosis.

LINE 21: See note to line 13 above.

LINE 35: My convent: according to Cornejo, the convent of Rabachino outside Siena (see introductory note above).

Preaching to Birds

In a letter dated 10 October 1995, novelist Narcís Oller (1846–1930) told Verdaguer that "Preaching to Birds" was one of his favorite poems.

LINES 7–8: Cònsul (2001, 200) reminds us that banishment from the celestial homeland and longing (*enyorança*) to return is a recurring theme in mystic poetry.

LINES 25–27: Cf. Matthew 6:26–32.

LINES 31–34: Cf. ibid.

LINES 51–58: This well-known Verdaguerian caricature of birds has been much popularized.

LINE 61: On the significance Verdaguer attaches to the nightingale, see "A Nightingale's Death" (from *Caritat*) and related notes.

LINE 64: The holy sign he makes: the sign of the cross when blessing them.

LINE 72: Seraphic Order: the Friars Minor (Franciscans).

The Pilgrim

Cònsul (2001, 214) notes that in St. Francis's earlier biographers Tomasso da Celano and St. Bonaventure, the anecdote described in this poem is unconnected with Christmas 1223; Verdaguer's association is based on his reading of Damián Cornejo, Pio da Bologna, and Candide Chalippe.

LINES 1–2: Anadiplosis renders the verse popular in tone (cf. note to line 25 below, "Rosalia," and "The Turtledoves," where Verdaguer uses epanadiplosis).

LINE 25: On Verdaguer's use of epanadiplosis, see note to line 7 in "Rosalia."

LINE 54: The fatherland: heaven (cf. note to lines 7–8 in "Preaching to Birds").

LINE 56: Afield: according to Cònsul (2001, 218), reference to the crèche at Greccio.

Saint Teresa

The alternating feminine-masculine heptasyllables feature assonant *o*-sounding
rhyme at masculine lines.

TITLE: Santa Teresa de Jesús, or St. Teresa of Ávila (1515–82), influential Spanish
mystic and Catholic reformer, honored since 1970 as Doctor of the Church.

Poverty

The three quatrains feature alternating feminine-masculine decasyllables rhyming
abab.

TITLE: Cf. "The Pilgrim" (from *Sant Francesc*) on poverty.

Simile

The two quatrains feature alternating feminine-masculine heptasyllables rhyming
abab.

Soon

The three quatrains feature alternating masculine-feminine heptasyllables with as-
sonant *e*-sounding rhyme at feminine lines.

To a Detractor

The alternating masculine-feminine heptasyllables feature assonant *o*-sounding
rhyme at feminine lines.

Shaped like a Cross

The hexasyllables are predominantly feminine, with assonant *o*-sounding rhyme at
even-numbered lines; only the first and penultimate are masculine, spotlighting
creu and *cel* ("cross" and "sky/heaven") as the means and desired end—the cross
(suffering) is the way to heaven (salvation).

Sum vermis

One of Verdaguer's few poems in blank verse, all decasyllables are feminine with a
predominant caesura after the sixth syllable (6 + 4).

TITLE: From Psalm 22:6–7: "But I am a worm, and not human; scorned by others,
and despised by the people." Verdaguer's allusion to this psalm, a messianic
prophecy of Christ's death (customarily read during the Good Friday service),
suggests the dignity he found in his suffering by seeing it in the light of Christ's.

By the Sea

Torrents has argued that in this poem, more than any other, Verdaguer's "conception
of poetic creation" can be glimpsed. Written in Caldetes (or Caldes d'Estrac, a
late-nineteenth-century upscale seaside resort town north of Barcelona) in 1883,
"nel mezzo del camin" of his literary career, the poem reveals "an accumulation
of all the conflictive forces" the poet harbors within as he "turns against poetry,
accusing it of having deceived him," prefiguring the personal crisis and conflict to

come (1995b, 143–62). Torrents also examines Verdaguer's innovative use of metrics, alternating feminine decasyllables in the Italian style (6 + 4) with masculine hexasyllables in quatrains rhyming *abab*.

LINES 5–12: As Torrents points out, the outer landscape of the initial block of three stanzas reflects the interiorization, or inner landscape, of the poet.

LINES 6–8: The sea and the sky: cf. lines 38–40, where the sky/heaven is a sea with stars on its shore; their immensity contrasts with the poet's smallness yet motivate his reflection.

LINES 13–28: Torrents notes how this four-stanza-long single sentence, the poem's middle block, formulates the poet's reflection on his past.

LINE 22: One morning in May: cf. "What Is Poetry?" (from *Aires del Montseny*), line 33.

LINES 29–40: According to Torrents, the poem's final block of three stanzas reveals the poet's sense of dissatisfaction, culminating in the unanswerable question of existence and the final expression of *enyorança*, or yearning, for the celestial homeland.

LINE 36: Deceitful poetry: Torrents (1995b, 159) notes the sharp contrast here with Verdaguer's habitual notion of poetry.

LIV

Verdaguer used this short poem to preface a letter from La Gleva (25 September 1894) to his cousin Narcís Verdaguer i Callís, an attorney/politician who sided with Church authorities against him; cf. "To a Detractor." The poem's six heptasyllables are feminine at the first, second, fourth, and fifth lines, rhyming at the second and fifth and masculine (third and sixth) lines.

LXX

The alternating masculine-feminine heptasyllables feature assonant *o*-sounding rhyme at feminine lines.

XCVI

The alternating masculine-feminine heptasyllables feature assonant *e*-sounding rhyme at feminine lines.

EPIGRAPH: From Thomas à Kempis's *Imitation of Christ*.

Martyrdom

The alternating masculine-feminine heptasyllables of this romance feature assonant *a*-sounding rhyme at feminine lines in the first section, shifting to *o*-sounding in the second and *u*-sounding in the third; the final section reverses the pattern, alternating feminine-masculine heptsyllables now with *a*-sounding assonance occurring at masculine lines to produce more striking, conclusive couplets.

EPIGRAPH: In "La Perla" (not included in this selection) St. Eulària is depicted as a pearl carried by waves to Barcelona's shoreline. Eulària (or Eulàlia) is Barcelona's patron saint, martyred in the year 304 during the Diocletian persecutions.

LINE 12: Tabor: Tabor Hill, behind the present-day cathedral, highest point in the old Roman city.

LINE 14: Golgotha: Calvary.

LINES 19–20: On the summit of Tabor Hill was the forum surrounded by a colonnade.

LINE 25: Desert: According to Codina and Pinyol (1995, 103n4), the district of Sar-
rià was so named after the founding of its sixteenth-century Capuchin convent
("desert" or "wilderness" commonly referred to out-of-the-way religious centers);
St. Eulària was born in Sarrià.

LINE 30: Datian: legendary Roman governor.

LINE 35: Ungulae: instrument of torture consisting of iron hooks or talons.

LINE 66: The world's greatest gift: the love of God.

What Is Poetry?

This poem was first published in *L'Atlàntida* (15 May 1896), a literary magazine
founded by Verdaguer that same year. The quatrains alternate masculine-
feminine decasyllables featuring *e*-sounding assonant rhyme at feminine (second
and fourth) lines.

LINE 9: Nightingale: on the significance of the nightingale in Verdaguer, see notes to
lines 28, 29, and 31 in "A Nightingale's Death" (from *Caritat*); cf. also line 6 in
"Preaching to Birds" (from *Sant Francesc*) and "To a Nightingale from Vallvi-
drera" (from *Barcelonines*).

LINES 13–14: Verdaguer seems to allude here to his own spiritual transformation and
subsequent conflict as the Comillas' family chaplain and almoner; cf. also "To a
Nightingale from Vallvidrera" (from *Barcelonines*).

LINES 33–36: On "one morning in May" and the sentiment of *enyorança*, or longing,
see headnote to this section; cf. also headnote to *Pàtria* poems in this selection.

The Milky Way

Modern in form, this poem combines blank verse with occasional six-syllable lines,
all feminine, alternating in the final five-line stanza for a conclusive effect.

LINE 7: Phaëthon: son of Phoebe who, according to Ovid, unable to control his
father's chariot—the sun—was struck down by Jupiter when it veered too close to
the earth.

LINE 30: Núria: mountain valley (6,430 ft.) north of Ripoll and site of Catalonia's most
popular devotional shrine to the Blessed Mother after Montserrat; according to
tradition, a pilgrim from Dalmatia, Amadeus—who searched in vain for the image
of the Madonna left by St. Giles of Athens (who had formerly preached the gospel
to shepherds in the valley)—erected the chapel devoted to the Blessed Mother of
Núria, whose image was to be discovered shortly after Amadeus's departure.

The Moon

The five-line stanzas feature alternating feminine-masculine decasyllables with an
unrhymed hexasyllable at the fourth line (*abacb*).

LINE 23: Saturn's ninth moon, Phoebe, was discovered in 1898, after the poem was
written.

LINE 28: Ariadne's crown: crown of stars (Corona Borealis or Northern Crown)
promised to Ariadne by Dionysus, whom she married after being abandoned on
Naxos by Theseus.

To a Nightingale from Vallvidrera

The alternating masculine-feminine heptasyllables feature assonant *a*-sounding rhyme at feminine lines.

TITLE: Vallvidrera: small town and surrounding woodlands in the mountains rising behind Barcelona, today the site of the Verdaguer Museum at Vil·la Joana, the house where Verdaguer died.

DEDICATION: Antoni Rubió and Lluís Carles Viada: friends of Verdaguer who stood by him during his confrontation with Church authorities.

LINE 1: Nightingale, fine nightingale: the formulaic use of epanadiplosis renders the verse popular in tone (cf. line 7 in "Rosalia" and lines 13 and 21 in "The Turtle-doves").

LINE 4: Valldaura: in Verdaguer's day a wooded area below Vallvidrera, today part of Barcelona.

LINE 15: Month of May: most likely an allusion to Verdaguer's poetic calling, described in "The Harp" (cf. also "By the Sea").

LINE 19: The city-countryside contrast suggests the worldly-heavenly divide.

LINE 24: They only put in cages: allusion to Verdaguer's removal from Barcelona and confinement to La Gleva (near Vic) in 1893–94.

REFERENCES

Amades, Joan. 1982–83. *Costumari català*. Barcelona: Salvat Edicions 62.

Beltran, Abel. 1999. "La gènesi de Santa Eulària." *Anuari Verdaguer*, 1995–96, 277–88.

Bernal, M. Carme. 1999. "*Roser de tot l'any*, cruïlla en la producció poètica i periodística de Jacint Verdaguer i banc de proves d'un nou ideari." *Anuari Verdaguer*, 1995–96, 211–23.

———. 2003. "Eulària Anzizu (Mercè Anzizu i Vila): A propòsit de dos poemes de *Roser de tot l'any, dietari de pensaments religiosos*, de Jacint Verdaguer." *Anuari Verdaguer*, 2002, 239–57.

Boix, Maur M. 1997. "Estudi preliminar." In *Montserrat II: Llegenda de Montserrat*, by Jacint Verdaguer, edited by Maur M. Boix. Vic: Eumo Editorial/Societat Verdaguer.

Boix, Maur M., and Ramon Pinyol i Torrents. 2004. "Estudi preliminar." In *Montserrat I: Llegendari, cançons, odes*, by Jacint Verdaguer, edited by Maur M. Boix and Ramon Pinyol i Torrents. Vic: Eumo Editorial/Societat Verdaguer.

Codina i Valls, Francesc. 2003. "Verdaguer (1865–1883): De fadrí de muntanya a mitificador de Barcelona." *Anuari Verdaguer*, 2002, 83–114.

———, ed. 2006. *Barcelona: Textos per a un llibre*. Vic: Eumo Editorial/Societat Verdaguer.

Codina, Francesc, and Pinyol i Torren[t]s, Ramon. 1995. Notes in *Verdaguer i Barcelona*. Barcelona: Ajuntament de Barcelona.

Cònsul, Isidor. 2001. "Estudi preliminar" and headnotes. In *Sant Francesc*, by Jacint Verdaguer, edited by Isidor Cònsul. Vic: Eumo Editorial/Societat Verdaguer.

———. 2003. Introduction to *Sant Francesc*. In *Poemes llargs/Teatre*, vol. 2 of *Totes les obres de Jacint Verdaguer*, edited by Joaquim Molas and Isidor Cònsul. Barcelona: Proa.

———. 2005a. Introduction to *Caritat*. In *Poesia, 1*, vol. 3 of *Totes les obres de Jacint Verdaguer*, edited by Joaquim Molas and Isidor Cònsul. Barcelona: Proa.

———. 2005b. Introduction to *Flors del Calvari*. In *Poesia, 1*, vol. 3 of *Totes les obres de Jacint Verdaguer*, edited by Joaquim Molas and Isidor Cònsul. Barcelona: Proa.

Cortès, Francesc. 1999. "Jacint Verdaguer: Més que un text per a bastir-hi música." *Anuari Verdaguer*, 1995–96, 189–207.

Duran Tort, Carola. 2003. "'Amor de mare,' hipertext hipotextificat." *Anuari Verdaguer*, 2002, 301–19. Vic: Eumo Editorial.

Farrés, Pere. 2002. "Estudi preliminar." In *L'Atlàntida*, by Jacint Verdaguer, edited by Pere Farrés. Vic: Eumo Editorial/Societat Verdaguer.

———. 2003. Introduction to *L'Atlàntida*. In *Poemes llargs/Teatre*, vol. 2 of *Totes les obres de Jacint Verdaguer*, edited by Joaquim Molas and Isidor Cònsul. Barcelona: Proa.

Garolera, Narcís. 2003. "*Flors del Calvari*, un tombant en la poesia de Verdaguer." In *Flors del Calvari: Llibre de consols*, by Jacint Verdaguer, edited by Narcís Garolera. Barcelona: Columna.

Garolera, Narcís, and Curt Wittlin. 2002. *Jacint Verdaguer: Del Canigó a l'Aneto*. Lleida: Pagès Editors.

Jorba, Manuel. 1995. "Aproximació a l'obra de Jacint Verdaguer." In *Jacint Verdaguer: 150 aniversari (1845–1995)*. Barcelona: Institució de les Lletres Catalanes.

Molas, Joaquim. 1986. "Jacint Verdaguer." In *Història de la literatura catalana*, vol. 7. Barcelona: Editorial Ariel.

———. 1988. "Els poemes llargs de Verdaguer: Ideologia i forma; Notes per a una primera aproximació." *Anuari Verdaguer*, 1987, 19–31.

———. 1999. "Jacint Verdaguer: Un poeta en crisi; Notes per a una primera lectura dels *Aires del Montseny*." *Anuari Verdaguer*, 1995–96, 11–26.

———. 2003a. Introduction to *Jesús Infant*. In *Poemes llargs/Teatre*, vol. 2 of *Totes les obres de Jacint Verdaguer*, edited by Joaquim Molas and Isidor Cònsul. Barcelona: Proa.

———. 2003b. "Sobre la poètica de Verdaguer." *Anuari Verdaguer*, 2002, 25–43.

———. 2005a. Introduction to *Idil·lis i cants místics*. In *Poesia, 1*, vol. 3 of *Totes les obres de Jacint Verdaguer*, edited by Joaquim Molas and Isidor Cònsul. Barcelona: Proa.

———. 2005b. Introduction to *Roser de tot l'any*. In *Poesia, 1*, vol. 3 of *Totes les obres de Jacint Verdaguer*, edited by Joaquim Molas and Isidor Cònsul. Barcelona: Proa.

Pinyol i Torrents, Ramon. 2002. "Estudi preliminar." In *Pàtria*, by Jacint Verdaguer. Vic: Eumo Editorial/Societat Verdaguer.

Riba, Carles. 1922. "Pròleg." In *Jacint Verdaguer: Antologia poètica*, edited by Carles Riba. Barcelona: Edicions 62.

Soldevila, Llorenç. 2002. Introduction to *Canigó*, by Jacint Verdaguer, edited by Llorenç Soldevila. Barcelona: Proa.

Terry, Arthur. 2003. *A companion to Catalan literature*. Woodbridge, UK: Tamesis.

Tió i Puntí, Pere. 1999. "De la poesia religiosa de Verdaguer (La Gleva) al retrobament amb el poeta (Vallcarca): A propòsit d'*Al Cel*." *Anuari Verdaguer*, 1995–96, 289–303.

Torrents, Ricard. 1995a. "Estudi preliminar." In *Dos màrtirs de ma pàtria, o siga Llucià i Marcià*, by Jacint Verdaguer, edited by Ricard Torrents. Vic: Eumo Editorial/Societat Verdaguer.

———. 1995b. *Verdaguer: Estudis i aproximacions*. Vic: Eumo Editorial.

———. 1995c. *Verdaguer: Un poeta per a un poble*. Vic: Eumo Editorial.

———. 2002a. Headnotes in *Autobiografia literària*, by Jacint Verdaguer, edited by Ricard Torrents. Vic: Eumo Editorial.

———. 2002b. "Les Sagrades Famílies de Verdaguer i de Gaudí." Opening speech for the academic year 2002–2003. Institut Superior de Ciències Religioses de Barcelona. Archbishopric of Barcelona.

———. 2003a. "Famílies nosagrades de Verdaguer i Gaudí." *Anuari Verdaguer*, 2002, 45–79.

———. 2003b. Introduction to *Canigó*. In *Poemes llargs/Teatre*, vol. 2 of *Totes les obres de Jacint Verdaguer*, edited by Joaquim Molas and Isidor Cònsul. Barcelona: Proa.

———. 2004. *A la claror de Verdaguer*. Vic: Eumo Editorial.

———. 2006. *Art, poder i religió: La Sagrada Família en Verdaguer i en Gaudí*. Barcelona: Proa.

Verdaguer Pajerols, M. Àngels. 2003. "Sobre els lemes i les citacions a *Flors del Calvari*." *Anuari Verdaguer*, 2002, 281–99.

Vilamala, Joan. 1999. Notes to *Antologia poètica: Jacint Verdaguer*. Barcelona: Biblioteca Hermes.

INDEX OF TITLES AND FIRST LINES